Why Am I So Anxious?

Why Am I So Anxious?

Powerful Tools for Recognizing Anxiety and Restoring Your Peace

Dr. Tracey Marks

Publisher Mike Sanders
Senior Editor Brook Farling
Art & Design Director William Thomas
Assistant Director of Art & Design Rebecca Batchelor
Development Editor Elizabeth Bryson
Proofreader Monica Stone
Indexer Celia McCoy

First American Edition, 2022
Published in the United States by DK Publishing
6081 E. 82nd Street, Indianapolis, Indiana 46250

Note: Neither the publisher nor the author is engaged in rendering professional
advice or services to the individual reader. The ideas, procedures, in suggestions
contained in this book are not intended as a substitute for consulting with your
physician. All matters regarding your health require medical supervision. Neither
the author nor the publisher shall be liable or responsible for any loss or damage
allegedly arising from any information or suggestion in this book.

Published in the United States by Dorling Kindersley Limited

Library of Congress Catalog Number: 2022931012
ISBN: 978-0-74405-704-1

DK books are available at special discounts when purchased in bulk for sales
promotions, premiums, fund-raising, or educational use. For details, contact:
SpecialSales@dk.com

Printed and bound in the United States of America

Author photo © Dr. Tracey Marks

For the curious
www.dk.com

Acknowledgments

I chose electrical engineering as my college major mainly because I've always been more skilled at math than language arts. But a secret reason was that I wanted a major that required a minimal number of books to read and papers to write. I've never been a good reader, and I loathed writing assignments. I fell asleep during the SAT reading comprehension section.

If you told me then that 30 years after making that decision, I would script online educational content and write a book, I would say you've mistaken me for someone else.

My introduction to psychiatry changed my life trajectory and set me on a path that I could not have foreseen when I chose medicine as a career. I want to acknowledge a few key people and experiences that shaped me into the psychiatrist I am today.

William H. Campbell, MD, a resident physician on my psychiatry rotation in medical school, opened my eyes to psychiatry as a fascinating science and gave me the courage to forego my plan to specialize in internal medicine.

Josepha Cheong, MD, was my medical school class sponsor and an extraordinary psychiatrist who made it possible for me to switch out of the Internal Medicine residency program to which I was assigned.

The New York–Presbyterian Hospital, Cornell Campus, Department of Psychiatry, did the work of transforming me from an analytical engineer who had never heard of Sigmund Freud to a psychoanalytically informed, curious psychiatrist.

Elizabeth Auchincloss, MD was my residency training director. I greatly admired her for her intellect and leadership. Having her invest in my personal and professional development was a privilege.

William Sobel, MD, was a supervising psychiatrist in my residency program who taught me by example to be unapologetically exceptional.

Finally, my parents, Bernard and Thelma Irvin, continuously pushed me to do my best and use my brain to do great things. They paved the way for all the others who came after them to take the baton and lead me toward the finish line.

I thank all of you for your roles in inspiring who I am today. I am forever grateful.

I also thank my patients whose collective experiences form the basis of my love for psychiatry and my online community whose thirst for knowledge keeps me creative and current.

Contents

Introduction

Sometimes, anxiety is like the sea: it ebbs and flows, but it's always there. Other times, it's like a chameleon: it can take many forms, some of which may not be obvious. We all experience anxiety at some level. What matters most is how it affects you and how you manage it.

I wrote this book during the COVID-19 pandemic, which is an unprecedented time that has universally affected us. If you didn't struggle with distressing anxiety symptoms before, COVID might have introduced you to the experience.

So for many people, the answer to the question "Why Am I So Anxious?" could be summed up in one word: COVID. But anxiety is so much more than the effect of a situational disaster. While disasters can make anxiety worse, anxiety is part of the human experience; it will persist, independent of an infectious outbreak or other natural disaster.

As such, I purposely left COVID out of my explanations of the origins of anxiety. Part of me had hoped that by the time I finished writing, COVID would be over. As of the date of this writing, it's not, and that doesn't change the book's message. It may make the need for tools to manage your anxiety even more essential.

I wrote this book to give you a deeper understanding of the different factors that can influence how anxious you feel. Not all anxiety is a disorder, and sometimes anxiety stems from your personality. If you've been diagnosed with a disorder or wonder if you have one, the chapters discussing anxiety disorders can help you see if you should seek further professional help. I also help you understand how much anxiety is normal and when it might be appropriate to take medication.

I hope this book eases some of the frustration of figuring out how to manage your anxiety. As a psychiatrist, I mainly prescribe medication for anxiety disorders, with psychotherapy to address specific issues. I have found over the years that by the time someone comes to see me (the prescriber), they are fed up with natural interventions and want an end to their suffering—yesterday. The prescribed medications often work as expected to reduce or eliminate their anxiety, and all is well until the side effects appear. Usually, the best-case scenario is a little weight gain and mild fatigue. But as you will see in Chapter 5, where I talk about prescription medicines, there are a lot of downsides to taking medication.

Often, when I try to introduce complementary and alternative therapies like diet and lifestyle interventions, the person will inevitably say, "I tried all that, and it doesn't work." In reality, a person may feel too overwhelmed to sort out all possible interventions on a trial-and-error basis. Like my patients, I got frustrated with the many options that are supposed to work but don't.

Then it hit me. My patients and I were expecting the alternative approaches to work the same way as medication with one solution to handle all the symptoms. But that's too much to expect from a nonprescription option. It's not even realistic for the medications to address all anxiety symptoms. That's why most people don't have 100% improvement with the medications.

What's the answer to this dilemma? How do you address anxiety without medication?

The answer is avail yourself of a variety of tools that address different aspects of anxiety and layer the tools to get the maximum effect. In the second half of the book, I equip you with several tools to address your anxiety.

Many options can still leave you feeling overwhelmed if you try to apply all of them. I suggest you read through the book to get the big picture and then return to the chapters that resonates with you the most. In the appendix, I present some summary tables and additional information to help you focus on the tools that will work best for you in diverse situations.

Happy reading, and I'll see you on the other side.

PART 1
Anxiety Origins

CHAPTER 1

Understanding Different Aspects of Anxiety

The Biology of Anxiety

Everyone has experienced anxiety at some level. Even if you are the calmest, most nonreactive person in the world, you have been anxious. It's a physiological fact. We all are wired to experience a hyperarousal state in response to an environmental stressor. When we perceive a threat, we instinctively respond with apprehension and caution.

This apprehensive response is why some people think of anxiety as being synonymous with fear. After all, fear is scary and being afraid causes distress. But fear is only one aspect of anxiety. Fear is your emotional response to a perceived threat that is imminent. The threat may be hypothetical, like something you imagine happening, or it can be real and forthcoming.

On the other hand, anxiety is the anticipation of a future threat. This threat can be real or imagined, but it's not immediate. An example of anxiety triggered by a nonimminent threat is worrying that you may lose your job if your company doesn't generate enough business.

The physiological reaction your body has to a threat is not pathological anxiety. It's a normal hyperarousal state. Typically, once the threat has passed, the hyperarousal state subsides. But for some people, the vigilance can develop into fear and trepidation and persist beyond the threat. Or worse, it can appear in the absence of any recognizable threat. This persistent fear creates pathological anxiety.

A Brief Tour of the Brain

Scientists refer to the normal hyperarousal state—your automatic stress reaction—as the flight, fight, or freeze response. These responses originate deep inside the brain and help you mobilize the energy you need to deal with a dangerous situation.

Imagine that your brain is a theater. It has an upper level, a lower level, and an orchestra pit. The lower level houses the subcortical structures, like the amygdala and thalamus, which handle instinctual drives (safety, sexual needs, etc.). They are encased inside the brain and out of view. Some people call this your "lizard brain," as it acts on instinct and learned memories rather than logic. Your subcortical structures also store emotional memories.

In the upper level, you'll find the cortex. This includes the outer surface of the brain, which you see in pictures as wrinkled grey matter. Just as you get a higher-level view of a performance from this level, the cortex handles higher-order functions, like thinking and interpreting the emotions created by subcortical structures.

In the orchestra pit sits the conductor and the musicians. This is your midbrain: a conductor coordinating complex signals from the cortex and subcortex down through the brain stem, spinal cord, organs, and periphery.

Before I was old enough to go to school, my grandmother would watch me while my parents worked. Her style of punishment was to spank me with a flyswatter when I misbehaved. I wasn't one to misbehave defiantly; I just kept myself occupied by taking things apart. (How else do you find out how something works?) She never told me ahead of time that she didn't want me to touch her sentimental trinkets. I only learned that my curiosity was unacceptable when I saw her stomping in my direction with the flyswatter in hand.

The rubber end of the swatter wasn't hard enough to hurt much, even when my grandmother hit my bare legs. But my disgust at being touched by something that had smashed an insect dwarfed any pain I felt. She never cleaned the swatter, so it always had at least one crushed fly stuck in a hole. The sight of the swatter alone was enough to keep me in line.

Today, I live in the South. Even with the most diligent door-closing, we need to rid our home of flies sometimes. After all these years, I still have trouble looking at our flyswatter without feeling a couple of seconds of angst.

My logical mind (the upper level) knows that a flyswatter is harmless to humans, but my emotional mind (the lower level) remembers my childhood disgust, it and won't let me forget.

The Physiology of Stress

The amygdala is an almond-shaped structure in your lower brain. There is one on each side of the brain. Most people refer to both as "the amygdala." Your amygdala is constantly scanning the environment to help you detect even the slightest threat. Once it does, it sends messages to other brain structures. The brain chemicals norepinephrine, acetylcholine, dopamine, and serotonin are used as the messaging system.

The activation of the other structures, like the hippocampus, hypothalamus, and pituitary, triggers a cascade of body reactions called *sympathetic activation*. This response increases your heart rate, blood pressure, and breathing. It also shuts down your digestion and releases glucose stores from the liver. (This is why it's not a good idea to engage in strenuous activity soon after eating; it diverts resources away from your digestive tract.)

As your body gets ready for action, the prefrontal cortex and other higher-level cortical structures gather more information about the threat.

If this analysis yields a false alarm or the threat has passed, your parasympathetic nervous system slows everything back down and returns you to your resting state.

How does your amygdala identify a threat? We instinctively interpret certain things as threatening, like snakes or insects. Other threats are taken from things we're taught, like not walking into the street without looking both ways. Through life experiences, the amygdala creates a database of emotional memories that it draws upon in stressful times.

As you can see from this process, your amygdala mobilizes your body's emergency response before you even know what the emergency is about. Therefore, your first response to a threat is unconscious. Knowing that the initial sympathetic response is an automatic process becomes relevant later, when you'll begin to determine how to address your anxiety.

Here's how anxiety develops from this automatic process.

The amygdala is a central structure in emotional expression. It's connected to the prefrontal cortex, which gives it feedback on whether the threat is real. Early exposure to highly stressful experiences (e.g., parental neglect, abuse, or bullying) alter the connection between the amygdala and prefrontal cortex. Some people are born with disrupted connections in this circuit and have overactive amygdalae. When this happens, the amygdala gets less feedback from the prefrontal cortex on whether it's overreacting. It can sound the alarm on something it perceives as a threat and keep you on alert even when it's unnecessary.

The Role of the Default-Mode Network (DMN)

There's another area of the brain that contributes to anxiety. This area is a group of brain regions called the *default-mode network* (DMN). The DMN communicates through direct channels, sort of like being in a group messaging chat. If you're neuroanatomically inclined, know that the primary brain structures that chat with each other are: medial prefrontal cortex, posterior cingulate cortex, precuneus, and lateral prefrontal cortex.

The DMN works like this: When you are not actively thinking about something, your brain's default state is to think about things from the past and present. Letting your mind wander in this way is called stimulus-independent thought. It's like having a video running in the background that doesn't get your attention but fills your mental space. When you turn your attention to something, the default thoughts turn off while your mind processes your intentional thoughts. This automatic process turns on and off throughout the day.

People with a very active DMN spend lots of time daydreaming and otherwise letting their mind wander. They might also excessively rehash the past or worry about the future. This is called *ruminating*. The literal definition of ruminate is to chew repeatedly. If you've ever watched a cow chew the cud, you've noticed its jaws move up and down in a slow rhythm. Similarly with rumination you chew on thoughts for a long time in slow contemplation.

Researchers have found that people with anxiety have an overactive DMN, though it's not clear which comes first: the anxiety or the overactivation. We do know that brain structures in the DMN bring about self-reflection and emotional appraisal. Emotional appraisal is the forming of judgments about particular situations. Therefore, a common rumination theme is forming judgments about yourself or your performance. If this takes an adverse turn, your overactive mind creates and perpetuates distress as you overfocus on these negative themes.

An uncontrolled amygdala and overactive default-mode network are two of the biological bases of anxiety. Some people are genetically predisposed to these issues, while others endure highly stressful experiences that make them more likely to be anxious. The good news is that you can change your wiring no matter what created it. The ability of the brain to remodel itself over time as we learn new things is called *neuroplasticity*.

Think of the brain as a complex electrical circuit comprising a network of linked nerves. From my days of taking apart objects in my grandmother's house, I learned that a circuit won't activate if a wire isn't twisted tightly to the adjacent wire. Similarly, the tighter the connections between the nerves, the better the nerves transmit information. Some anxiety states cause loose connections, while others cause overly tight connections. Both result in overactivation states.

Medication, diet, and meditation are a few interventions that improve the quality of nerve connections through the neuroplasticity remodeling process. We'll delve more into these interventions in Part 2 of this book.

Why Are Some People Anxious and Others Not?

In the previous section, I explained what happens in the brain when you experience anxiety. But what is normal anxiety, and what makes it pathological?

Normal Anxiety

Everyday anxiety is usually adaptive—that is, it's a reasonable response to a stressful situation, and it resolves once the stressor has passed.

For example, if I hear that my neighborhood has had a rash of home invasions, I might become terrified that my home will be next. I could have trouble sleeping for several nights.

This fear will motivate me to have an alarm system installed in my home. Once we install the system, I'll experience significant relief, but I still might be vigilant about checking the doors at night and ensuring the alarm is active before I go to bed. If weeks pass without another home invasion, my vigilance will subside. Even better, if I hear that the police securely locked the culprits away, I might feel that I'm no longer at risk. This response is an example of normal reactive anxiety.

Pathological Anxiety

If your anxiety response is abnormal, it isn't proportional to the stressor, lasts well beyond the stressor, and has some effect on your personal life, relationships, and/or ability to function at work.

An example of an abnormal response to the home invasions would be if my worry about being the next victim extended past the point of getting an alarm. In this scenario, I develop a nightly routine of checking the alarm three or four times before bed. If I notice that my husband is still awake watching television, I can't fall asleep until he comes to bed and reassures me that he turned on the alarm. Even with that reassurance,

I'm still only able to sleep 5 hours a night. The sleep loss makes me cranky, and I lash out at my family. My body feels tense most of the day, and I have headaches, which I remedy with four glasses of wine each night. Because I'm always on edge, I now wake up every time the neighbor's dog barks. I don't feel rested on most days, and I forget important work deadlines.

Anxiety like this rarely results from a single threat. It's a pattern responding to a variety of threats. Normal anxiety will produce a reaction proportionate to the threat. But an anxious person can expect threats or feel anxious when faced with a minor threat. Today, it's news of a possible home invasion; tomorrow, it might be a presentation at school or work. Next week, it's the possibility that you won't get the promotion you've been wanting.

Stressors are a part of daily life, and there will always be another one. The person prone to anxiety can have a continuous experience of angst that becomes unmanageable. If exposed to enough stressors, the person who is not prone to anxiety can cave under pressure and develop anxiety that persists past their usual experience.

The Genesis of Anxiety

How does one become prone to responding to life anxiously?

Anxiety starts early, usually in childhood. Many children don't recognize that what they feel is anxiety. It's not until they get older and see that other people around them don't feel or think the same way that they realize what they had was anxiety all along.

Anyone can be predisposed to anxiety. We call this predisposition *trait anxiety*. In contrast, *state anxiety* is your current anxiety experience. Everyone is born with a temperament which is genetically hard wired. Twenty to fifty percent of people inherit an anxious temperament from their parents.

The way you view the world and how you react to it depends on your temperament. Personality and temperament are similar and are often used interchangeably. You can think of temperament as the emotional core that stays with you throughout your life. Several factors influence your personality, including your temperament, your upbringing, your parents' personalities, and your life events. People commonly refer to this concept as *nature versus nurture.* Your temperament is your nature, and your early life experiences are how your caretakers nurtured you.

Researchers have developed several models to describe temperament, each with their own terminology. All the models have terms that describe the trait of anxiety-proneness. Harm avoidance and neuroticism, which are discussed below, come from two popular temperament theories.

Harm-Avoidance Temperament

Harm avoidance refers to the tendency to worry about negative outcomes. A high harm-avoidance individual worries and expects failure or harm. Generally, they're anxious and uncomfortable in unfamiliar situations, and they're shy around strangers. They're also unassertive, which means they don't make their needs clear. People who score high on harm avoidance also struggle with mental toughness and resilience. Because of this, they decompensate easily and have trouble recovering after hardship.

The lack of mental toughness even extends to how you respond to physical illness. Some people get sick and can't move for weeks. They might miss school or work because they're sick. Someone else who gets the same illness can manage to get through their workdays despite feeling sick. This same person seems to bounce back quickly after getting sick.

When you have trouble recovering from an illness or setback, it can affect your self-esteem and self-concept. If you don't recover from adversity quickly, you can feel weaker than other people. This is especially true if you have a sibling who isn't harm avoidant. You might hear your parent or siblings say: "What's the matter with you? Johnny's not complaining. Why can't you pull it together?" And if you're an adult, you might hear, "Stop acting like a baby."

Let's say you're the opposite of harm avoidant. If that's the case, you tend to feel more confident and secure in most situations, are more assertive in your relationships, and recover from problems faster. Fast recovery makes you resilient.

Neuroticism Temperament

Neuroticism is similar to harm avoidance but also includes general negative thinking. It's how vulnerable you are to negative emotions like anxiety, depression, and anger. People high in neuroticism tend to be tense, excessively worry, have trouble handling stress, and get upset easily.

You've probably heard the saying, "What doesn't kill you makes you stronger." That may be true for some people, but it's not always the case for people with anxious temperaments. Because you're more likely to decompensate under stress, trying times can beat you down and leave you scarred. Less intense stress that is repeated or persistent can have the same effect. Not being able to return to your usual state or elevate to a stronger normal can leave you feeling inadequate.

A person with a harm-avoidance or neurotic temperament is more likely to develop an anxiety disorder later in life. While it's not definite, it's as if you have the groundwork for an anxiety disorder if you're faced with difficult circumstances.

The Effects of Your Environment

Think back to the way your primary caregivers dealt with stressful situations. How did they respond to their own stress? How did they respond to you when you were stressed?

You can learn to be anxious from your primary caregivers. Children model their parents' behavior as part of their development. Observing how your parents deal with stressful situations may teach you to be fretful or fear the unknown. Fearing the unknown conditions you to become intolerant of uncertainty.

Parenting style is another way our parents affect how we experience anxiety. How our parents react to our feelings shapes how intensely we experience and manage anxiety. Cold, critical, controlling, and overprotective parenting styles tend to cause anxiety in children.

When a parent is warm, they respond to their children positively, such as with praise, smiles, and terms of endearment, like "sweetie." A parent who suffers from anxiety may be stifled from expressing warmth. You can experience them as cold because they don't (or can't) reciprocate your positive emotions.

Consider this example. A young boy, Tim, comes home and is excited to tell his father about his school award. A warm response would be "That-a-boy, Tim! I knew you could do it. Show me the award." A cold response is

"That's nice. Hey, you're getting mud all over the carpet. I told you to check your shoes before you come in the house." In the second scenario, Tim's father has a lot on his mind and doesn't have time to talk to him about school. He may even be frustrated about something that happened earlier that day, and the dirty carpet becomes the final trigger to release his feelings. Tim is superexcited about his award, but his dad isn't and won't even look at him. In Tim's mind, his dad's comment means the carpet is more important than his achievements.

Constant criticism and disapproval can lead children to feel insecure and incompetent. Feeling insecure can make one feel as if the world is unsafe. Parents can be controlling in many ways. They make too many decisions for you, are overprotective, discourage independent thinking, or don't let you express yourself. If you're raised with a parental style like this, it can be hard to develop your sense of mastery and autonomy.

These are a few of the ways your home environment can make you vulnerable to anxiety. Other factors include exposure to trauma, neglect, and extreme poverty.

Being predisposed to anxiety doesn't have to mean that you will be overwhelmed by anxiety for the rest of your life. It simply means that you may anxiously react to things by default, but you can still learn how to manage those reactions. Understanding the source of your anxiety is part of the process of overcoming it. We will discuss techniques to manage your anxiety later in the book beginning in Chapter 5.

Recognizing Anxiety

Anxiety is an intense emotion that takes many forms, but most find it easy to recognize the more common physical symptoms:

- Rapid heart rate
- Chest pain
- Choking or difficulty swallowing
- Sleeping problems
- Sweating
- Tremors
- Nausea

- Decreased appetite
- Heavy breathing
- Lightheadedness
- Numbness and tingling
- Heat sensations or chills

These symptoms directly result from an overactive sympathetic nervous system. A rise in epinephrine speeds up your heart and breathing leaving you ready to fight, run, or freeze. Although you can experience these symptoms with other physical conditions, if they follow a stressor, it's easy to associate them with the stressor and conclude they are part of your stress response.

However, there are also less obvious physical symptoms, like head-aches, visual changes (such as flashing lights or spots), and skin or finger picking. Let's take a closer look at some of the less common symptoms.

Brain Shocks

These are a common side effect of discontinuing an antidepressant, especially if you do so abruptly, without tapering it down. The sensation can feel like the brain is turning on and off or like a surge of electricity through your head. Some describe this experience as "brain shivers," because it feels like their brain is shaking. The experience rarely lasts long, but it can happen several times in a row. There is no specific frequency for brain shocks. You may experience a series of shocks in one day and not have them again for weeks or even months.

Brain shocks can be highly distressing when they first start, and many fear that they have developed seizures or a tumor. Rest assured that although the symptom is distressing, it doesn't cause brain damage. It is, however, a scary experience, and that alone can add to your anxiety.

Hyperventilation

Breathing too quickly is common in people who suffer from anxiety. When you hyperventilate, you exhale lots of carbon dioxide, lowering your calcium levels. Low carbon dioxide and calcium can cause muscle spasms in your hands or feet. The clinical term for this is carpopedal spasms. The nonclinical term is "claw hand." These spasms can be painful. and if severe enough, can look like the hand of someone who's had a stroke. I have personal experience with this frightening symptom....

Claw Hand

My son sets very high expectations for himself and becomes overwhelmed if he believes he won't have enough time to finish his schoolwork. This work ethic became a problem when he transitioned from the light workload of elementary school to the nightly homework of middle school.

One day, I heard a gasping noise from his room. I dismissed it, thinking he was being overly dramatic—sometimes I hear him screaming one minute and laughing the next. But a few minutes later, I heard a choking sound that sent me running up the stairs. I could barely breathe. *Has he swallowed something? How long has he been without oxygen?*

I found him sitting stiffly upright, staring straight ahead. His arm was bent at the elbow, his hand bent at the wrist. His fingers were spread apart and fixed like claws. *Oh my God, my child has had a stroke! Or maybe a seizure? But he's not moving. What's going on? Is he dead?* I called his name, and he slowly looked up at me, only moving his eyes. *Okay, he's not dead.*

I moved closer and massaged his stiff arm. It slowly straightened, with some resistance. It took at least 5 minutes for him to respond to me as I rubbed his back and tried to soothe him. After he relaxed, he told me that he didn't understand a school assignment and feared he would fail his test. After hearing this, I concluded that he'd had a very severe panic attack.

Because of my medical training, I knew about tetanic muscular con-tractions that follow hyperventilation. Reading about that phenomenon in a textbook is one thing, but it was quite another to witness it in a loved one. I later felt guilty for dismissing his cry for help as "adolescent drama," and the image of him sitting in that chair with a claw hand remains hauntingly etched in my mind. (Thankfully, he has no recollection of it.)

Common Mental Symptoms

Not everyone experiences anxiety physically. Anxiety is predominantly an emotional experience, with common mental symptoms like these:

- Feeling on edge
- Worry
- Concentration problems
- Memory problems
- Catastrophizing (assuming the worst)
- Fear

Anxiety can produce many fears. You can become preoccupied with the thought that something terrible will happen, even if you can't pinpoint it. Sometimes, this can be a nonspecific sense of foreboding. For example, some fear that they've missed a deadline even though they have none looming. Another common fear is thinking that you're losing your mind.

The Airport

While I'd like to think of myself as a seasoned traveler, in reality, I'm not. I find the preparation for travel very stressful, but the worst part for me is the trip to the airport. Living in the suburbs of Atlanta, the drive can vary between 45 minutes and infinity, depending on traffic. We usually leave 3 hours before boarding time to give ourselves 1 hour of travel and 2 hours to park and get through security.

During our last trip, to a family wedding, we traveled to the Atlanta airport in the rain. Rain often means longer, unpredictable driving times, so this triggered my travel anxiety. And it was already pretty high.

My husband knows that I don't like to spend the 45-minute trip hearing his ominous predictions about missing our flight and other unpleasant consequences. So wisely, he elected to keep his thoughts to himself. I also kept my angst to myself, but I just couldn't stop envisioning a 10-car pileup that would make us miss our flight.

After sailing through the drive without incident, the next issue involved figuring out a way to stay dry so as not to end up sitting in a cold airport wearing wet clothes. We decided not to park our car in the long-term economy parking lot, which would require us to walk 10 minutes in the rain. But naturally, we weren't the only ones with this bright idea. After seeing the long line of cars turning into the parking deck, my husband couldn't contain his worry any longer. He said, "I bet the only spots available will be the ones on the roof that aren't covered, and we'll get wet anyway."

Like a flower blooming in time-lapse, his version of our future unfolded before us. We'd have to sit at the airport gate for 2 hours, shivering, our clothes stuck to our skin. We'd catch the flu on the trip, and since we were staying with family, they'd also get sick. My older, immune-compromised family members would end up hospitalized. No one would be able go to the wedding, the whole point of the trip.

As ridiculous as this trail of calamities seemed to me, it's a practical example of just how far catastrophic thinking can go. Here, one afternoon of rain would cause an entire extended family to miss my nephew's wedding, and vulnerable relatives would end up on life support.

Other Mental Symptoms

Mental symptoms that you may not associate with anxiety include irritability, indecision, perfectionism, and reassurance seeking. People with anxiety can also have intrusive thoughts: unpleasant or otherwise unwanted thoughts that unexpectedly pop into your head. A prime time for them to appear is when you're trying to sleep or are fully awake but alone with your thoughts. The default-mode network plays a role in inserting these thoughts into your awareness when you're not actively thinking about something else.

Some people with anxiety experience dissociation, a broad term that refers to mentally separating from the present moment. Traumatic experiences can often trigger dissociation as a response to anxiety. These are two types of dissociation:

1. **Depersonalization:** a feeling of detachment from your thoughts, sensations, and actions

This feels as if you're observing yourself and your thoughts from a distance—a fly on the wall. Here are a few examples:

- Looking in the mirror and not recognizing yourself.
- Seeing yourself as if you're an observer in the room.
- Feeling numb all over.
- Feeling like your body isn't real.

2. **Derealization:** a feeling of detachment from your environment

   You might feel as if you're looking at the space around you through a glass window, or as if you're in a dream. Time might feel like it's passing unusually fast or slowly. You might have trouble seeing things in your periphery (tunnel vision). Some people have told me that the world seems a little off-axis or that colors aren't as bright.

   Dissociation is a psychological defense mechanism used to ward off unconscious anxiety. It's your mind's way of keeping you from being aware of the disturbing thoughts that make you anxious.

   We will go over psychological defenses and unconscious anxiety in Chapter 4.

The Negative Effects of Anxiety

A birth deformity of my leg delayed my ability to walk. At around 18 months old, doctors broke my leg and reset it. I still have the tiny, 10-inch cast that covered my entire leg, from hip to foot. I spent several years wearing ugly corrective shoes to keep my feet straight. I was like Forrest Gump without the metal braces. When I was four years old, my parents enrolled me in ballet classes to help me become more graceful.

I excelled in ballet and advanced to a role in the performing company. Although I enjoyed performing, I found the preparation very stressful. Most afternoons after school and every Saturday, I went to dance practice. This busy schedule left little time for me to complete the crush of work from my advanced classes, so I stayed up late to finish my assignments.

There were two or three performances a year, and I would always catch a cold a few days before each one. My ballet instructor put it together when she saw me taking cough medicine in the changing room.

"Are you sick again?" she once asked me. "It seems like you're always sick." Her comment stung a little; it didn't feel very compassionate. I didn't understand what she was trying to accomplish with her observation, but in the end, it prompted me to reflect on the connection between my stressful schedule and my physical health.

We discussed earlier how anxiety causes a wide range of physical symptoms. But chronic anxiety can cause even more serious health problems. Here are some long-term effects:

- Trouble concentrating
- Headaches
- Fatigue
- High blood pressure
- Increased resting heart rate
- Lower immune system
- Worsening of respiratory problems
- Insomnia
- Body aches
- Low sex drive
- Irritability
- Gastrointestinal problems
- Depression

Concentration Problems

Anxious people have a hard time concentrating. If anxiety makes it difficult to focus, you may mistakenly believe that you have attention deficit disorder (ADD). To remember something, you have to focus on it long enough to encode it in your memory. Because of this, anxiety can lead to forgetfulness and disorganization.

Compromised Immune System

Your immune system is your first line of defense against infections and illnesses. When anxiety strikes, your body produces high levels of cortisol, which suppresses your immune system, making you more susceptible to infection.

Problems Related to Muscle Tension

When you're anxious, you tense your body muscles—typically without realizing it. Tension in your face, head, and neck can cause headaches.

Tension in your jaw muscles can cause you to grind your teeth. Sometimes, you may notice yourself clenching your jaw. But the grinding can also happen while you're asleep, so you don't realize you're doing it. You can sleep with a mouth guard to protect your teeth, but it doesn't always prevent you from clenching your jaw. Chronic jaw clenching can lead to temporomandibular joint problems.

Tension in your neck and back can leave you feeling exhausted at the end of the day. If you spend the day sitting at a desk, you may feel tired from this type of muscle tension. When muscles contract for a long time or remain still, they secrete lactic acid. You can experience muscle pain if you accumulate excessive lactic acid, such as after a strenuous workout. Stiff or contracted muscles can cause similar muscle pain as strenuous activity.

Cardiovascular Disease

Cardiovascular disease and anxiety are closely linked. In the short term, anxiety increases heart rate and blood pressure, but continuously elevated blood pressure can weaken the heart muscle. Anxiety also increases chemicals in the body that cause inflammation. The coronary arteries, which are the blood vessels that supply blood to the heart, may suffer damage from inflammation.

Anxiety also affects your cardiovascular health by reducing your heart rate variability, which is how much your heart rate changes based on what you're doing. If you're sitting comfortably and reading in a chair, your heart rate will be close to your regular resting rate. If you hear your phone ring or receive a text message, your heart will beat faster as you grab your phone. When you return to your reading, your heart will slow back down. When the heart is beating efficiently, it will speed up to meet increased energy demands and slow down as soon as possible to conserve energy—that is, your heart only works as hard as it has to. Anxiety causes your heart to beat more rapidly at rest, decreasing your variability and reducing your ability to conserve energy. Low heart rate variability increases the risk of heart attacks.

Although there is no timeline for these cardiovascular effects, it generally takes months, if not years, of chronic changes to see the more serious consequences. You can take steps now to reduce your anxiety and improve your cardiovascular health.

Respiratory Problems

When you're anxious, your breathing becomes shallow and rapid. Because of this, you don't exhale enough carbon dioxide compared to your oxygen intake. Excess carbon dioxide constricts blood vessels, causing breathing problems for people with asthma or chronic obstructive pulmonary disease (COPD). As a result, someone with COPD who is anxious could end up in the hospital more often.

Low Sex Drive

A high cortisol level can lead to low libido or low sex drive. This low sex drive happens because cortisol suppresses testosterone, which controls sex drive. Testosterone is primarily a male hormone, but women produce small amounts of it as well. It's not just cortisol that suppresses libido, but angst and fear can also kill your desire. It's hard to feel intimate if you can't relax.

Insomnia

Insomnia involves trouble falling asleep or staying asleep at least three nights a week for at least 3 months. Preparing for my ballet performances didn't cause insomnia. Instead, I self-imposed a poor sleep pattern because I needed more hours during the day to finish my work.

Anxiety can make it difficult to relax and fall asleep. Many people manage to ignore their anxiety during the day because they have a busy, distracting schedule. The problem comes when they're alone with their thoughts at bedtime.

Another sign of anxious insomnia is a broken sleep pattern. You may have no trouble falling asleep within the usual 15 to 20 minutes but then wake up several times and fail to fall back asleep. Your body acts like it's on alert and won't let you sleep.

Gut Problems

Irritable bowel syndrome (IBS) and gastroesophageal reflux disease (GERD) are the two most common bowel disorders associated with anxiety. IBS causes chronic abdominal pain, gas, bloating, and irregular bowel movements. An irregular pattern can range from having a bowel movement several times a day with loose stool to going several days without a bowel movement and feeling constipated.

Even if you don't feel anxious all the time, a single episode of anxiety may aggravate existing GERD and IBS symptoms. Studies show that anxiety traits like neuroticism, catastrophizing, and somaticizing (a tendency to focus on physical problems) worsen IBS. We will discuss the effect of anxiety on gut health more in Chapter 9.

Depression

Anxiety and depression are highly comorbid—that is, they occur together much of the time. In fact, it's estimated that almost half of people with generalized anxiety disorder will also have depression at some point in their lives.

Anxious depression can present itself in many ways. Consider a person with generalized anxiety. They throw up every morning, and all day, they feel like a heavy weight is pressing on their chest. There isn't any obvious reason for this, which leads them to constantly think things like *What's wrong with me?* and *Why don't I feel normal?* They feel shame about being unable to control their anxiety symptoms and start to lose hope for their future. Eventually they develop depression as a result of persistent anxiety.

Some people experience anxiety symptoms concurrent with their depression. Their symptoms may not reach the level of a full-blown anxiety disorder like panic disorder or generalized anxiety disorder, but the anxiety alters the quality of the depression. Clinicians call this combination "depressed with anxious distress."

The Diagnostic and Statistical Manual of Mental Disorders 5th edition (DSM-5) defines anxious distress as experiencing at least two of the following symptoms for most of the day while depressed:

- Feeling on edge or tense.
- Having unmanageable restlessness.
- Worry that makes it difficult to concentrate.
- Fear that something terrible may happen to you.
- Fear that you may lose control.

Being anxious can make you feel as if you have lost control or are losing your mind. You can also lose control in more subtle ways, such as being unable to hold back from insulting someone who has made you angry.

Anxiety combined with depression makes both conditions more difficult to treat. As a result, you will probably need the help of a health-care professional, such as a primary care doctor or psychiatrist, to address your symptoms. To fully recover from anxious depression, most people need more than one medication. In Chapter 5, we will discuss anxiety medications.

CHAPTER 2

Introduction to the Disorders

How Many People Have An Anxiety Disorder?

In the previous chapter, we talked about normal versus pathological anxiety. Pathological anxiety causes anxiety disorders, the most common form of mental illness in the United States. Many people have anxiety, but not all anxiety is a disorder.

Clinicians rely on the Diagnostic and Statistical Manual of Mental Disorders, currently on its 5th edition, to define the various illnesses. The DSM-5 presents lists of symptoms that serve as criteria to diagnose a particular illness. Doctors and therapists use the manual to form their opinion about your diagnosis.

Here are eight anxiety conditions listed in order of most to least common. The percentage represents the proportion of people who will have the disorder at some point in their lives.

Specific phobia	18.4%
Social phobia (also called *social anxiety disorder*)	13.0%
Post-traumatic stress disorder	10.1%
Generalized anxiety disorder	9.0%
Separation anxiety disorder	8.7%
Panic disorder	6.8%
Agoraphobia	3.7%
Obsessive-compulsive disorder	2.7%

According to the National Comorbidity Survey, 41.7% of people will develop an anxiety disorder. As you can see from the table, the two most common anxiety disorders are specific phobia and social phobia (more commonly known as *social anxiety disorder*).

Separation anxiety disorder and social phobia both start earlier in life. Separation anxiety starts in childhood, and social phobia begins in adolescence, between ages 15 and 17. Panic disorder and generalized anxiety disorder appear for the first time a little later, between ages 23 and 30.

Even though they cause a great deal of anxiety, posttraumatic stress disorder (PTSD) and obsessive-compulsive disorder (OCD) are no longer in the anxiety disorders section of the DSM. Therefore, they will be discussed in Chapter 3, alongside other anxious conditions.

In this section, I break down the features of the various anxiety disorders.

Specific Phobia

I have a roach phobia, but for years, I didn't think of it as a phobia. I saw it as a necessary and justified avoidance of a universally despised bug. I attribute this fear to growing up in Florida, where palm trees are the standard yard vegetation. While they offer a pleasing aesthetic, their dark side is that they are roach motels. Even worse, they house the flying roaches—in my mind, they're roaches with superpowers.

Whenever my dad performed his annual branch trimming, the newly homeless roaches invaded our house, transforming nighttime into a zombie apocalypse. If I got up in the middle of the night and turned on the light, I had to duck out of the way of the massive flight of displaced bugs scrambling to safety. I can still hear their wings buzzing past my ears. With that experience, who wouldn't hate roaches and not want to look at them? I thought everyone felt similarly until my recent experience with a pest control company.

One night, I saw a roach skitter across my floor. I ran to get my handy spray can, but I couldn't find the roach when I returned. Not seeing the dead body before I went to bed ruined my sleep. The next day, I called a pest control company to request that they spray inside the house. There was a long silence before the customer service agent said, "You saw *a* roach?"

I knew I wouldn't be able to make her understand that, for me, seeing even one roach is like taking a bullet in the chest. It can leave me feeling disturbed and unsettled for a week. I spared her that disclosure, and instead, I used the tip of the iceberg analogy to convey that one visible roach meant many others were lurking in the shadows. She reluctantly accepted my request to bring in the troops.

The 5 years I spent in New York City for my psychiatry training provided a healing respite from those Florida experiences. I even considered living permanently in the northeast to avoid ever seeing another flying roach. While I'm less reactive to the sight of a roach now, I still can't watch them on television (not even a cartoon roach). I go to great lengths to avoid them and am perfectly fine with never feeling comfortable around them.

Specific phobia is the most common anxiety disorder. It's characterized by the fear and avoidance of a specific situation or object. It typically starts in childhood, but many people around midlife can also develop it for the first time. The phobia usually lasts years, even decades. Most people with phobias have more than one. Here are some features of specific phobia:

- You immediately become anxious when you encounter the object or situation.
- You put great effort toward avoiding the situation, or you endure it with much discomfort (some people will have panic attacks).
- The level of fear or anxiety does not match the actual danger you face from the object or situation.
- The fear, anxiety, or avoidance lasts at least 6 months.
- The fear, anxiety, or avoidance causes a lot of distress, or it causes problems in specific areas of your life, like your work or social life.

There are six subcategories of phobias: animals, natural environment, situational, blood-injection injury, other situations, and unspecified. Heights and animals are the two most common phobias.

Fear Versus Disgust

My dad used to tease me about being afraid of roaches. They don't bite. I know they can't harm me. Still, I fear them touching me. I'm not afraid of roaches; I'm disgusted by them. The disgust runs deep, right to my core. Seeing one crushed is a horror show for me. So, my roach phobia is not based on fear; it's based on disgust.

Disgust differs from fear, but it's just as strong of a phobic trigger. Evolutionary psychologists theorize that disgust is the body's way of protecting itself from harmful substances. Not all cultures are disgusted by the same things, however, and this has led scientists to conclude that disgust is a learned behavior.

Disgust sensitivity develops throughout your life. There's some evidence that children as young as 4 may fear contamination. But other studies have shown that after exposing children to a variety of disgusting things, like certain foods and imitation poop, most children under age 8 were not cognitively mature enough to appreciate what should and should not be disgusting. In the developmental stage from ages 2 to 8 we learn what things in our environment to find disgusting.

Some researchers believe that disgust is the emotion at the root of many psychiatric disorders, such as phobias and obsessive-compulsive disorder (OCD). High disgust sensitivity is a component of neuroticism, and people who have it have a higher risk of animal and contamination phobias.

Let's take a closer look at seven of the more common phobias.

Acrophobia (Fear of Heights)

A fear of heights typically begins in childhood. For some, it can last a lifetime. This fear often starts with an instinctive fear of falling. Watching movies that depict people falling off buildings or cliffs can instill this fear in younger impressionable children. As with all phobias, irrational fear and avoidance behaviors transform the instinctive fear into a phobia. People with acrophobia fear many different kinds of high places, such as mountains, bridges, ladders, and stairs. The condition can make it hard for them to do everyday things, like take public transportation or even go up the stairs in their own home.

People with acrophobia are sensitive to body sensations and interpret them as threatening. This negative bias reinforces their anxiety. A height-phobic person might be afraid that if they look down from a high place, they'll get dizzy, lose their balance, and fall. And if they feel any lightheadedness or even a slight increase in their heartbeat, they might become even more anxious. They may experience a cascade of other sensations, like dizziness, nausea, and disorientation, that confirm their fear and reinforce their phobia.

Zoophobia (Fear of Animals)

The common fears that fall under this category are arachnophobia (spiders), ophidiophobia (snakes), and cynophobia (dogs). Of these three, arachnophobia is the most common, affecting 3–5% of people. About half of people are afraid of snakes. But only about 2–3% of people have a fear that reaches a phobia level.

Some people believe that spider phobia is an exaggerated response to an instinctual fear. Others think it occurs because of the way the media portrays spiders. Even people without a phobia can be afraid of spiders, especially if a spider has bitten you or if you know someone who has been bitten. But for arachnophobes, anything that reminds them of spiders is a trigger. People with spider phobias can get anxious from seeing an empty spider web on their doorstep. They might be afraid to go to places where spiders live, like their own backyard. And there's a good chance they won't show up to your summer barbecue.

Interestingly, even with negative media portrayals of spiders, a 2019 study by Hoffman and colleagues found that watching *Spider-Man* movies reduced arachnophobia symptoms. This could be because these movies personify spiders and show them in a positive light.

Claustrophobia (Enclosed Spaces)

This fear can take the form of avoiding elevators or crowds. Claustrophobia doesn't always have to involve a tight space. Wearing a mask or helmet with a shield can make a person with claustrophobia feel short of breath or experience intense anxiety.

Trypanophobia (Needles/Injections)

This fear can affect people's ability to work if their employment or school requires vaccinations or lab work. In worst-case scenarios, a person with trypanophobia may refuse certain types of medical treatment, which could put their overall health at risk. For example, a person with diabetes who needs injections to treat their condition is at risk of complications if they refuse to use needles.

People with trypanophobia can even be affected by things associated with needles. For example, they might have a strong anxiety response to things that remind them of needles, such as the smell of rubbing alcohol or the sight of cotton swabs.

Aerophobia (Flying)

People who fear flying and manage to get on a plane may spend the flight fretting about many things, like the possibility of crashing or what would happen if they needed to use the restroom during takeoff. They may convince themselves that they suddenly smell smoke or see flames engulfing the plane.

Sometimes, people will miss important family events to avoid having a panic attack on the plane. People whose job depends on flying may take a sedative medication to ease their anxiety, but the flying experience will still be somewhat distressing.

Emetophobia (Vomit/Vomiting)

Emetophobics forecast the kinds of experiences that may expose them to vomit. Examples include parties where people are drinking, amusement rides, and consuming certain foods. More extreme avoidance behaviors include refusing to travel abroad or to areas where they believe the food may not be safe to eat. Some people with emetophobia may avoid getting pregnant for fear of morning sickness. They can also become consumed with checking behaviors, like checking the expiration dates on food or avoiding eating any food that might spoil or cause food poisoning. The result can be a severely restricted diet and suboptimal nutrition.

Nausea is a very common anxiety symptom. With emetophobia, if you become anxious and nauseous, your anxiety can escalate because of your fear of vomiting. This intensification of your nausea can make you refuse to eat. Some people are hospitalized with dehydration and malnutrition because of their emetophobia.

Iatrophobia (Doctors/the Medical System/ Medical Treatment)

The origin of iatrophobia is not well understood, but like many phobias, it often starts with a traumatic experience. Going through a painful procedure or fearing that doctors will always bring bad news can make people with iatrophobia avoid treatment. Unfortunately, this avoidance frequently leads to poorer health outcomes than they would have had if they'd engaged in preventative care.

Only about 10–25% of people with specific phobia get treatment. For many people, the phobia doesn't interfere with their life (like with my roach phobia). People with phobias of flying, closed spaces, and heights are more likely to seek treatment, probably because these fears have more potential to interfere with everyday life.

Social Anxiety Disorder (Social Phobia)

Social anxiety disorder can cause a lot of shame and significantly interfere with daily functioning. The name has changed from social phobia in the DSM-3 (published in 1980) to social anxiety disorder in the DSM-5 (published in 2013). This name change considers the deeper fears people have that go beyond fearing social situations.

Here are some features of the disorder:

- Fear of specific social situations because of a belief that you will be judged, embarrassed, or humiliated.
- Avoidance (or anxious endurance) of social situations that you know will make you anxious.
- Excessive anxiety that's out of proportion to the situation.

There are some situations in which it's normal to be anxious, like taking a test or giving a speech. Even experienced speakers can feel nervous before they give a speech. The difference between social anxiety disorder and normal anxiety is that with the former, you may hyperventilate, pass out, or vomit before the event. Chances are you have developed a pattern of avoiding these situations so that you don't have to experience this degree of anxiety.

With social anxiety, your anxiety or distress interferes with your daily living. It can interfere with going to networking events, speaking up in class or meetings, or participating in recreational activities.

Jeff and the Soccer Games

Jeff has suffered from social anxiety for as long as he can remember. School was a harrowing experience, especially around sports. His father had played lacrosse in college, and because he expected Jeff to be similarly athletic, he enrolled Jeff in a community lacrosse team. Jeff loathed the practices and didn't perform very well. He was stricken with diarrhea before every game, and after three missed games, his coach removed him from the team. His coach encouraged him to join the next season when he "feels better." After that, Jeff's parents recognized his low aptitude for sports and left him alone to explore other interests.

Years later, Jeff's son took an early interest in soccer. His wife brought their 4 year old to all the practices without Jeff, but she expected Jeff to be there to support him on game days. Jeff felt intensely anxious about going to the games for fear that the other fathers would want to "talk sports." He convinced himself that everyone would immediately recognize him as a fraud who knew nothing about soccer. Jeff initially agreed to go to the game but had to stay home because of an explosive bout of diarrhea.

After the third missed game, his wife became angry with him and told him to "man up and go." Jeff made it to the next game with the aid of an antidiarrheal agent, but he spent the entire game answering "important" emails (on a Saturday). On the drive home, his son kept asking, "Daddy, did you see when I made the goal?" "Did you see me block Tommy's kick?" Jeff feigned excitement but could feel the scorn of his wife, who knew he hadn't watched any of the game.

Jeff's apparent disinterest in his son's sport became a source of arguments between Jeff and his wife. Before every game, Jeff downed a shot of vodka to make it easier to talk to the other parents. Then, he followed up with "a couple" of drinks at home.

Jeff's example illustrates a few key points about social anxiety. First, his marital conflict would be considered a personal impairment. Jeff had more than a reluctance to go to his son's game. He experienced intense anxiety and attacks of diarrhea. His wife excused him the first time it happened, but she didn't accept his anxiety as an excuse to miss the other games. Even if his wife knew that he had social anxiety, she, like other loved ones, set limits on Jeff's avoidance. She expected him to work through his anxieties for the sake of supporting their son.

Second, Jeff's story shows how people who have social anxiety can use avoidance behaviors to take control of a situation and lessen their anxiety. Under the guise of responding to important emails, Jeff used his phone to occupy himself so that he would not have to talk to other parents at the game. Other avoidance strategies he could have used include keeping a list of talking points (regardless of their relevance to the game) or asking the parents so many questions about themselves that they had no time to reciprocate.

Third, excessive alcohol use is a common complication of social anxiety. A person with social anxiety may not complain about participating in the social situation. Instead, they may use alcohol to manage their distress when they need to engage with other people. Jeff resorted to alcohol to loosen him up before the games and recover from the humiliation afterward.

Finally, social anxiety affects how you interpret what people say. When Jeff started engaging with other parents, he concluded that most of what they said was rejecting and humiliating. People with social anxiety can take a neutral statement and see it as a personal attack. The problem might lie in the brain's medial prefrontal cortex, which controls self-image. It's also part of your default-mode network (remember that?), which becomes active when your mind is at rest. When you're not actively thinking about something, the medial prefrontal cortex and other structures fill in the dead airspace for you. With social anxiety, the narrative your mind offers you to reflect upon is all the negative (or seemingly negative) feedback you've received from other people.

Shyness Versus Social Anxiety

Shyness differs from social anxiety, although both can make you feel insecure. Shyness is feeling awkward or uneasy in unfamiliar situations. However, shy people usually aren't debilitated by their discomfort around others. Socially anxious people are extremely sensitive to being humiliated, embarrassed, or rejected by others. This sensitivity takes the form of being preoccupied with what other people are thinking. Instead of listening to what someone is saying, you might be asking yourself, "Am I boring this person?"

If that's what you're thinking about while someone else is talking, you're bound to miss important points in the conversation, and you may even look preoccupied or zoned out. If someone notices that your eyes have glazed over and you're not paying attention, they may stop talking to you or confront you about not listening. Their reaction to your inattention will likely reinforce your fears of being criticized and rejected.

This behavior differs from that of a shy person, who may be slow to warm up but becomes more at ease as their confidence grows. This ability to adapt socially is what sets shyness apart from social anxiety. A socially anxious person has more intense reactions to social situations that don't improve with more exposure.

Performance-Only Type

This is a subtype of social anxiety that can make you avoid performing or public speaking altogether, even if you're not the center of attention. You may also have trouble speaking in everyday situations—not just formal ones. The stress of speaking in front of a large group of people can make you stutter or speak rapidly.

Performances that might cause anxiety include public speaking, singing, playing an instrument in front of others, presenting at work, or performing in skits. Individuals who have the performance-only subtype don't have any other type of social anxiety.

How Social Anxiety Develops

Adults rarely experience social anxiety for the first time unless they suffer an impactful event, like being publicly humiliated. It may also happen if they change social roles later in life, such as marrying someone from a different social class. Most often, social anxiety starts in childhood and adolescence, between the ages of 8 and 15. Shy children are more likely to develop social anxiety. Being raised by overprotective or rejecting parents also increases the risk of social anxiety.

Children learn how to interpret facial expressions by age 6. In this early stage of socialization, young children are at their most vulnerable. When children see an abundance of negative emotions expressed by their parents or older siblings, they can assume those negative emotions are how people feel about them. Because of these assumptions, they develop a negative self-image.

Social anxiety continues to develop during the transition from adolescence to adulthood. Peer groups and friendships play an influential role in the transition. Around age 15 to 17, adolescents become more interested in their peers and frequently compare themselves to them. Adolescents who see they are different from their peers interpret these differences negatively. The negative self-perceptions get stored in the prefrontal cortex for later use in developing social anxiety.

When children don't feel accepted by their peers, they become socially anxious. Even if the child has just a few friendships, feeling validated and accepted reduces their risk of later developing social anxiety. Therefore, healthy peer relationships protect against social anxiety.

Generalized Anxiety Disorder (GAD)

This is a worry-based disorder, making it different from fear-based phobias. Fear is an instinctive reaction to an imminent threat, whether it is real or imagined. Worry concerns itself with future events where you are uncertain of the outcome and expect negative consequences.

Worry is like rumination in depression. Rumination is where you run past or present events or situations over in your head, usually thinking about them in a negative light. The word comes from the behavior of cows when they eat. They regurgitate previously swallowed food to chew it again. Similarly, with rumination, you "chew" on thoughts repeatedly in your mind. With worry, you are chewing over future possibilities and imagining undesirable outcomes, and these outcomes can scale up to catastrophic consequences. Thinking about catastrophes all day long makes it easy to believe that the world is not a safe place.

Normal Versus Pathological Worry

When life is stressful and you're facing many challenges, it's natural to feel uncomfortable with uncertainty and worry about the future. But the person with GAD keeps their worries top of mind. When one situation resolves, another one follows. You also have worries that continually run in the background and never resolve.

The following chart presents a comparison of pathological and normal worry.

Pathological Worry	Normal Worry
Based on perfectionistic tendencies (concern over making mistakes and having high standards)	Reaction to a threat or expected danger
Causes procrastination	Capable of breaking through apprehension to take action
Needs lots of evidence	Able to tolerate some uncertainty
Ruminative (repetitive) thinking of "what if's"	Thoughts are reasonable given the danger
Uncontrollable and intrusive	Able to control and divert attention away
Nonspecific and multi-focused	Focus limited to specific/relevant situations
Tendency to catastrophize	Able to consider less extreme possibilities

With GAD and pathological worry, you feel on edge about nothing in particular. You can have nonspecific, free-floating anxiety. With GAD, you have excessive, uncontrollable, and often irrational worry about everyday things. You may not be able to stop thinking about potential problems. For example, when someone you love is late getting home, you'll worry that they were in an accident and cannot feel settled until you know their whereabouts. You may also try to stop others from doing things you fear will have a bad outcome.

Worriers procrastinate more than other people. Procrastination is putting off or avoiding something within your control. The reason worriers procrastinate might be that they have a high standard for evidence. They need more information to be absolutely convinced they are making the right decision.

Researchers have seen a link between certain aspects of perfectionism and pathological worry. They found that excessive concern over making mistakes and having high personal standards were positive predictors of pathological worry.

To demonstrate how these symptoms can manifest, let's look at Beth. Friends and family would describe Beth as a perfectionist: she's careful, detail-oriented, and dislikes presenting anything other than her best effort. She lives with a fear that she has always missed something, like an important deadline or appointment. Even if Beth checks her calendar, she can't shake the feeling that she's going to find out she dropped the ball somewhere and that someone will be angry with her.

She doesn't worry intensely every day. Beth can often distract herself with work, and during less stressful times, she may barely worry at all. But if she has downtime—especially when multiple sources of stress converge—the feeling of impending doom hits her like a pile of bricks. This feeling leads her to avoid or prohibit certain activities. For instance, she won't let her young son play football because she fears that he will suffer a paralyzing injury. She also dislikes unwinding before bedtime because this gives her too much time alone with her worries. The result is many nights spent tossing and turning.

When I interview people about their anxiety, I always ask about their sleep. Sleep is a very sensitive barometer of your distress level. A person with "normal" reactionary anxiety can feel stressed after a tough day but still sleep their usual amount. Once your anxiety reaches a certain level, it's bound to break up your sleep throughout the night or make you struggle to fall asleep because you can't stop your racing thoughts.

Here are other physical symptoms you can experience with GAD:

- *Heart palpitations.* This is where you can feel your heart beating in your chest. At rest, you should not feel your heart muscle contracting.
- *Shortness of breath.* You may feel that you can't catch your breath or can't breathe deeply.
- *Lightheaded or dizziness.* This experience differs from vertigo. With vertigo, you feel as though your environment is spinning. Vertigo is usually a sign of an inner ear disturbance. The lightheadedness that results from anxiety makes you feel like the room is getting dark or that you are on the verge of losing consciousness.
- *Weak legs.* Some people say that they feel their legs are going to "give way" and don't feel secure enough to stand up. Their legs may feel like rubber or jelly.

- *Chest and back pressure.* This is the sensation of someone pressing down on your chest. It can also feel like someone wedged you into a tight wall space and is crushing you.
- *Neck and shoulder pain.* This is usually from muscle tension, but it can be so painful that you may not associate it with anxiety. The muscle tension can leave you feeling exhausted in the evenings.
- *Headaches.* The quality of these headaches is often a dull ache throughout your head. It doesn't localize to a spot in your temples or scalp that you can massage, like with a tension headache. It doesn't have the throbbing quality of a migraine headache.
- *Heat emanating from the top of your head or your ears.* This is an atypical symptom that can make some people think, "Something is seriously wrong with me."
- *Lump in the throat.* This symptom can be very frightening, especially if the lump interferes with swallowing food. However, it most commonly manifests as a minor nuisance where you feel the back of your throat when you swallow.
- *Cloudy, blurry, or tunnel vision.* This can look like someone pulled a clear frosted shade over your eyes or darkened your peripheral vision, like a photograph with extreme vignetting. Your environment may appear slightly out of focus.

If you're experiencing any of these symptoms for the first time, it's important to see your doctor to rule out a medical cause before assuming that it's anxiety. For example, sometimes acid reflux can cause you to feel a lump in your throat, and changes in vision are associated with a variety of medical conditions, such as diabetes and cataracts.

For a diagnosis of generalized anxiety disorder, you must have at least 6 months' worth of constant and excessive worry about two or more areas of your life. The condition must also result in adverse effects on daily life and wellbeing. GAD starts later than many other anxiety disorders. The median age of onset is 30 years old. People may worry early in adolescence, but the complete disorder usually develops in early adulthood. People with anxious temperaments are at risk of developing GAD.

People with GAD often feel ashamed about their anxiety. They may feel slighted by family members who tell them they worry too much. Because of this, they may be reluctant to share their feelings or seek professional help.

It's important to understand that GAD is a chronic disorder that worsens and improves at different times but never completely disappears. In certain seasons of your life, you may be able to manage your symptoms without professional help. Then, stressful events may render your anxiety unmanageable, causing functional problems in your personal or professional life. There is nothing shameful about seeking help from people who can ease you through the difficult times.

Panic Disorder

Panic attacks are episodes of intense anxiety that are usually orders of magnitude greater than "ordinary" anxiety. The DSM-5 defines a panic attack as having a minimum of 4 out of 13 symptoms simultaneously. The manual divides these symptoms into a physical cluster and a mental cluster:

Physical

- Pounding or racing heart
- Sweating
- Trembling or shaking
- Feeling as if you are choking
- Chest pain or pressure on your chest
- Feeling short of breath or like you can't breathe
- Nausea or other types of gastrointestinal distress like heartburn
- Dizziness, lightheadedness, or feeling faint
- Numbness or tingling sensations
- Hot flashes or chills

Mental

- Derealization or depersonalization
- Fear of losing control or losing your mind
- Fear of dying

Panic attacks come on abruptly and peak within minutes. A true panic attack is short-lived and may last anywhere between a few minutes and half an hour. An unwanted social situation can trigger a panic attack, or the attacks can pop up without a trigger.

A *triggered* panic attack can occur when you are already anxious. You may be in a worry cycle or in a situation that stirs up your social anxiety. Then, your anxiety intensifies to the point of a panic attack. Once the panic levels off, you return to your previous state of worry. Patients have told me that their panic attacks last hours, but this usually means that they view the panic attack, the precipitating anxiety, and the subsequent anxiety as a single event.

A panic attack will feel *untriggered* if it begins from a relaxed state. When this happens, you might not connect the experience to anxiety, because the physical symptoms don't match how you feel or what you're thinking.

Panic at the Restaurant

I belong to a book club of nine women. Each month, one person chooses a book that we all read. Then, we meet to discuss the book, socialize, and share a meal. We call ourselves Books and Bubbles, because our discussion always includes alcohol—typically champagne. We usually meet at someone's home, but one month we met at a Mexican restaurant. It was when the country saw a window of hope that the COVID-19 pandemic was finally under control, and our leaders encouraged us to go forth and socialize. Even though we enjoyed meeting in each other's homes, it was exciting to get back into the world and enjoy dining in a restaurant. I love Mexican food and was excited to have my favorite drink, a margarita.

Other recently liberated people crowded the restaurant, so the server stuffed the nine of us into a tight corner at the back. The restaurant's front opened up to a patio with ample airflow, but this air fell off before it reached our corner. Despite the low oxygen levels, we engaged in our usual activities, catching up on one another's lives while we ate and imbibed.

Shortly after I finished my drink, I felt a wave of heat and nausea. I looked up from the table, and it seemed like the room was moving like a boat, slowly rising and falling. It also felt as though the room was closing in. I dreaded the idea of throwing up at the table. I have never thrown up in public and, without question, did not want to throw up at a table where everyone was eating.

I stood up and hurried off to the restroom. I have a strong aversion to public restrooms that has not reached the phobia level, but the disgust factor is still pretty high. My fear of vomiting at the table largely dwarfed the restroom aversion, allowing me to dash into the small one-person room. I immediately sat on the floor in front of the toilet and prepared myself to throw up. Even though my face was dreadfully close to the toilet seat, nothing happened. I gave it a few minutes, and my nausea improved.

I stood up and splashed cold water on my face. I then steadied myself on my feet and returned to the table. My friends asked if I was okay, and I told them I felt nauseous. "Oh, it must be something you ate," one offered. Feeling confused about what was happening, I agreed it must have been the spicy enchiladas. After all, it had been over a year since I'd eaten at a restaurant. Within a few minutes, the feeling returned, except this time I felt the imminent threat of diarrhea. As before, the table and my friends subtly swayed from side to side. It even seemed like the lights were dimming. I thought, "I will be forever embarrassed if I pass out at the table and eject loose stool all over myself for everyone to see." So I stood and returned to the bathroom.

This time, as I prepared myself to sit on the toilet, I no longer felt I had to go. My stomach still didn't feel completely normal, but I didn't need to use the restroom immediately. I decided my body must be warning me that it needs to expel whatever I'd ingested, but it was giving me time to get home so I could be in the comfort of my own bathroom.

I exited the bathroom and told my friends I had to leave because I wasn't feeling well. I hurried to the front door and out to my car. I felt confident to drive because, I thought, if I had to throw up, I'd rather do it on the side of the road than in that tight restaurant bathroom—or worse, on the floor in front of all of those people. Five minutes into my trip, everything I felt at the restaurant lifted. The cool outside air felt nourishing, and I inhaled it as if I were taking my first breaths.

I arrived home within 10 minutes, and there was no need to run to the bathroom. I felt the same way I did before I left my house. However, as a caution, I went to my bedroom and waited just in case I got another surge of nausea. Two hours later, and still, nothing. One of my friends called to check up on me, and I told her how I felt fine as soon as I left the restaurant and got some fresh air. I blamed the experience on something I ate and on feeling trapped in that small corner with little air circulation.

But my nausea and bowel issues disappeared and didn't return. So how could it be something I ate?

I churned that experience over in my head for a while and concluded that I'd had a panic attack. It was hard for me to come to this conclusion because I hadn't been anxious, and everything I experienced was physical (except for the derealization experience of the room swaying). When my son suffered his "claw hand," his panic intensified the anxiety he'd had about his schoolwork. But not so for me. I was having a great time, laughing with my friends, happy to be out in public again.

So in some ways, untriggered panic hardly feels like panic. Panic implies angst and distress, but I was hardly in any distress. This mismatch of experience and emotion is why many people with panic disorder will believe they have a physical problem, sometimes for years, before seeking help for an anxiety disorder. It's a typical story that someone with panic disorder has been to the emergency room four or five times for their panic attacks. Or they've had thousands of dollars in medical workups, like gastrointestinal studies or heart stress tests, before someone concludes that they have panic attacks.

The term "panic" is sometimes misleading, because it implies that you are aware of your fear. But in this context of panic attacks, it's your sympathetic system that panics. Your amygdala responds to a threat that doesn't exist and triggers a false alarm. My panic attack didn't feel triggered by anxiety; my high-salt meal and strong margarita probably triggered it. Salty food and preservatives like monosodium glutamate (MSG) can increase lactic acid levels in your cells. Alcohol also increases lactic acid. The acidic environment activates a fear response from your amygdala.

So, upon reflection, my experience *was* from something I ate.

Nocturnal Panic Attacks

The most extreme form of untriggered panic attacks occur while you're in the deepest phase of sleep. We call these nocturnal panic attacks. When a nocturnal panic attack awakens you, you can wake up very confused and disoriented. Unlike daytime panic attacks, when you are fully aware of your surroundings, nocturnal panic attacks can create significant fear and terror.

Some researchers consider nocturnal panic attacks to be a more severe form of panic disorder. We don't know why some people panic while they're sleeping, but there seems to be a connection between nocturnal panic attacks and sleep terrors. Sleep terrors happen as you are transitioning from deep sleep to lighter stages of sleep. You awaken abruptly and feel confused. Sleep terrors are more common in children, and they usually grow out of them, but many adults with nocturnal panic attacks also have a history of night terrors.

Panic Attacks Versus Panic Disorder

You can have isolated panic attacks that don't have many long-term consequences. It's estimated that 20% of people have a panic attack at some point in their lives. But only a minority of those people progress to having panic disorder.

Panic disorder is an anxiety disorder that entails recurring panic attacks. Their repetitive nature instills fear and distress. Sometimes, people develop agoraphobia where they do not want to leave their home or avoid certain places that they fear will not provide a place to escape to safety. Agoraphobia is a separate anxiety disorder that I will discuss in the next section.

To be considered to have a panic disorder, you need to have more than one panic attack within a short time frame—days or weeks—followed by at least a month of worrying that you will have another attack. You may obsessively worry about what will happen if you have another attack.

That worry can lead you to make extensive changes to your routine to avoid having another attack or avoid being in an unsafe or unfamiliar place when you have an attack. For example, you may cancel an upcoming trip because you fear you may have an attack on the way to your destination or once you arrive.

Panic disorder typically starts in a person's early to mid-twenties. Some people have attacks daily or multiple times a day. I would consider an attack that occurs once a week to be moderately frequent, and infrequent attacks would be one to two per month.

Panic attacks can come and go and vary in their frequency. Another presentation is an outbreak of frequent attacks that lasts for weeks or months before going into remission for several years. Stressful events can trigger a relapse in symptoms, as can an illness like a severe case of pneumonia or stomach flu.

You can have panic attacks as part of other disorders, like post-traumatic stress disorder, obsessive-compulsive disorder, and generalized anxiety disorder. But with panic disorder, it's all about the panic attacks and the things you do to avoid them.

Agoraphobia

In previous versions of the DSM, agoraphobia was an add-on qualifier of panic disorder. If you had panic disorder and developed agoraphobia with it, your diagnosis was panic disorder with agoraphobia. With this construct, agoraphobia was seen only as a complication of panic disorder.

Although about 30% of people with panic disorder develop agoraphobia, researchers made two important observations:

- Some people experience agoraphobic symptoms before they start having panic attacks.
- Agoraphobia is a feature of other anxiety disorders.

In 2013, the DSM-5 promoted agoraphobia to an independent anxiety disorder. With this change, if you have panic disorder and develop agoraphobia, you have two diagnoses: panic disorder and agoraphobia.

Agoraphobia is the fear of being in places that trigger your anxiety and where you cannot easily escape or get help. For the diagnosis, you must have an extreme amount of fear or anxiety about two out of five of these situations:

- Taking public transportation, like buses and planes.
- Being in an open space, like a parking lot, park, or bridge.
- Being in enclosed places, like a supermarket or theater.
- Waiting in line or being in a crowd.
- Being alone outside the house.

With agoraphobia, you fear or avoid these situations because you may not be able to escape if you become panicked or have an incapacitating or embarrassing symptom. In more severe cases of agoraphobia, you can become anxious at the thought of these places without ever going to them.

Agoraphobia causes a lot of distress and impairment in everyday life. People suffering from it may become entirely housebound, relying on others when they need to leave their homes. Unfortunately, agoraphobia is chronic and rarely resolves on its own. Without treatment, more than a third of the people become entirely homebound and unable to work.

People with agoraphobia can feel demoralized, hopeless, and helpless. Depression is a common outcome in people with moderate to severe agoraphobia. Some people cope with the anxiety by using alcohol, pills, or other substances and develop a substance-use disorder.

Agoraphobia is persistent and progressive. Long-term sufferers have a hard time breaking away from their symptoms, especially once they become homebound.

The avoidance is not always an active process, like refusing to leave the house or arranging grocery delivery. It can involve more subtle planning behaviors like rearranging your schedule to avoid encountering a feared situation or keeping your residence close to family members so that you don't have to use public transportation to visit them.

My father has a fear of flying. Because of this, we limited our family vacations to drivable destinations. "Drivable" included only one overnight stop. That meant, as Floridians, we could never visit our family in California, because 3 days of driving with bickering children in the back seat is listed in the dictionary under "mental torture." Visiting Europe or any other place out of the country was never a consideration for us.

As a child, I didn't know that my father was afraid to fly. I thought he liked to drive and "sightsee," as he would call it. It wasn't until years later, when friends invited my parents to attend a party in Las Vegas, that I saw just how phobic he was of airplanes. He refused to go, and my mother refused to go alone.

I don't know what threats my mom used on him, but at age 58, he flew on an airplane for the first time in his life. He survived the trip and even managed to enjoy himself in Las Vegas. But the gains were short-lived, because after he returned home, he resumed his insistence that airplanes are unsafe. He justified surviving the trip as "the grace of God" and had no intentions of "testing" any more airplanes.

Some fears that underlie the avoidance may change depending on your life stage. Although agoraphobia is rare in children, children can show early signs of fearing being alone outside. Adult fears are related to having panic attacks or any level of anxiety in a place where they can't get to safety or privacy. Older adults can develop a fear of falling and begin to avoid standing in lines or being in crowded places where someone may cause them to lose their balance. On the surface, avoiding these situations may seem prudent for someone who is a fall risk. But the person who develops agoraphobia will overestimate the fall risk and avoid any situation where they fear they may fall and can't get help.

A person who is already having panic attacks is more likely to develop agoraphobia in late adolescence. If you don't have panic attacks, agoraphobia more typically arises in your mid- to late twenties.

Separation Anxiety Disorder

Separation anxiety is not just a disorder of a child missing their mother. It can first appear in children, but it can also start in adults, especially after a life-altering event like the death of a loved one, marriage, or the birth or adoption of a child. A 2014 study by Pini and colleagues concluded that separation anxiety disorder is more common in adults than in children.

Separation anxiety is a form of excessive fear or anxiety concerning separation from attachment figures. We expect a one-year-old child to be anxious around strangers or become anxious when pulled from their caregiver's bosom. However, this anxiety disappears as you mature. When anxiety continues past this point, we consider it developmentally inappropriate—and, therefore, a disorder.

According to the DSM-5, you must have three out of eight of the following characteristics:

- Excessive distress when you anticipate or experience separating from home or important attachment figures.
- Fear of losing or harm coming to significant attachment figures.
- Worry about harm coming to you, such as via accident or kidnapping, and that event separating you from your attachment figure.
- Refusal to go to essential places like school or work or reluctance to leave home because of the separation.
- Fear of being alone or without attachment figures, at home or elsewhere.
- Refusal to sleep away from home or without your attachment figure nearby.
- Recurrent nightmares on the theme of separation.
- Distressing physical symptoms like headaches, stomachaches, nausea, or vomiting from anticipated separation.

These fears must last 4 weeks for children and 6 months for adults.

Separation anxiety looks different across the lifespan. Young children with separation anxiety feel helpless without their mother or surrogate. They worry about abandonment or harm afflicting their parent. As a result, they'll often cry out for them, follow them around the house, and only eat food that their parent prepares. Sometimes, the child's distress leads their parents to feel incredibly guilty when they have to leave the child with a babysitter or go to work.

Older children can feel extreme distress when around unfamiliar people, places, or things, similar to someone with social anxiety. They may fear for their safety, as if someone may kidnap them or fall victim to an accident. They may feel "sick" every morning before school or refuse to go to summer camp. A teenager who goes to a sleepover may need to call home or text several times to check in with their parents.

Adults with separation anxiety focus less on parents and caregivers and more on other close relationships, such as romantic partners, children, and pets. Young adults may not want to go away to college or only seek out jobs that allow them to work from home.

Separation anxiety can lead to overprotective parenting. You may become overly concerned about your children's welfare and restrict their freedom. That said, separation anxiety is not always at the root of overprotective parenting. One way to tell the difference between parental overcontrol and separation anxiety is that the person with separation anxiety will be overprotective of their spouse. Overprotective behavior can lead to marital issues if the spouse resents you treating them like a child.

Separation Anxiety and Attachment

Some have theorized that separation anxiety is a root cause of panic disorder. But later studies didn't confirm the link. Instead, they showed that separation anxiety disorder might be a precursor to many disorders, including personality disorders.

However, there is a relationship between anxious attachment style and separation anxiety. Attachment refers to the bond you form with people in close relationships, such as your parents, children, close friends, or romantic partners. Psychologists John Bowlby and Mary Ainsworth first developed attachment theory, but other researchers have since expanded it. According to Bowlby's model, there are three attachment styles:

- Secure

- Insecure-Anxious

- Insecure-Avoidant

An individual with a secure attachment style feels comfortable letting people know them and is confident that the other person will always be there when needed. With the two insecure styles, people are anxious about being abandoned or avoid intimacy with others.

If you have an anxious attachment style, you are clingy in relationships and always on alert for the subtlest sign of rejection. Trust is difficult for you, and relationships are a roller coaster of emotions. You can drive people away with your suspicions. Your fear of rejection can lead you to prematurely end relationships to avoid being rejected or abandoned by your partners.

If you have an avoidant attachment style, you can appear aloof in relationships. Essentially, you're not very reactive to people. When you feel threatened in a relationship, you may ignore the threat and rely on your own resources to get you through the crisis. It's as if you are entirely independent of everyone else. Your partner or friend may feel that you don't need them.

How Do We Become Attached?

Attachment begins between a newborn and its primary caregiver and continues through childhood. As you develop, you rely on your caregiver for reassurance and safety.

A parent builds attachment with the infant through physical closeness, touch, reassuring facial expressions, and establishing a sense of security. In the infant stage, you can see this attachment building when the baby coos and the parent responds with a smile and a kiss. In the toddler stage, you see this when the child explores a new environment by taking a few steps away from the parent, then returns to the parent and holds on to their leg. After venturing away again, the child looks back to ensure that things are still okay at home base. They may even bring you a stick they picked up off the floor. This offering helps them gain reassurance that the parent is still there after they leave.

The back-and-forth behavior of exploring the world and returning to safety creates a strong bond. The parent acts as a safe base for the child to explore the world and a safe place to retreat to when distressed. As you get older, your important attachment figures shift from parents to close friends and romantic partners.

Some parenting styles can interfere with this process and lead to insecure attachments. If your parent is inattentive and unresponsive, you may become overly self-reliant. This self-reliance can lead to an insecure-avoidant style. Being an unresponsive parent is more than simply being too busy cleaning the house to talk or not wanting to play the same game for the eighth time. Instead, the unresponsiveness is more on the level of neglect or absence. A depressed parent, for example, may not engage with their child, and this emotional absence can have a ripple effect that leads to attachment difficulties.

A child may develop an insecure-anxious attachment style as a response to harsh and critical parents. Contrary to the insecure-avoidant person who felt invisible and ignored, the insecure-anxious person received too much negative attention, and this affected their view of themselves and others.

But trauma and less-than-ideal parenting aren't always the culprits behind insecure attachment styles. Some people are just hardwired to be anxious or avoidant when relating to others.

Some attachment studies found children identified as insecure-avoidant would explore their environment and appear to forget their parent was around. When the parent left the room, they continued to play with toys and seemed unfazed. Children who were insecure-anxious cried when their parents left the room, and the parents couldn't console them when they returned. Securely attached children would cry when their parents left them alone, but they accepted the comforting gestures and returned to exploring when their parents returned. All the children had similar upbringings, and their behavior was not related to poor parenting.

Insecure attachments and personality disorders share some features. People with personality disorders experience problems in relationships, and some of these problems relate to bonding and intimacy. People with avoidant and dependent personalities show insecure-anxious attachment. But just because you have an insecure attachment style does not mean you will have a personality disorder.

Separation anxiety in adults is an underdiagnosed condition, and because of this, we don't have standard treatment protocols. I think this is because separation anxiety often pairs with other disorders that receive more attention, such as social anxiety, panic disorder, and post-traumatic stress disorder.

People with separation anxiety can feel too embarrassed to talk about their problems with others, so they may never get help. Even if they have another problem, they may seek help but never discuss their separation fears. The upside, though, is that most people who develop separation anxiety disorder recover within 10 years.

Anxiety Due to a Medical Condition

Your mind and body are intimately connected, and sometimes anxiety is caused by a medical problem. Here, you only experience anxiety when the medical disorder is active; when the medical issue resolves, so does your anxiety.

We know that certain medical conditions generate pathological anxiety. If you first had the medical condition and then developed anxiety, you would be diagnosed with anxiety due to this medical condition. Sometimes, anxiety is the squeaky wheel that draws attention to the medical problem. You may not realize that you have a medical condition, and it's the anxiety that sends you to your doctor for a workup. Panic attacks are the most common anxiety symptoms related to medical conditions, as they can lead to worry, sleep problems, and a cascade of other issues.

It's possible to develop another anxiety disorder after experiencing a medical illness. Let's say you have panic attacks, and a physical examination reveals that you have asthma. You had asthma as a child and grew out of it—that is, until you moved to an area with asthma-triggering allergens. Now, you have asthma attacks that you can't get under control no matter what you do. Once while alone on your back deck, you suffered a sudden asthma attack, and you didn't have your inhaler with you. Your neighbor saw you struggling for breath and called 911. Emergency medical services transported you to the hospital, where you received breathing treatments.

This near-death experience was so terrifying that you are now afraid to go outside because you believe the tree pollen triggered this attack. You never want to be left alone and insist a family member always stays with you. After 8 months with no attacks, you allow yourself to be alone, but you remain housebound.

In this scenario, asthma triggered the panic attacks. Therefore, your primary diagnosis would be anxiety due to asthma. While your asthma was hard to manage, you continued to have sudden-onset breathing difficulties. Because of these unrelenting asthma attacks and the trauma of nearly dying from one of them, you developed agoraphobia and separation anxiety disorder.

Here are some medical conditions that can cause anxiety.

Endocrine Diseases

Hyperthyroidism arises from an overproduction of thyroid hormones by the thyroid gland.

Grave's Disease is the most common hyperthyroid condition.

A *phaeochromocytoma* is a benign tumor of the adrenal gland. It's an uncommon condition in which the adrenal gland secretes excessive amounts of adrenaline and noradrenaline.

Hypoglycemia refers to low blood sugar levels. This is most commonly associated with diabetes, but other conditions and medications can cause you to experience a drop in blood sugar as well.

Cushing's syndrome happens when your body produces too much cortisol. As cortisol is a stress hormone, your body responds as if it is under high stress.

Cardiovascular Disorders

Congestive heart failure is a condition in which your heart muscle weakens and doesn't keep up with the body's blood flow needs. It can result from a temporary condition, like a viral infection or from a progressive condition.

A *pulmonary embolism* occurs when a blood clot breaks off, usually from your leg veins, and travels to your lungs. The clot gets lodged in an artery in your lung and causes tissue damage.

In *atrial fibrillation*, the top portion of your heart beats uncontrollably. You can still have a regular heart rhythm with atrial fibrillation since the bottom part of your heart muscle (ventricles) controls your heartbeat. With the irregular atrial activity, you might still feel faint or anxious or have palpitations.

Respiratory Illnesses

Chronic obstructive pulmonary disease (COPD) causes progressively less airflow in the lungs.

With *asthma*, your airways become inflamed and cut off your airflow.

Pneumonia is an infection of the lungs that causes your air sacs to fill with fluid.

Metabolic Disturbances

Vitamin B12 plays an essential role in red blood cell production, cellular DNA, and nerve cell function, so *vitamin B12 deficiency* is a serious problem. Plants don't contain vitamin B12, so vegans and vegetarians are at risk of deficiency if they don't take supplements. Since B12 absorbs into the body in the small intestine, people who undergo gastric bypass surgery need to take B12 shots to maintain normal B12 levels.

Porphyria is a metabolic disorder that is caused by a buildup of a chemical called porphyrin, a building block of hemoglobin. A milder version affects the skin, but the acute version affects the nervous system and can make you anxious.

Neurological Illness

Your vestibular system, in your inner ear, controls your balance. *Vestibular dysfunction* can make you feel unsteady, disoriented, and even nauseous.

Encephalitis is an inflammation of the brain caused by either an infection or an autoimmune reaction. The severity of symptoms depends on which part of the brain is affected.

Disorganized electrical activity causes *seizures* in the brain. Since the nerves are activated in a disorganized fashion, if you have a seizure that affects your motor pathways, you'll get uncontrollable jerking. When the seizure affects your emotional or cognitive parts of the brain, you might experience unstable moods, anxiety, or psychosis.

Whether you suffer anxiety associated with a medical condition or anxiety that occurs due to a medical condition, you need to know that medical conditions may cause anxiety. Typically, anxiety begins in adolescence, but it can begin later in adulthood. If you have unmanageable anxiety as an adult, see your primary care doctor for a general checkup and blood work to ensure that a physical condition isn't causing your anxiety.

This chapter discussed several different types of pathological anxiety that the DSM-5 categorizes as anxiety disorders. Next, you'll learn about other conditions not considered anxiety disorders but that can cause anxiety.

CHAPTER 3

Other Anxious Conditions

I discussed in the previous chapter how the DSM-5 anxiety disorders can cause anxiety. There are also conditions that aren't in this category that still generate a lot of anxiety. In this chapter, I focus on eight of these conditions.

Obsessive-Compulsive Disorder (OCD)

Most parents instinctively know that they should not choose favorites among their children. At least, they shouldn't express it or treat their children differently because of it. Similarly, as a psychiatrist, I believe that all patients are equal; everyone's distress is unique and significant to them.

Still, if I had to choose one disorder that locks you into the most mental distress, I would choose obsessive-compulsive disorder. Hollywood movies depict OCD as a disorder involving rituals like checking, cleaning, or avoiding stepping on a crack. As a result, I think many people believe that's the gist of OCD. But it's so much more than checking, and the obsessions can be haunting.

The Airport Ritual

As I mentioned earlier, driving to the airport causes me significant anxiety. I'm a checker when I'm anxious. I always worry that I'm going to leave something important behind, like my ID or phone. As I ride in the car, I check these two things multiple times. My checking process usually involves digging into my purse and touching the phone, but when I'm really uptight, I'll need to pull it out of my purse to look at it. I also pull out my overstuffed wallet and touch the top of my ID, tightly wedged in a card slot. I only need to touch the ID once. For future checks, I feel satisfied by peeking inside my purse, visualizing the ID tucked neatly away in its slot.

Usually, the first round of checking takes place in the driveway before I get into the car. But once in the car, I think, *What if my ID fell out of my purse and onto the driveway as I stepped into the car?* I've never seen that happen, but my mind thinks it could have happened. Therefore, once I sit down in the car, I must check again to ensure I didn't leave my ID on the driveway.

As we pull out of the driveway, I need to see the garage door completely close. We have an electronic garage door opener with a safety feature that will not allow it to close if it senses an object in its path. While I appreciate that this protects us from being crushed by the door, it becomes one more thing for me to check. Fortunately, though, seeing the door close is a one-time check. I've also learned to trust my husband's word that he saw it close.

My obsession with leaving behind my ID began when I lived in New York City and traveled to Florida to visit my family for the holidays. On one of these visits, I had to catch a taxi in the rain. As I watched cars pass with their "available" light turned off, I worried I might miss my flight when a car finally stopped for me. I quickly jumped into the car with my wet umbrella and struggled to close it before it broke. I felt extremely pressed for time and needed every single minute. As a time-saving measure, I had the taxi fare ready in my hand. When we pulled up to the drop-off area, I quickly handed the driver the money and bounced out of the car. It was still raining, and my umbrella was useless, so I grabbed my bag and ran for cover. It wasn't until I entered the security line that I realized I didn't have my driver's license. I must have dropped it in the taxi when I pulled the money out of my wallet. Not having my driver's license could mean spending Christmas alone without my family, and I was desperate to see them.

I begged the security person to let me use another form of ID. I told him I must have lost my license on the trip to the airport in the hopes he'd feel sorry for me. He made me step out of line to speak to a security agent, who turned his back to me as he made a phone call. Time was ticking— I only had about 30 minutes to get through the gate. My anxiety soared. After a few minutes of mumbling to someone, he allowed me to pass through the security line using my hospital photo ID and a bank card. I was so relieved. As I nearly ran for the gate, it felt like his eyes were boring into my back. I didn't look back for fear that if I met his gaze, he'd change his mind and snatch me back through the line or, worse, turn me into a pillar of salt.

You're probably thinking, *That's some weird stuff you do. You must have OCD!* I agree that I have obsessive-compulsive tendencies that emerge when I'm stressed, but the checking behaviors are limited to traveling. Fears of leaving something behind don't intrude into my thoughts when I'm not traveling. Most importantly, though, my checking rituals don't come close to causing the misery that people with moderate-to-severe OCD endure.

What is OCD?

In the DSM-5, OCD was pulled out of the anxiety disorders category and given its own: obsessive-compulsive and related disorders. With OCD, you either have obsessions, compulsions, or both. Most people with OCD have both.

Obsessions

Obsessions are repeated unwanted thoughts, images, or fears that get stuck in your head and cause mental distress. You don't always feel in control of your thoughts. They pop into your mind at inappropriate times, and you're not able to dismiss them and think about something else. The spontaneous, uncontrollable nature of the thoughts makes them intrusive.

An important criterion for the disorder is that the obsessions and compulsions are time consuming, often taking an hour or more. This distinguishes OCD from ordinary intrusive thoughts and repetitive behaviors. For example, after accidentally leaving my garage door open a few times, I now check it every time I leave the house. This would be considered a normative response to my mistake of leaving it open. An excessive response would be spending 30 minutes in the driveway, lifting the door up and down several times, then spending another 30 in the car worrying if it had spontaneously reopened.

People with moderate OCD may spend 3 to 4 hours engaged in obsessive thinking or compulsions. Those with severe OCD may spend most of the day thinking about their particular obsessions or engaged in rituals to reduce the anxiety related to these obsessions.

Obsessions are the hidden part of the disorder, because the torment is entirely in your head. If you don't use compulsions to cope with them, you're left managing the distressing thoughts on your own. Although it's not an officially recognized term, some people will refer to OCD with only obsessions as *pure-OCD*.

There are common obsessional themes with OCD:

- Contamination (with or without cleaning compulsions)
- Symmetry or precision
- Forbidden or taboo thoughts
- Religious thoughts
- Harm

Contamination OCD can take many forms. There is the usual obsession with dirt, germs, bodily fluids, or infectious agents. It can also take the form of feeling physically or spiritually unclean. Spiritual contamination overlaps with religious obsessions, which some people refer to as *scrupulosity*. With this focus, you get overwhelmed with concerns about displeasing God or not engaging in enough spiritual activities, such as praying.

People with the symmetry theme focus on counting and having things in order. Perfectionistic obsessions also fall under the precision theme, as they worry about being correct or living within a particular set of rules. With forbidden or taboo thoughts, people become overwhelmed with thoughts or images of perverse sexual acts or desires. Some worry about their sexual orientation.

With the harm obsessions, people fear bringing harm to themselves or others. Harm obsessions can generate disturbing images. For example, a new mother may have intrusive images of seeing herself drop her baby from a window. Some see flashes of themselves decapitating someone. These images are traumatizing because they can make you feel as though you actually performed the act.

People with OCD are sometimes ashamed to tell others about these thoughts. They can develop superstitions around this—for example, that telling someone will cause the thoughts to come to pass. I once had a patient tell me about a harm obsession years into treatment. He feared that if he spoke about it, one of his children would die unless he counted to 50 four times. He felt safe to tell me because he'd already completed three counting cycles before the session.

These superstitions are an example of dysfunctional beliefs common to people with OCD, who have trouble distinguishing between beliefs and facts. OCD makes it difficult to know whether your concerns are realistic. An example of this is believing that if you don't turn your faucet on and off 20 times, it will leak and flood your home. If you ask this person, "How can your house flood from turning off the faucet less than 20 times? If it's off, it can't leak, right?" The person may reply, "I don't know how it can happen, and it probably won't, but I can't make myself stop thinking that it will."

In this scenario, if the person can't be convinced that the feared outcome isn't possible, their belief would be considered *delusional*. A delusion is a fixed false belief that's held even in the face of contradictory evidence. If you have OCD with delusional beliefs, this is one of the few instances where it would not be considered a psychotic illness. The term "delusional beliefs" would be a course specifier, providing additional information about your OCD symptoms.

Compulsions

Compulsions are repetitive behaviors employed to offset the anxiety caused by an obsession. You don't have to develop a compulsion for every obsession. In my checking example, my obsession is that I will not have essential travel items when I need them. I deal with that fear by repeatedly checking for these items. Even when I know the items are there, touching them and seeing them helps ease my general anxiety about getting to the airport.

Examples of compulsions are opening and closing your car door five times before you can get in the car. Someone with a symmetry obsession may walk into a room that has tiles on the floor and count all the tiles before they feel comfortable in the room. The compulsions are hard to resist performing and will typically give you a lot of anxiety if you don't follow all the steps. As I previously mentioned, for a diagnosis of OCD, the compulsions need to be time-consuming. So if you're someone who checks that you locked your door twice before you leave every morning, that's compulsive, but it's not a disorder. There's a certain degree of normal compulsivity or obsessional thinking that anyone can have.

Even if you recognize that your compulsions are unreasonable, you'll need to perform them to relieve your anxiety. For example, let's say you fear getting an HIV infection. Logically, you know that the infection is transmitted through human fluid exchange. You can't get it from touching a doorknob or shaking someone's hand (if neither of you has an open sore). But then you go to a crowded party and someone sneezes behind you. You imagine their nasal drops penetrating your shirt and seeping into a hair follicle on your back, giving you HIV. You come to see me, and I tell you that's not a way to contract HIV. You leave my office feeling somewhat reassured, but you can't stop feeling anxious until you get tested … twice.

The gold standard treatment for OCD is cognitive behavioral therapy (CBT) with exposure and response prevention. This therapy exposes you to situations that trigger fears or urges to do your rituals and then helps you avoid performing them. You'll learn more about exposure therapy in the chapter on behavior tools.

OCD is a chronic condition that develops in early adulthood, although some people show signs as early as childhood. It's usually a gradual onset.

Sometimes, the symptoms can get so severe that you can't work or maintain a relationship. When your symptoms are severe, medication treatment may be the best option. We also have neuromodulation treatments, which are nonmedication options such as transcranial magnetic stimulation and electroconvulsive therapy. You'll learn more about the medication and neuromodulation treatments in Chapter 5: Prescription Medications.

Body-Focused Repetitive Behaviors

Body-focused repetitive behaviors is a broad term that refers to specific types of compulsive behaviors that cause self-injury. The two most common compulsive behaviors are hair pulling (trichotillomania) and skin picking (excoriation disorder).

Trichotillomania

This is a condition in which you repeatedly pull out your hair, usually strand by strand. Even though trichotillomania has "mania" in the name, it has nothing to do with the mania of bipolar disorder. In fact, trichotillomania was listed under impulse control disorders in earlier versions of the DSM, and now it's listed under obsessive-compulsive and related disorders. This categorization is a better match for these behaviors because they really are more compulsive than impulsive. You don't randomly do them; you can't stop doing them.

Trichotillomania is much more than that behavior. It's a complex sensory experience. First, anxiety or a buildup of tension precedes the urge to pull hair. Pulling the hair relieves that tension. Sometimes, random hairs satisfy the urge to pull, but the hair needs to meet specific criteria, like being the right texture or length. Some derive intense pleasure from seeing the root bulb, and you have to pull just right to get that root. This specificity is one reason a person may need to pull many hairs until they get the "right" one.

Once a person secures the hair, it's common to manipulate it. They may like the way it feels rolling between their fingers or between their teeth. Some will suck on the root. There's usually a lot of relief or gratification from this ritual, but the relief is short-lived, because the behavior causes significant distress. Sufferers can feel shame for needing to do this or frustration about feeling out of control. They may attempt to stop pulling and succeed for a while. Then, something triggers them to do it again.

People with trichotillomania can pull hair from anywhere on the body. The usual places are the scalp, eyebrows, and eyelashes. Because they typically want to hide this behavior from others, they will rotate sites to pull to avoid creating prominent bare spots. If they are picking a noticeable area, like the scalp, they may wear hats or scarves to hide them.

Usually, negative emotions like anger or frustration drive the behavior, but sometimes it's an automatic behavior with little conscious awareness. An example of this is pulling your hair while you're watching television. Here, hair pulling can be a soothing behavior similar to a child's thumb sucking. The hair pulling still serves the purpose of calming mental tension, but you're not intentionally pulling the hair to get relief.

Some people with trichotillomania may pull hair from another source, like hair from a pet or fibers from a sweater. Here, pulling foreign hair is an extension of pulling their own hair and a progression of the disorder. The problem starts with pulling one's own hair first and advances to other pulling behavior.

Excoriation Disorder

Skin picking shares many characteristics of hair pulling. The most common picking places are the face, hands, and arms. Most people with excoriation disorder use their fingernails, but some use tweezers or bite their skin (often on the hands and cuticles). Sometimes they focus on a pimple or bump, but often they pick at healthy skin until they make a sore. Then later, they pick at the scabs. Similar to the rituals with trichotillomania, some people will play with the scabs or even chew them.

People can spend hours doing this and usually hide these rituals from others. You may be able to hide how compulsively you engage in the behavior, but it's hard to hide the evidence of chewed fingers or sores. Outward evidence of the problem can make you anxious around others and fear they will discover your problem.

You may think, *If I chewed my fingers, I would be self-conscious, too.* This may be so, but the shame and embarrassment of excoriation disorder go beyond vanity concerns. Because this disorder makes you feel out of control and flawed, you fear your private pain will be exposed once someone sees the evidence. You assume people will connect the dots between your skin picking and your mental issues. A close friend or acquaintance may see your chewed fingers as a sign that you struggle with anxiety, but it's a stretch to assume that your inner pain will be obvious to ordinary acquaintances. Referential thinking assumes that all external clues point to you, and it shares characteristics with other compulsive disorders, like OCD.

Both disorders usually start in adolescence, right around puberty. They are chronic disorders that come and go in spurts. You can struggle with them for weeks, then stop or do it at a less intense level for months or years at a time. An example of a mild form is when you spend a little time engaged in hair pulling or skin picking, but you still punish yourself or think less of yourself for doing it. You may have a few chewed fingers or a thin area of hair in your temple that's not very noticeable. You may go long periods without doing it, allowing your skin to heal and your hair to grow back. With a severe case, you can spend hours skin picking or hair pulling for weeks or months at a time. Severe skin picking or hair pulling can lead to serious infections like cellulitis or permanent skin scarring.

Those are the two body-focused repetitive behaviors that are listed as disorders in the DSM-5. Often, a person with either of these will engage in other repetitive behaviors. Some other body-focused repetitive disorders include nail biting (also called onychotillomania), lip biting, and nose picking.

These are not separate disorders, but behaviors anyone can engage in under stress, but not to the extent that it becomes uncontrollable. A person with trichotillomania or excoriation disorder may add these to their repertoire of compulsive behavior that they engage in with little control.

Treatments

People with mild cases often go without treatment, and the problem can resolve on its own. Since it's a compulsive disorder, the obstacle to overcome is controlling your urges. If you have a mild case, you can learn to recognize and avoid triggers that make you want to resume the behavior or find ways to distract yourself. If you have been doing these things for a while, you probably also need to strengthen your self-image.

When you can't control it on your own, there's therapy. One therapy used to help this condition is a type of cognitive behavior therapy called habit-reversal training. There's a self-help technique called *decoupling*, where you substitute the compulsive behavior with something else. Whenever you feel the tension that triggers your compulsion, you perform a different predesignated behavior instead of the compulsion. The other behavior decouples or disrupts the connection between the emotion and the compulsion. Engaging in the other behavior allows you to gain some control over the compulsive behavior.

We don't have any medications that are standardly used for this disorder. There is some evidence that inositol and N-acetylcysteine (NAC) might be helpful. Both are supplements that you can get without a prescription. Since the FDA doesn't regulate supplements as drugs, it's always a good idea to speak with a trusted healthcare provider about which brands and dosages to try. They can help you determine if the supplement is working and avoid interactions with any medications you may be taking.

Other alternative therapies include yoga, aerobic exercise, acupuncture, biofeedback, and hypnosis.

Hoarding

Compulsive hoarding and obsessive-compulsive disorder (OCD) are closely related and often occur together. In fact, in previous editions of the DSM, hoarding was a subtype of OCD. A person would have persistent thoughts of collecting or acquiring things or rituals of holding onto items.

But research using functional brain imaging shows that hoarding affects different areas of the brain than OCD. Therefore, with the DSM-5, hoarding and OCD were established as separate disorders under the obsessive-compulsive and related disorders.

The two core features of compulsive hoarding are excessively acquiring items and being unable to discard items. The result is a collection of clutter that reaches hazardous proportions and causes severe impairment in daily functioning.

First, let's look at the acquisition process. The most common acquisition method is buying, which often causes people to overspend and get into debt. Another method is collecting free items, like pamphlets and flyers. An example of this kind of hoarding is going to an event and taking all the programs. A smaller percentage of people with compulsive hoarding will steal items as part of the acquisition process. Because this is a compulsion, the need to acquire things is so strong that it's very difficult to disrupt it. If someone tries to stop it or circumstances make it difficult to collect things, they become intensely distressed.

The second feature is an insurmountable difficulty in discarding these possessions. The amassment of goods accumulates to the point of congesting key living areas. The congestion keeps sufferers from using the space as it was intended. Intended use is an important distinction, because it separates clutter in a basement or attic from the clutter in a living room. Filling areas of a home intended for storage would not count as hoarding activity, as it doesn't interfere with a person's ability to function.

On the other hand, people who compulsively hoard will fill their bedroom with stacks of old newspapers or collected items and not sleep in their bed. Similarly, they may not use the bathtub or kitchen because of clutter filling the usable area. If you visit a person who hoards, you will have difficulty finding a walking path or place to sit unless someone comes before you and clears a space.

Hoarding is not a disorder that exclusively affects prosperous communities. People acquire and retain whatever objects are available, regardless of their value across cultures. Also, the psychology of hoarding goes much deeper than the value of the object.

Some researchers have proposed that insecure attachments are a psychological cause of hoarding. We all have an instinctive need to attach to others, and the strength of those attachments determines how psychologically secure we feel. Early in development, we attach to our caregivers, and as we grow older, those attachments extend to other relationships, like significant others, children, extended family, and friends. We also assign sentimental value to objects because of the relationship we associate with those items.

With compulsive hoarding, you have a distorted view of the importance of ordinary objects. As a result, you compensate for your insecure attachments by overattaching to them. You need to save the objects from being destroyed. Your attachment can become so intense that you treat the items like living beings. Throwing away a newspaper from 1982 causes the same upset as having your dog taken away.

Hoarding Versus Collecting

Collectors acquire related things of value, like figurines or race cars. The accumulation is not considered clutter. Clutter is an unorganized jumble of unrelated or slightly related objects piled in a space meant for something else. Collectors often index and organize their possessions. The possessions are not just strewn about or thrown in piles. Some people have so many collected items that their homes feel cluttered, but their active living spaces are still functional, even if they're messy.

There are other reasons that people who hoard having difficulty discarding items. Researchers have found that hoarders have trouble with executive functions. Executive function is a term used to describe tasks such as making decisions, organizing, completing tasks, being attentive, and remembering things. Attention deficit hyperactivity disorder (ADHD) is a common co-occurring illness with hoarding disorder.

Therefore, it makes sense that if you have trouble making decisions, the path of least resistance is to keep something rather than assess its merits. If you lack good organizational skills, you won't know how to arrange your items in a way that optimizes your home's functionality.

Animal hoarding is an unofficial subtype of hoarding where people accumulate many animals but cannot provide a minimum standard of nutrition and sanitation. It's more than just having a lot of pets because they love animals. They acquire the animals but don't take care of them. The neglect is because of their poor executive function. They don't have the organizational skills to meet their needs or the vision to plan out how to take care of them. When you hoard animals, the urine and feces that accumulate in your home create even more health hazards than hoarding other items. Some even keep dead animals around, unwilling to dispose of them. This level of squalor becomes a community health threat.

Hoarding symptoms start early, between ages 11 and 15. But since children don't control their living spaces, having a parent who cleans up after them can mask the problem until around their mid-20s. As the years progress, so does the illness, with symptoms peaking in the mid-30s. It runs in families: 50% have a relative who also hoards.

Therapy is the best approach to treat hoarding disorder. A therapist will address the thoughts around acquiring and holding onto the items. Because the hoarder has an uncontrollable need to acquire and accumulate, it's not helpful to send them on a weekend getaway while you get rid of their stuff. That will only send them into a downward spiral of distress over the loss of their items. And it won't take long for them to accumulate more things.

We don't have medications specifically to treat hoarding disorder. In my experience, some medications, like antidepressants or antipsychotics, can help, but therapy is still needed to address the compulsive behavior.

Post-Traumatic Stress Disorder (PTSD)

Post-traumatic stress disorder occurs from exposure to extreme life-threatening stress, severe injury, or violence. A variety of emotions accompany PTSD, like guilt, shame, anger, and anxiety. Trauma and its aftermath are complex topics deserving of their own book. Here, I will focus on the way trauma creates anxiety.

Similar to the changes we saw with the DSM-5 and the compulsive disorders, PTSD was also considered an anxiety disorder in previous versions of the manual. The authors included PTSD in a new section called "Trauma and Stressor-Related Disorders."

As the name implies, PTSD starts with trauma. Trauma is something that poses an imminent threat to your life or harm to your physical or mental well-being. Examples of threats are sexual violence, physical harm, a natural disaster, or a life-threatening accident. Something like getting yelled at by your supervisor or being humiliated in front of your friends wouldn't cause PTSD. Although those situations are upsetting, they are not of the same magnitude as the trauma of a threat to your physical or mental integrity. Having a terminal illness, like cancer, does not qualify as trauma that causes PTSD. But you can have a traumatic response from a medical catastrophe that's sudden and unexpected, like waking up from anesthesia during surgery. The trauma doesn't have to result from your own experience. It can be something you witness—for example, as a bystander or first responder.

Suppose you are sitting on the front deck of your house reading a book and drinking a tall glass of lemonade when you see a car drive across your neighbor's lawn and hit their dog before crashing into the side of the house. The dog appears dead, and the car's front is so crumpled that you can only assume the driver is also dead. You call 911, and after they arrive, you witness them extract the unconscious driver from the car. The medics cover the person's face with an oxygen mask and put them in the back of the ambulance. You watch the ambulance sit in the driveway with the door closed for at least 15 minutes. As it drives away slowly, without a siren, you can only assume that the driver didn't survive.

You didn't know your neighbor very well, and you had no attachment to their dog, because you're not a dog person. But you can't stop picturing how the sleeping dog was startled by the sound of the car, similar to how the car startled you. You saw the dog move in your direction to get to safety before the car plowed him over. If only you could have reached out and pulled him toward you. But you were too far away, and it happened before you could react.

Before the accident, you didn't see the driver's face; after, you only saw glimpses as the paramedic put on his oxygen mask. But after seeing his picture in the local newspaper the next day, you have dreams of him driving into the wall with precise details of his face.

In the first weeks after witnessing the accident, you recognize that the experience upset you, and you'll need some time to get it out of your mind. But 3 months later, you're still having those dreams and not sleeping very well. The dreams aren't as frequent, maybe once a week, but they have expanded to include the dog. You decide to take a weekend trip to the beach with your family to speed up your recovery.

Before the trip, you avoided drinking lemonade, your favorite beverage, because it reminded you of the incident. But you know you can't avoid lemonade forever, and you want to get back to your life. So you sit on the back porch of the beach house your family rented and watch the kids play in the sand. While you unwind, you think, "this is exactly what I needed." As you close your eyes and sip your lemonade, you're jolted from your reverie by the sound of a yelping dog. Your heart pounds in your chest, and you feel faint and nauseous. "Did someone bring a dog to the beach?" You think, "Were we unlucky enough to get a house next to a family with a dog?"

You force yourself to breathe in slowly as you gather your thoughts when you hear the sound again. It's not the same sound, but it's similar. You look toward your children. It looks like you are watching them through a telescope. You can't tell if you have neighbors or if anyone else is on the beach. You only see your children throwing dirt at each other while your daughter squeals (or yelps) with delight.

PTSD Symptoms

PTSD symptoms are grouped into four categories.

Intrusion

Intrusion symptoms can involve memories of the event popping into your mind at unwanted times. You can experience these memories as nightmares of the event or daytime thoughts. The intrusive nature of the memories can make you feel retraumatized by forcing you to visualize the experience you desperately wanted to forget.

You can also re-experience the event as a dissociative experience. With dissociation, you experience parts of the trauma as if it were occurring in the present day. In the example of the car accident, you thought you heard the dog yelp. But your mind morphed your daughter's squeal into the sound the dog made when the car hit him. Because your daughter did squeal, what you heard what a misinterpretation of an existing sound.

Some re-experience the trauma with hallucinations of the event. Hallucinations are sensory perceptions you have when your senses aren't being stimulated. For example, a person who was sexually assaulted may continue to smell the body odor of the attacker. Someone witnessing an explosion may randomly smell smoke or hear crunching metal. These intrusive experiences can make people feel helpless and retraumatized.

Avoidance

This is going out of your way to avoid reminders of the trauma. You can avoid activities like driving a car if you've been in an accident, or you can avoid conversations around topics related to your trauma.

Sometimes, the avoidance is subtle. For example, few would remark on the fact that you stopped drinking lemonade after the car accident. The lemonade did not cause you harm, nor was it involved in the accident, but you connected it to the accident in your mind. The connection is so strong that when you resume drinking the lemonade in a similar situation of being relaxed and enjoying your downtime, the drink triggers you to re-experience part of the event.

Negative Thoughts or a Negative Mood Associated with the Trauma

An example of this would be someone who feels that they will not live very long or who always thinks something ominous is about to happen. In the car accident example, you develop what some people refer to as survivor's guilt. War veterans commonly experience survivor's guilt. For you, the most traumatic part of the experience was the dog. Even though you don't like dogs, you felt a connection with the dog in the way you both were relaxing on a lazy afternoon. You could have easily been the victim of the rogue driver. Instead, you remained comfortable in your chair while you watched the unsuspecting dog struggle to save himself.

It's not rational to punish yourself for not saving the dog. And most times with survivor's guilt, people rewrite the narrative and add a negative, self-loathing spin that makes them assume responsibility for the event. This thinking is part of the "negative cognitions" category of PTSD. Some thoughts can reach a nearly delusional level. For example, you can believe that the driver intentionally hit your neighbor and spared you and obsess over what factors the driver considered in making this arbitrary decision. Your thoughts can spiral into existential ruminations about the meaning of life and the certainty of death.

You may wonder, "In this hypothetical example, why didn't I feel worse about the man's death, especially if I don't like dogs?" Good question. For one thing, you didn't see the man's face until well after you experienced the traumatic event. You saw the oxygen mask, but by that point, you were already in such shock that his face and, therefore, his humanity didn't register. By contrast, you had a "bonding" moment with the dog who was engaging in a relatable relaxing activity before the car hit him. You met his eyes as he desperately attempted to escape harm. Even though he was an animal, you related to that instinctive drive to live. While the driver also died, he is the "adversary" who could have "chosen" to invade your yard instead of your neighbor's. Because you may not consciously understand these feelings, you can experience anxiety and guilt about your focus on the dog.

Vigilance or Hyperreactivity to Things Associated with the Trauma

The vigilance can take the form of feeling on edge, irritability, or broken sleep. You may have anger outbursts with little provocation. Some people who have been victims of a crime may keep the house lights always on or spend the night checking locks and sitting on the couch with a weapon. I've seen people who have reversed their sleep schedule to sleep in the daytime so that they can be on guard at night.

For the PTSD diagnosis, you need one or two symptoms from all four groups co-occurring. Many people don't qualify for the full diagnosis because they only have some symptoms. But even a few of the symptoms can cause considerable anxiety and disruption.

Not all exposure to trauma results in PTSD symptoms. People who work in jobs that expose them to traumatic situations, like veterans, police officers, and first responders, have higher PTSD rates. How likely you are to develop PTSD depends on the type of exposure. Combat, captivity, genocide, and sexual assault cause PTSD at the highest rate, estimated to be 33%–50%. Researchers have found that people who develop PTSD have different gene patterns from those exposed to similar traumas but do not get PTSD. This genetic research is still in the early phases, but eventually, we may be able to predict who is more likely to develop PTSD versus those who will not.

Complex PTSD Versus PTSD

Complex PTSD (cPTSD) is not an official diagnosis in the DSM-5. Instead, it's a psychological construct that refers to the long-term effect of multiple traumatic experiences. The process usually starts in childhood as abuse and neglect. This abuse could be physical, emotional, or sexual. The trauma shapes your development and personality because the neglect or abuse occurs during highly vulnerable developmental years. The multiple traumatic experiences create a fractured self-identity. People suffering from cPTSD can spend years trying to mend the fracture.

Because of the vigilance, a person with PTSD may check locks, have flashbacks, refuse to drive, or jump every time they hear a loud noise. But the person with cPTSD lacks this hyperreactivity and, instead, has long-standing interpersonal problems like relationship difficulties, poor self-esteem, anger problems, or mood instability. A person with cPTSD can develop depression or anxiety as secondary problems. Still, the core issue is the fractured self that resulted from a severe emotional disruption that occurred during formative years. The baggage from that trauma gets hardwired into the personality. As we previously discussed, hardwiring affects how you respond to your environment.

A person with PTSD can also have personality changes because of the negative thinking they develop. Their negative outlook can linger and impact their decisions and how they interact with people. This negativity may also affect how they view themselves, which is similar with cPTSD. However with cPTSD, the hardwiring change occurs early in development; if the event that causes the PTSD occurs in adulthood, personality changes will be more subtle. This is because the core of the personality has already been formed.

Treating PTSD usually requires specialized, trauma-specific therapies, like eye movement desensitization reprocessing, somatic therapy, cognitive processing therapy, cognitive behavior therapy, and others. These therapies treat the underlying traumatic reaction. Addressing the trauma response will also help your anxiety. However, since trauma-based disorders like PTSD and cPTSD are so multifaceted, it's valuable to use tools to help your anxiety while addressing your trauma symptoms simultaneously.

Conversion Disorder

Conversion disorder is not very common, but it can cause a lot of emotional distress and physical problems. It's listed under the DSM-5's "Somatic Symptom and Related Disorders" category. The term *somatic* means "related to the body." With these disorders, there are physical symptoms that are thought to have a psychological cause. A common term for this is *psychosomatic*, which some people believe is code for "it's all in your head." Not all the symptoms you experience with somatic disorders are *only* in your head, but the mind and body are closely connected. And, as we saw in Chapter 2, the mind can express itself physically when it's under duress.

Another name for conversion disorder is *functional neurologic symptom disorder*. This name is more descriptive of how the disorder presents with medically unexplained neurological symptoms. The symptoms are thought to have a psychological basis since medical tests do not verify the symptoms and don't fit how the disorder manifests.

An example of a conversion symptom is pseudoseizures, also called nonepileptic seizures. A pseudoseizure is convulsions, jerks, or falling that resemble seizures but don't cause abnormal electrical activity in the brain, as an actual seizure would. A seizure test called an *electroencephalogram* (EEG) would come back normal. Sometimes though, an EEG doesn't detect seizure activity, even in a person with an established seizure disorder. Therefore, a negative EEG is not definitive proof that you had a pseudoseizure.

But here's another way to tell the difference between an actual seizure and a pseudoseizure. During a seizure, you experience uncontrolled electrical activity in your brain that travels through your nerves in a disorganized manner. If the electrical activity affects the nerves that control your left arm, only your left arm will shake, resulting in a focal seizure. Many times, the abnormal electrical current spreads to both sides of the brain, causing multiple body parts to shake or jerk out of control. Once the electrical activity crosses from one side of your brain to the next, you lose consciousness. We call this a generalized seizure, because it affects your entire brain instead of focusing on one part of the brain. Therefore, it's a pseudoseizure if you have abnormal movements on both sides of your body while remaining awake. People with conversion disorder don't intentionally produce their symptoms. The movements are involuntary and a reaction to unconscious anxiety.

The term conversion disorder is based on the work of Sigmund Freud, an Austrian neurologist who founded the theory and practice of psychoanalysis. He theorized that conversion disorder creates pseudoneurological symptoms when your mind converts an unconscious psychological conflict into a physical representation of that conflict.

Consider this example: Judy is holding her 2-month-old baby when she hears the doorbell ring. She rushes down the stairs and slips on the carpet. She tries to grab the handrail, but because she's also carrying her cellphone, she misses the rail, falls backward on the stairs, and lands on top of the baby. The baby screams with such force that her body jerks back and forth.

Though the baby isn't injured, this experience leaves Judy a wreck. She blames herself for not being more careful. The pediatrician and Judy's family reassure her that accidents happen, and they encourage her not to blame herself. Their support makes her feel a little better, but she can't get the image of her daughter's screaming face and jerking body out of her mind. Weeks later, Judy develops a spastic twitch in her arm and a hand tremor. These episodes last hours, and afterward, her arm is weak and numb for days. Judy's symptoms convince her that the fall caused a head injury.

Judy sees a neurologist and has a brain scan and EEG. While both come back normal, this changes nothing for Judy. The episodes get so out of control that she doesn't feel safe taking care of her child. Her mother-in-law comes to the rescue as Judy gets worse. Judy spends most of her day either spastically twitching or completely immobilized from complete left-sided weakness. Her neurologist refers her to a psychiatrist for treatment.

The psychiatrist finds Judy to be depressed and anxious, with lots of worries about the cause of her symptoms. Judy believes she has an undiagnosed brain injury that has escaped detection by all her doctors. She also believes that the brain injury is progressive and that she will soon require a wheelchair.

The psychiatrist prescribes an antidepressant, which only helps a little with her low mood and anxiety. She continues to have the attacks that made her poorly functional and unable to take care of her daughter.

Association 1

In the course of therapy, the psychiatrist learns that Judy and her husband had argued about her phone use the night before the fall. He thought she spent too much time on her phone. She remembered him saying, "You're a mom now. You need to get off Instagram, and pay attention to our daughter." His comment made Judy feel guilty and like she was a terrible mom. But she felt social media was a necessary outlet. She didn't think she used it to excess.

This was Judy's first association between her mental conflict and her symptoms. Her phone was a sign of parental negligence.

Association 2

Just before the doorbell rang, she'd posted a cute picture of herself holding the baby. She took the phone downstairs so that she could immediately check people's responses to her post after she answered the door.

Judy's second association was if she'd listened to her husband and put down the phone, she would have had a free hand to catch herself on the stairs.

Association 3

Judy recalls that the worst part of her fall was watching her baby cry because of the pain Judy had caused her. She had never seen her baby cry that hard, and when she saw her body jerk, Judy had been afraid that the baby was having a seizure. Even though the baby never jerked like that again, Judy believes that it was evidence of brain damage. Therefore, Judy's third association was that her negligence caused her baby brain damage.

The psychiatrist helped Judy make these connections between her guilt, her belief that she'd witnessed her daughter have a seizure, and her belief that she'd caused her daughter permanent brain damage.

Judy had converted all those unacceptable thoughts about her daughter into physical symptoms that looked like a seizure and brain damage in herself. The hand that had twitched and jerked was the same hand that held the phone that failed to grab the handrail.

When Judy made these connections, she came to understand that her anxiety and worries had caused her symptoms, but this didn't make them disappear entirely. Self-hypnosis helped her relieve most of the symptoms, apart from an occasional hand tremor she still gets when she's stressed.

Judy's condition was severe and dramatic: her jerky movements and weakness made her unable to care for her daughter. Not everyone has such impairing symptoms. Also, not all conversion symptoms connect to a psychological cause. Sometimes the conflict or traumatic event occurred in the distant past. In these cases, the feelings around the event are often buried too deep to connect to the current situation.

There are eight types of conversion disorder symptoms:

- Weakness or paralysis
- Abnormal movements like tremor, stiffness, or walking problems
- Swallowing symptoms or throat closure
- Speech symptoms, like slurred speech or trouble producing speech
- Nonepileptic seizures or attacks
- Sensory loss, like numb body parts
- Special sensory symptoms, like smelling unusual odors or seeing flashing lights or spots
- Mixed symptoms (a combination of the above)

Judy's situation is an example of conversion disorder with mixed symptoms: she had a combination of weakness, abnormal jerking movements, a tremor, and numbness.

You can think of the anxiety that accompanies conversion disorder as *silent anxiety*. Sufferers don't necessarily feel subjectively anxious; rather, the neurologic symptom is a manifestation of unconscious mental distress. But the pseudoneurologic symptoms can cause so much dysfunction that you develop an anxiety disorder on top of the conversion disorder. For example, suppose you develop a swallowing problem where you experience random attacks of your throat closing. You can't consistently identify a trigger. You then become agoraphobic and afraid to leave your home for fear of having an attack in a place where you can't get help. If you also have trouble producing speech, you could develop performance anxiety and become very anxious speaking around people.

You can develop conversion disorder at any age, from childhood to later life. Conversion disorder can spontaneously appear under certain circumstances and then disappear just as suddenly. It can also come and go or persist for most of your life.

Health Anxiety

Health anxiety is a term that combines two disorders from the DSM-5: somatic symptom disorder and illness anxiety disorder. Previous versions of the DSM called it *hypochondriasis*. Out of this term was born the pejorative label, *hypochondriac*.

People with health anxiety obsess over bodily functions, like breathing or their heartbeat; physical imperfections, like skin blemishes; or physical complaints, like headaches, stomachaches, and lightheadedness. Health anxiety entails catastrophizing even minor discomforts. Sufferers might focus on a specific organ system and believe that they have the most serious disorder of that system possible.

Consider Bob: He reads a post about one of his three thousand Facebook friends having a rare muscular cancer. Bob has never heard of this type of cancer, so he researches it. He finds out that people with this cancer have muscle and joint aches that pass as overactivity. When they complain to their doctors about the aches, the doctors tell them to lose weight and improve their diet. It's not until they have trouble performing daily operations that doctors do more tests and find out that the cancer is too advanced to treat.

After reading this information, Bob notices that his shoulders have felt stiff and painful the past few days. He assumes it was because of the extra yard work he's been doing over the weekends. Bob monitors his progress, and after a few days, his shoulders feel better. But he notices pain in his right calf that he could not connect to any activity. This additional pain makes him worry. He reads that people with cancer form blood clots easier than people without cancer. The blood clots are called deep vein thromboses (DVT), and they commonly form in your calf when you haven't been active. Bob has been lying on the couch more because of his shoulder pain. Maybe this new DVT is one of the hidden signs that he has cancer. Bob worries his DVT will break off and travel to his lungs, causing a pulmonary embolism. Bob takes himself to the emergency room to have his sore calf evaluated. He hopes that once the doctors see he has a DVT, he can convince them to fast-track a cancer workup.

It's as though Bob's body has manufactured these symptoms in response to his worry. Once the illness was top of mind, he began having symptoms that matched the condition he believed he had.

Another version of health anxiety manifests in the form of overreactions to bodily sensations. Sufferers fixate on sensations and analyze them in order to assign them an illness. Because they're anxious, they may experience some of the physical symptoms of anxiety, like heart palpitations or dizziness. But instead of connecting these sensations to anxiety, they worry that their dizziness signals a brain tumor.

When a medical workup shows no clear physical reason for the symptoms, they start to believe that the doctors missed something, leading them to seek second and third opinions. People with health anxiety will often see multiple doctors and get many unnecessary medical tests, feeling that the medical establishment isn't taking their concerns seriously.

Here are some examples of misconceptions people with health anxiety have:

- "My general anxiety symptoms (e.g., feeling on edge with some heart symptoms) will escalate to something that kills me in my sleep."
- "Normal medical test results mean that my illness is undetectable."
- "Even if my exam is normal today, the disease could still materialize tomorrow."
- "Doctors can't know what's wrong without running all available tests."
- "I continuously check for new symptoms, so I will know when the illness is getting worse."
- "The more I learn about the illness, the better I will be at helping doctors find the cause."

People with health anxiety usually don't seek mental health treatment, because they don't believe that they have a mental problem. Seeing a therapist or psychiatrist is typically a late-stage intervention when the doctor evaluating the physical condition reaches a dead end. Or they may decide to get mental health treatment if their anxiety is so great that it interferes with their medical workup.

The Conditioned Response

Recall that anxiety is strongly linked with physical symptoms, like sweating, shakiness, and the sensation of a lump in the throat. A person with health anxiety will handle these symptoms differently from one without. Someone who experiences the physical symptoms of anxiety but doesn't have health anxiety can recognize the mind-body connection taking place. If a doctor searches for a physical reason for the symptoms and concludes that they were caused by anxiety, this person will be reassured. With health anxiety, medical workups don't typically lead to reassurance. So why does one person feel reassured and not the other? Because the person with health anxiety has a *conditioned response*.

You may have heard of the story of Pavlov's dogs. Ivan Pavlov was a Russian scientist who studied learning theory and classical conditioning. Pavlov's dog experiments showed that you could trigger a physiological response with a neutral stimulus if you pair it with a potent stimulus. He used a bell as a neutral stimulus in his dog experiment and meat as a potent stimulus.

First, he showed the dogs a piece of meat. The dogs salivated. When he rang the bell, the dogs had no response. Then, he showed the meat while ringing the bell, and the dogs salivated in response to the meat. By continuously pairing the meat with the bell, the dogs learned to associate the meat with the bell. Finally, when Pavlov rang the bell without the meat, the dogs salivated.

Similarly, with health anxiety, people associate feeling anxious with physical sensations and conclude that all physical sensations are dangerous and represent hidden signs of catastrophic disease. People with health anxiety develop a conditioned response to their symptoms through research, seeking reassurance, and body surveillance.

This is the life of a person with health anxiety. It's exhausting. It's highly distressing for the person affected and exasperating for the people around them who try very hard to reassure them.

Existential Anxiety and Life Crises

It's a natural process to wonder about life's meaning and whether you have a greater purpose in the world. Many people have these existential thoughts, but some experience so much anxiety from these fears that it causes a life crisis.

Existentialism is a philosophy that teaches that life doesn't have meaning by default but that we assign meaning and execute it through our own free will. Existentialism teaches that each person is responsible for their life choices and outcomes. Our freedom allows us to assume this responsibility and has two components: agency and will. Will is the decision to be free. Agency is the action taken to exercise that will.

This theory has been around for centuries and was initially developed by the European philosophers Søren Kierkegaard, Friedrich Nietzsche, Jean-Paul Sartre, and Martin Heidegger. Modern theorists have further developed the concept. In his 1980 book *Existential Psychotherapy*, Dr. Irvin Yalom identified four human fears that he referred to as the four givens. These "givens" are death, freedom, existential isolation, and meaninglessness.

You might occasionally think about these fears, or specific events could trigger you to worry more intensely about them. Here are some examples of life transitions that commonly trigger existential fears:

- Graduating college and starting a career, which signals the end of your safety net (unwanted freedom)
- Getting married and questioning the permanency of your choice (loss of freedom, isolation)
- Having children and feeling your youth disappear (death)
- Watching your parents die and realizing you're the next wave (death)
- Ending a long-term relationship and worrying you won't find another partner (isolation)
- Selling a business you spent 20 years building with the plan to relax and enjoy your money (meaninglessness)

There are also certain life stages that generate crises for many people. Graduation is one example. Someone graduating from college may delay the transition to adulthood by continuing to pursue advanced degrees. Here, the academic institution is an authority and a substitute parental figure that shelters this person from being fully responsible. As long as they're in school, they don't have to make a "final" decision about who and what to be.

Once you finish school and start working, you can enter a quarter-life crisis. Two issues that arise at this stage are feeling locked in and locked out. You can feel locked into a course you can't change if you have a job that you hate. You may feel that you are in that job because you chose the wrong major or graduate school program. Because of the time and money you've invested in this career path, you can feel locked out of other opportunities.

In their late 30s and 40s, people spend more time contemplating the impact their decisions have made on their life and whether or not it has meaning. You can feel angst if you believe that you've failed to reach certain life milestones. Many then have a late-life crisis when they retire from a career that had consumed their adult life. The career exit leaves a huge void to fill with a new purpose. At this life stage, you may be divorced, have adult children who no longer live with you, or have medical issues that limit your mobility. It's common to feel anxiety about facing death as you realize that you have fewer years ahead of you than behind you.

My Old Maid Crisis

I have a soft spot for my female patients who are in their mid- to late 30s or older who have never married. I relate to them because I was there, and I remember what it felt like to question if I'd ever find the right person or if I'd spend the rest of my life alone. I had some prospects beginning in college, but one of the major obstacles was my transient existence. I never lived in one place for more than 4 years. I lived in a different city for college, medical school, and residency. Since I wasn't on the premedical track in college, I spent one year working, followed by 2 years completing premedical coursework. So in the time between my hometown and where I now live, I lived in five other cities. And at each stage, I knew my time in that place was temporary.

My undergraduate and medical schools were both in small Southern towns. I felt suffocated by them and believed I was missing something big "out there." The feeling of being trapped influenced my residency choice, which led me to set my sights on New York City. This wasn't a permanent move for me, though, as I didn't want to settle myself so far away from my family.

Each time I landed in a new place, I was reluctant to get involved with someone. I knew that unless the guy was willing to follow me around, I would have to decide whether to abandon my training or leave without him and be heartbroken. As fate would have it, I always seemed to gain a love interest in my last year at each location.

I left New York City on a mission to find a man I could keep. I chose Atlanta as a metropolitan city with plentiful prospects that was closer to my home roots in Florida. But living in a city where women outnumbered men, it didn't take long for me to grow tired of the dating scene. I took myself off the market and had a midlife crisis.

With existentialist philosophy, life is made up of irreversible, irretrievable time segments. As I dwelled in that headspace, all of the missed opportunities in my 20s and early 30s passed before me. I blamed my position in life on my decision to go to medical school and burn a decade of my life moving around and being "too busy" for a man. I wallowed in regret that I could never get that time back.

I was anxious that I was in my late 30s with little to show for it. Friends my age had families and homes, and I was alone in an apartment because I had no savings and plenty of medical school debt. After some soul searching and prayer, I took an inventory of my values. I had friends, family, a satisfying job, and spiritual life that reminded me that God's grace was sufficient to sustain me. I decided I'd rather have a peaceful existence than be unhappily married. So I resigned myself to getting a dog and living happily ever after. As the crisis passed, I put my head down, settled back into my work routine, and enjoyed my friends and family.

Just before I got the dog, I met my husband-to-be.

Existential anxiety can appear randomly and either reach crisis proportions that disrupt your life flow or remain a passing contemplation that motivates you to make changes. Existential crises can produce self-improvement through self-reflection.

I believe that the threat of extinction from the COVID-19 pandemic activated these existential fears on a broader scale. COVID heightened everyone's awareness of our mortality and forced us to face individual and collective isolation. The pandemic also made us contemplate our freedoms and the need to assume agency over our health decisions. Other issues that may have triggered you to feel anxious were the threats to our freedom, international conflict, and political unrest, which intensified social division. Superimposed on all these issues is the impact of global warming that we see with climate change and increasingly devastating storms. It's no wonder there's so much unease.

Substitutes for Purpose

When you struggle with existential anxiety, you may find other activities to fill the void that isn't filled with purpose. In a 2006 paper on existential therapy, Dr. Aaron Keshen identified behaviors he termed "purpose substitutes" that you use to reduce your anxiety.

Here are some compensatory behaviors:

- Overindulging in substances (alcohol, pills, etc.)
- Excessive shopping
- Forming unfulfilling relationships
- Becoming overly involved in community service activities
- Zealously supporting a cause
- Excessively focusing on acquiring money, material items, or power
- Excessive media use (television, movie streaming, social media, etc.)
- Excessive work

Activities like these compensate for lack of purpose, but they're not adaptive or meaningful. If you recognize some of these activities from your own life, think about what they represent for you or what void they fill. These activities can help you identify areas in your life that you wish to improve. Finding purpose and value can remedy all types of existential anxiety. Values determine what you intend for your life, and they shape your decisions.

Mitigating Death Anxiety

Even though death is inevitable, meaning and value are powerful buffers against death anxiety. You can reduce death anxiety by aligning yourself with a worldview that shares your values. You gain symbolic immortality when you contribute to this worldview, because the cause you represent lives on beyond your mortal life. Through belief in a higher power, one gains literal immortality, which can ease the fear of death. If you believe that life continues after death, you don't have to fear death, because it's just a transition to a new life.

This chapter covered psychiatric conditions that can cause anxiety for you but are not primary anxiety disorders. In the next chapter, we will cover how certain personality features cause anxiety.

CHAPTER 4

Anxious Personalities

Everyone has a unique personality that takes shape and settles into its mature form during the late teens and early adult years. The DSM-5 considers personality a pattern of "inner experience" and behavior. To illustrate an inner experience, consider the classic example of the glass filled halfway with water. Your inner experience may be to see the glass half full and mine to see it half empty. Your perspective is more optimistic; mine is more pessimistic. They are both valid perspectives, but they differ based on our inner experience.

If your personality departs significantly from social and cultural norms, it might be considered disordered. In people with personality disorders, the pattern of inner experience and behavior is inflexible and runs through all aspects of life. The pattern traces back to late adolescence or early adulthood and causes internal distress, relationship problems, or conflicts at work or school.

To constitute a personality disorder, this pattern of inner experience and behavior must affect two out of four of these areas:

- Thought
- Emotional expression
- Relationships
- Impulse control

The DSM-5 groups 10 personality disorders into three clusters based on the characteristics they share:

Cluster A - Odd or eccentric
Paranoid personality

Schizoid personality

Schizotypal personality

Cluster B - Dramatic, emotional, or erratic
Antisocial personality

Borderline personality

Histrionic personality

Narcissistic personality

Cluster C - Anxious or fearful
Avoidant personality

Dependent personality

Obsessive-compulsive personality

In this chapter, we're going to focus on the three anxious personality types. Then, we'll talk about general personality traits like neuroticism and the psychological defenses we use against unconscious anxiety.

Avoidant Personality

Avoidant personality disorder is a pattern of thinking and behavior marked by feelings of inadequacy, extreme social inhibition, and marked sensitivity to criticism. It affects all aspects of your life and does not appear only after experiencing hard times, like a breakup. For example, if you were in a relationship where you felt emotionally exploited, it would be normal to feel inadequate for a short time after the breakup. By contrast, a person with avoidant personality disorder constantly anticipates criticism and rejection. This anticipation closes them off emotionally, and they have trouble showing vulnerability in relationships.

Most personality disorders, including this one, appear around late adolescence and early adulthood. Children can have a phase of being socially awkward and shy, but they usually grow out of it. With avoidant personality disorder, the shyness and social inhibition worsen as the child moves from adolescence to adulthood.

To be diagnosed with avoidant personality disorder, you'd need to have four of these seven characteristics:

1. Your fear of criticism, disapproval, or rejection prevents you from engaging in work activities that require a lot of interpersonal interaction.

   This resistance is more than saying "I'll pass" whenever you're asked to do something. You fear criticism so intensely that you risk being demoted or getting negative evaluations because you cannot follow through with responsibilities.

   Suppose you have a monthly activity that involves working closely with other people. You don't outwardly say, "No, I refuse to do it because it makes me uncomfortable." Instead, you miss meetings under the guise of being sick, late, or tied up with another obligation. You find a way to evade the meetings without looking like you're noncompliant. You may not get in trouble for your absence, but your work still suffers negative consequences because you're "M.I.A."

2. You won't get involved with people unless you know ahead of time that they will like you.

   This social separation puts you on the fringe of society. You skulk around the periphery of relationships to keep them superficial. Since you try to get reassurance that the person likes you beforehand, you rely on "vibes" and body language cues to know whether the person likes you. Ultimately, you make assumptions about what people think without direct evidence. Actual evidence comes from the content of what someone says and not from facial expressions or body movements. I emphasized "content" because when you have these fears, you rely too heavily on tone of voice to tell you how someone feels. And you usually misinterpret the tone.

3. You emotionally hold back in relationships to protect yourself from being mocked and demeaned.

You keep your inner circle at an emotional arm's distance. You can do this by refusing to go deep on a topic of conversation. A more subtle way is to work all the time or otherwise stay too busy to engage deeply with people. This process isn't entirely conscious, meaning you don't contrive this as a strategy to avoid intimacy. At a deeper level, you do want intimacy. But intimacy is too terrifying, so you gravitate toward work and other activities in your comfort zone. You tell yourself and others that you can't control how busy you are.

4. You assume people will criticize or reject you in social situations, and these thoughts stay top of mind.

Usually, your fixation on this is enough to keep you out of social situations. But if you do go out, it's a profoundly demoralizing experience. You can feel emotionally naked in front of everyone. You interpret almost any comment as a negative appraisal. Because of these insecurities, you're unlikely to say much; you fear you may say the wrong thing and suffer the wrath of all these critics.

5. You worry about how you appear to new people, in terms of both physical attractiveness and personal competence.

This aversion to being around new people can look like shyness, because you speak little around strangers or can't loosen up. To make life easier, you avoid dealing with unfamiliar people if you can help it. But if you can't help it, your inhibitions may make you look awkward. For example, you may stutter or have trouble clearly expressing yourself because you're overthinking how to say it or how the other person will receive it.

6. You see yourself as personally hideous, socially bungling, and positionally inconsequential.

   You may reach these conclusions from previous experiences where you became so anxious that you embarrassed yourself. You may have choked up and said the wrong things or started sweating in front of people. Instead of seeing these missteps as transient anxiety reactions, you see them as evidence that you are too deeply flawed to have close relationships.

7. You're afraid to take risks or try new things for fear that you will be humiliated.

   This risk avoidance can cause you to miss significant opportunities. For example, Paul is 38 years old and desperately wants to get married. He works with Sherry, who has been sending increasingly obvious signals that she's interested in him for months. Her overtures are the lowest hanging fruit he's ever received, but he's too inhibited to reach for it. He believes that once she has the chance to have a "real," personal conversation with him, his inferiority and ineptitude will become obvious. Watching her realize these truths would have disastrous effects on his emotional health, and he'd never recover.

As I noted above, people with avoidant personality disorder have at least four of these characteristics. But anyone can have one or two of them. Having some features of this personality can be a source of anxiety.

Avoidant personality shares many features of social anxiety. Some researchers have proposed that the two disorders are on a spectrum, two sides of the same coin. However with social anxiety, the fear and anxiety are limited to social interactions or performance. People with social anxiety also realize that their fears are unreasonable, even though they're still anxious about the situation. They can still have close personal relationships.

On the other hand, with an avoidant personality, people believe that they are deeply flawed. Because of this belief, they overfocus on subtle cues that people are rejecting or criticizing them. They have a low threshold for interpreting something as critical. Therefore, it doesn't take much for them to feel insulted or hurt by someone's remarks.

Their response to perpetually feeling on the receiving end of something negative is to avoid dealing with people in any way they can.

One approach to treatment for this disorder is addressing the distorted beliefs. I discuss cognitive therapy in more detail in Chapter 7, but while we're learning about avoidant personality, I want to mention some of the common, inaccurate assumptions that reinforce the problem:

- "People disapprove of me and want to criticize me."
- "I am inadequate."
- "If someone gets to know me, they won't like me, so I can't expose myself to them."
- "My feelings aren't safe around others because they will mock me."

If you can identify with these, write them down. Then, try to add more of your own thoughts by reflecting on interpersonal situations that cause you problems. For example, do you have trouble at work or school because you make too many assumptions about what people are thinking? Take an inventory of your relationships. Do you have close friends? Do you have a romantic partner? Most people with avoidant personality disorder are deeply lonely but don't take the necessary risks to develop closeness with someone because of how uncomfortable it makes them.

Identifying what is behind your behavior can help you understand what is holding you back. The next step is to challenge your assumptions. Challenging yourself is the hard part, and it works best with the guidance of a professional. But whether you hire a professional or try to make changes on your own, you have to be prepared for the fact that change can be uncomfortable. It's also a slow process that requires patience. There may be days when you easily recognize your distorted assumptions and days when you continue to repeat old patterns.

Skills training is another approach to helping avoidant personality disorder. This helps you start and maintain conversations. You can also learn how to nurture a relationship. One example of improving your conversation is asking people questions and later following up on the answers. Generally, people like talking about themselves, and if you later ask for follow-up on something they told you, it shows that you're interested in them. People respond positively when someone shows interest. Another skill to improve is learning how to reveal things about yourself so that people can feel close to you. If you're not used to talking about yourself, a professional or trusted person can give you feedback on appropriate things to share with people.

Dependent Personality

In his classic work, *Devotions Upon Emergent Occasions* (1624), the English poet John Donne wrote "No man is an island." The means no one is entirely self-sufficient. There is truth to this. With normal development, we begin with total dependence on caregivers for food, safety, and nurturance. As we grow older, we separate physically and emotionally from our caregivers but, hopefully, form lasting bonds with other adults.

As with all things disordered, somewhere along the line, some people struggle with developing autonomy. As they move from childhood to adolescence to early adulthood, they become clingy and fear separation from the people upon which they're dependent. This extreme need to be cared for is called dependent personality disorder.

Here are the eight symptoms of dependent personality disorder. You need five or more to qualify for the disorder. The traits form the handy pneumonic, **RELIANCE:**

"R" is for reassurance. It's hard for you to make everyday decisions without advice and reassurance from friends and family. These can be simple decisions, like whether you should wear a red or blue shirt. There's more to this than just being curious about what others think, though. Your need for reassurance is excessive. You may ask someone's opinion and then keep asking, "Are you sure?" Because you doubt yourself, you need to hear their answer more than once.

"E" is for expressing disagreement. It's hard for you to disagree with others because you're afraid that you'll lose their support. You may find disagreeing with anyone difficult, but it seems especially difficult to disagree with the people closest to you. Because you don't want to lose their support, you'll accept anything they say, even if you disagree with it. You also won't express your anger with them because you don't want to risk them abandoning you. It feels like speaking your mind means forfeiting everything that makes you feel secure.

"L" is for life responsibility. You need others to take the lead in most major areas of your life. This need can look different at different life stages. In adolescence, you might rely on your parents to tell you what to wear and choose your classes or hobbies. If your parent has a controlling parenting style, this combination of a dependent child with an overbearing parent forms a symbiotic dyad.

As an adult with dependency, you might rely on your parent or partner to choose your job, pick your friends, or even identify your preferences. It's not as though you have no preferences. You intentionally leave your options open so that your preferences are universally accepted. If someone makes these decisions for you, you don't have to feel responsible for a bad outcome or making the wrong decision.

"I" is for initiating projects. It's hard for you to start projects or complete tasks on your own. You have sufficient motivation, but you don't have the confidence to start or follow through with a task. You question your capabilities and believe that other people do things better than you. Similar to the person with an avoidant personality, you see yourself as inept and ineffective. The logical endpoint of these self-judgments is that you need someone else to "press start." Once the ball gets rolling, you can continue the effort only as long as someone more competent is around to make sure that you'll be okay.

Another manifestation of these symptoms is a low motivation to learn new skills because you don't believe you can sustain them. You fear that if you become good at something, people around you will leave you to your own devices. Then, when you lose those newly gained skills, you'll be alone and helpless. So you prefer to remain incapable and unskilled, because what you really need is the comfort of others taking care of you. Autonomy is distressing.

"A" is for alone. When you're alone, you feel helpless because you're afraid you can't take care of yourself. Isolation is terrifying for you. Because of this, you may hang around in places you'd rather not go to or get involved in things for which you have no interest, just to avoid being alone. You'd rather be bored out of your mind than be alone.

"N" is for nurturance. You go to great lengths to be nurtured by others, even if it means participating in undesirable activities. You'll submit to other's demands, even if they're unreasonable. Because of this, you can end up in very imbalanced relationships and make a lot of personal sacrifices just to stay connected. This willingness to submit to nearly any demand puts people with dependent personality disorder at high risk for abusive relationships.

"C" is for companionship. When a close relationship ends, you immediately seek another relationship to fill the void. Being without a relationship becomes a crisis. Being in a rush to find a replacement means you can end up in a low-quality relationship with someone who may not be a good fit for you.

"E" is for exaggerated fears. You're obsessed with the fear of being left to fend for yourself. You ruminate over the scary prospect of being alone and helpless. This fear is the opposite of what you see in someone with a schizoid personality. The person with a schizoid personality prefers to be untethered from relationships and experiences them as suffocating. The dependent person requires close relationships and experiences them as lifelines.

We don't know the cause of dependent personality, but some researchers have proposed that having a chronic medical condition as a child increases the risk of developing this disorder. Another potential cause is separation anxiety during childhood.

People with dependent personalities think negatively about themselves and have low self-esteem. Needing to decide something can trigger paralyzing anxiety.

Dependent personality rarely operates in a vacuum. It often comes alongside other disorders, like depression, social anxiety, panic disorder, and agoraphobia. One approach to helping people with a dependent personality is addressing any co-occurring depression or anxiety symptoms, because these problems worsen their dependency. Assertiveness training can help with some thinking patterns, but it's hard to break past the conditioned behavior of relying on others for your day-to-day functioning.

Being entangled in a relationship with someone who likes to be in control reinforces the helplessness. Many people with dependent personalities would rather be stuck in their dependency than face their fear of autonomy. On a more positive note, a person with a milder form of the disorder, who recognizes their neediness, can make incremental changes that allow them to feel good about progressively becoming independent.

Obsessive-Compulsive Personality Disorder

Because obsessive-compulsive personality disorder (OCPD) shares a name with obsessive-compulsive disorder (OCD), it is an oft forgotten disorder—and a misunderstood one. OCD is so pronounced with its quirky rituals and dramatic presentation that it overshadows the personality disorder.

OCPD shares some features with OCD, and they often co-occur. OCPD is a preoccupation with orderliness, perfectionism, and control.

For a diagnosis of OCPD, you need four out of the following eight features:

1. Rigidity and stubbornness

   The rigidity with OCPD manifests as an overfocus on having things "just so." The process is more important than the outcome. You must cross all the t's and dot all the i's. You don't make a great team player because you think way ahead of most people and develop a detailed plan of action. On the surface, this seems like a handy skill, but problems arise when you refuse to deviate from your plan and won't consider anyone else's point of view. If you are forced to incorporate someone else's ideas, you do so with great reluctance and anxiety. You value sticking to a principle over compromising.

2. Stinginess

   With OCPD, you adopt a hoarding mindset around material possessions. You hold on to money and possessions so that you're never in a situation where you don't have adequate resources. As such, you're reluctant to share wealth or good fortune with others. This miserliness is not just directed at others; you also withhold from yourself. You may live well below your means, because controlling your spending controls your anxiety about being without enough resources.

3. Hoarding

This feature overlaps with the former conceptualization of the OCD hoarding subtype. It entails resisting throwing away worn-out items like old clothes, because you see discarding things as wasteful. You might keep a shoe with a broken heel so that you can use it as a hammer.

This motivation to keep broken objects differs from a hoarder's motivation. The hoarder can't discard items because they've assigned them sentimental value. With OCPD, it's more about being unwilling to let any object go to waste.

4. Perfectionism

Perfectionism manifests as excessive concern about making mistakes and second-guessing your decisions. These concerns cause you to restart or redo things until you get them right. These extra efforts keep you from completing tasks. If you're consumed with a work or school project, you neglect "less important" personal obligations, like spending time with loved ones or doing chores around the house. You may have several personal projects you start with enthusiasm but never complete.

5. Fixation with details

A person with OCPD is one who, as the saying goes, "can't see the forest for the trees." For any activity, you overfocus on rules, minutia, schedules, and proper procedures to the extent that you forget the purpose of the activity. You take extreme care in all you do, with great attention to detail and repeated checks for errors. You don't let others' impatience with your thoroughness pressure you to move faster.

6. Reluctance to delegate

It's hard for you to pass things off to others because you don't believe that someone else can do that same quality work you can. If you're falling behind schedule, you'd rather turn things in late than get help from someone who may not do things the way you envision it. When you give someone a task that you don't plan to do yourself, you need to give them specific instructions for the one correct way to do it. You don't welcome any deviations from your instructions.

7. Excessive work productivity

OCPD breeds overwork. You value maximum productivity and neglect friendships and leisure activities. Your hard work isn't driven by a financial need (though it's essential for you to have considerable emergency savings). Despite pressure from friends or family, you find it very hard to take time off. Downtime feels like a waste of time and makes you anxious. This hard-driving work ethic spills over to your everyday work, like household chores. You pay meticulous attention to order in your home. Your perfectionism makes you competitive, and you prefer leisure activities that allow you to win at something.

8. Strict moral standards

You're very rigid with matters of morality, ethics, or values. Not only do you hold yourself to a high standard, you expect strict adherence from others. You exact harsh criticism on yourself when you fall short of these standards. You're a consummate rule follower and see no room for leniency or exceptions.

Here is an example of inflexibly adhering to a moral code you apply to yourself and others. You and your best friend work for the same company, and you both have an opportunity to receive an award that will give you a large bonus and an all-expenses-paid luxury trip. To qualify for the award, you have 3 months to give 20 sales presentations. The presentation is complex and lengthy, requiring several steps to coordinate. You also must generate your own list of prospects to attend the presentation.

You're not worried about meeting the quota, because you're skilled at planning. You start working immediately to achieve this goal. Your best friend procrastinates, as she always does, but once she gets started, she's on pace to finish only if she can do more than one presentation a day.

You finish your 20 presentations well before the deadline, and because the process goes so smoothly, you keep going and finish an extra five. A week before the deadline, your friend has a death in the family and must take a three-day leave from work. She returns 2 days before the qualification deadline and scrambles to complete her presentations. On the last day, she is short two presentations. She knows that you completed an extra five and that you can only report 20 certifications. The company doesn't grant extra credit for extra work. She asks if she could take two of your extra certifications to complete her 20. You refuse to give them to her because you feel it's a false representation of her effort. Although her family tragedy cut short her opportunity to complete the task, you believe she could have completed it if she hadn't waited to start the project.

You may wonder, *How could I treat my best friend like this?* It's because with OCPD, rules and principles supersede relationships. You're not only judging her for waiting a month to start the assignment. If she'd started on time, as you did, but got an illness that kept her bedridden for a month, you'd still refuse to do the work for her. In that situation, you'd see her illness as a misfortune that rightfully disqualifies her. She shouldn't get an award she didn't earn.

In some ways, OCPD is the polar opposite of dependent personality when it comes to self-efficacy. With OCPD, you have an extreme need for control and autonomy. With a dependent personality, you keep your anxiety under control by seeking the support and reassurance of others. But with OCPD, you defend against anxiety by resisting input from others and maintaining tight control of your decisions and circumstances.

Research has shown that OCPD is the most common personality disorder in the U.S. general population, followed by narcissistic and borderline personalities. You're more likely to have OCPD if you have social anxiety, obsessive-compulsive disorder, phobias, and generalized anxiety disorder. Having one of these anxiety disorders on top of the personality disorder gives you a double dose of anxiety, which requires more work to overcome.

What Does It Mean to Be "Anal"?

You may have heard someone say, "That guy's really anal." Here, "anal" is short for anal retentive or anal personality. Sigmund Freud established anal personality based on his libido theory. Today, we use the term *libido* to mean sex drive. But the original Latin word means "desire" or "lust." Freud broadened the term to mean any drive to fulfill instinctive wishes.

According to Freud's libido theory, we have an instinctual drive to satisfy bodily pleasures through erogenous zones, beginning at birth. The four erogenous zones are the oral zone, anal zone, phallic zone, and genital zone. These zones correspond to the developmental stage at which we seek to satisfy these needs. Freud proposed five psychosexual stages that incorporated the four zones.

Freud's Five Stages of Development

Stage	Erogenous zone
Oral (birth to age one)	Mouth
Anal (age one to age three)	Bowel and bladder function
Phallic (age three to age six)	Genitals
Latent (age six to puberty)	None (dormant sexual feelings)
Genital (puberty to death)	Genitals reawakened and applied to a sexual interest

During the first three stages, we have a conflict we must master. If we have difficulty mastering the conflict, we can develop a fixation around the erogenous zone corresponding to that stage. You find bodily pleasure from your mouth during the oral stage through drinking from either a breast or a bottle. When you're upset, you are soothed with a pacifier or by sucking your thumb. If you have trouble weaning from the breast or bottle, you can develop an oral fixation. This can manifest as smoking, overeating, or nail-biting, to name a few.

During the anal phase, you derive pleasure from exercising control over your bowel and bladder. Toilet training becomes the conflict to master, and successful mastery results in independence and self-control. Difficult toilet training, perhaps from an overly strict parent who uses punishment as "motivation," results in an anal fixation, or anal-retentive personality style. The anally fixated person is overcontrolled and inflexible, similar to the person with OCPD.

You can be "anal" about certain things and not others. In other words, being anal may not affect all aspects of your life. It's a way of responding to unconscious anxiety and is not a personality disorder.

Now, I'll shift from psychiatric disorders to nondisordered ways you can experience personality-based anxiety.

Neuroticism

During my last year of medical school, I shared a house with two of my friends. One night, we watched the 1989 movie *When Harry Met Sally*.

In one scene, Sally mailed envelopes using a blue United States post office mailbox stationed in her neighborhood. The mailbox's design includes a door about the size of a large envelope that you pull open to place your mail in. When the door closes, your mail slides into the box. If there's not much mail in the box, you can hear your mail hit the metal bottom; otherwise, you hear it land on a stack of mail. We, along with Harry, watched Sally take a stack of envelopes and mail them one by one. She placed each envelope on the door and closed it. She waited for a second, then opened the door to peek inside and make sure the envelope had slid down into the box.

My friend laughed and said, "She's so neurotic! This should be called *When Harry Met Tracey*." I was taken aback. "You think I'm neurotic?" Her eyes widened as she said, "God, yes!" I tried not to be insulted by such a resolute answer. But I had to admit that I did the same thing when I put mail in the box. The engineering of the door was a basic chute mechanism, but what if the door got stuck and trapped the mail before it slid down? The next person who opened the box could grab your mail and take it home. Of course, this presumes that grabbing mail is a thing. But at least I wasn't as bad as Sally. I would put the entire stack in at once.

As an early fourth-year medical student, I hadn't yet chosen to pursue psychiatry. I wasn't particularly psychologically minded, and I didn't understand what *neurotic* meant. I thought it meant someone with a lot of "hang-ups." I owned that I had hang-ups, but I thought I did a good job keeping them to myself. I didn't realize that they were so evident to other people.

The term *neurotic* means a tendency to experience negative emotions like anxiety and depression. There are several applications of the term, and here I will explore three of them.

Five-Factor Model

Psychologists Robert McCrae and Paul Costa developed the Five-Factor model to organize primary human personality traits. According to this theory, most personality traits can be placed into one of five categories, called "super traits": openness to experience, conscientiousness, extraversion, agreeableness, and neuroticism. Psychologists use tools to measure these factors and score them on the spectrum from low to high.

You can remember them using the acronym **OCEAN:**

"O" is for openness. If you score low on this scale, you're cautious and safety focused. Unfamiliar things cause anxiety. At the top end of the spectrum, you're very curious and like being outside your comfort zone. Boredom causes you stress.

"C" is for conscientiousness. If you score low on this scale, you like to live loose and carefree. You need maximum flexibility and get stressed when things are too rigid or black and white. If you're high on this scale, you're a rule follower. You prefer having conventions and standards, and your adherence to these conventions makes you very reliable. Also, when you're at the top end of the scale, having unclear expectations makes you feel anxious.

"E" is for extroversion/introversion. Scoring low on this scale puts you in the introversion range. You value privacy and draw energy from having alone time. Overstimulation from too much interaction leads to stress. At the high end of this scale is extroversion. For you, contact with others is an energy exchange, like being plugged into a recharging station. But isolation depletes you.

"A" is for agreeableness. People who score low on this scale (disagreeable range) are more competitive and mistrustful. When assessing someone's intentions, you don't give them the benefit of the doubt. If you're not sure, you assume that they have negative intentions. On this end of the scale, not getting what you want makes you anxious. People who are high on this scale (agreeable range) like to please others, put others' happiness before their own, and are very easygoing. You are stressed by disapproval and conflict.

"N" is for neuroticism. Neuroticism measures how vulnerable you are to negative emotions like anxiety, depression, and anger. People who score low on the scale have more self-confidence, are slow to become frustrated, and don't ruminate or worry that much. If something upsets you, you can calm down from it in a reasonable amount of time. People high in neuroticism are more emotionally reactive and easily stressed. Because of this, highly neurotic people are more prone to anxiety disorders.

Think of it as the difference between a bowl made of delicate china versus one made of stone. Both can break, but the fine china will break more quickly and with less effort. I use this china analogy because both materials have value. Some people prefer fine china over cheaper stoneware. If you're careful with china, it can serve you well and last a long time. But it's vulnerable. Similarly, being more emotionally reactive isn't necessarily negative. There's value to being in touch with your emotions or having them closer to the surface. People know where you stand and don't have to guess what you mean or how you really feel about something.

There are different tests—or inventories, as they're usually called—that measure these traits. One is the Big Five Inventory. It has 44 items that you rate according to how accurately they describe you.

These are the items corresponding to neuroticism:

- You see yourself as a depressed person.
- You are not very relaxed, or you don't handle stress well.
- You tend to be tense.
- You worry a lot about different things.
- You're easily upset.
- You can be moody.
- You get nervous a lot.
  [Source: Big Five Inventory]

If you're highly neurotic (meaning very prone to negative emotional states), you have to prioritize your self-care and optimize your coping skills.

Self-care describes the practices you partake in to promote your own physical, emotional, mental, and relational well-being. It means being aware of what your mind and body need. Examples of these activities or interventions include decluttering your home, taking a break from digital devices, setting limits with your work hours, saying no to requests that you don't have time for, exercising regularly, or reducing your junk food intake.

That's the Five-Factor model's conceptualization of neuroticism. Another is Freud's explanation of neurosis. Freud considered neurosis a disorder of the nervous system, and neurotic behaviors the things people do or think to manage unconscious anxiety. An example of a neurotic reaction would be to fixate on worst-case scenarios. Cognitive behaviorists call this *catastrophizing*. Evidence of this thinking might be that your speech is filled with absolute statements, like "always" and "never." "I'll never be able to get a good job" or "I'll always end up at the bottom of the list."

Neurosis was taken out of the DSM in 1980, with the third edition. But internationally, it's still used to describe mental conditions. For example, the International Classification of Diseases has a coding system that is used for research and insurance billing. That coding system still uses the term *neurosis* to describe a mild mental condition.

A third approach is a psychoanalytic theory used to describe personality organization. Otto Kernberg, an American psychiatrist and psychoanalyst, described three levels of personality organization: neurotic, borderline, and psychotic.

Neurotic is considered the highest level of functioning with intact reality testing, which means you know what's real and what's not. You also have mature defense mechanisms and a stable concept of yourself and others.

Borderline personality organization is called this because it falls in between the neurotic and psychotic levels. With this organization, you employ some primitive defenses and can slip into occasional psychotic states under stress.

A person with a psychotic personality organization has the lowest level of functioning, exhibiting many psychotic symptoms and using primitive defenses to respond to unconscious anxiety.

Psychological Defenses and Coping Skills

Freud was the first to posit that we use automatic psychological processes to defend against internal anxiety that occurs beyond our awareness, also known as *unconscious anxiety*. He called these behaviors *psychological defense mechanisms*. These are born out of his structural model of the mind, which he expanded to the concept of ego psychology.

Ego psychology divides the mind into three parts: id, ego, and superego. The id represents our most primal instincts and is entirely unconscious. It's controlled by the pleasure principle, the mental drive to satisfy instinctual impulses such as sex, hunger, thirst, and body elimination. The superego is your moral compass that is based on standards set by your parents and society. You can think of your ego as your self-representation that balances the unacceptable drives of your id against your rule-following, morality-abiding superego. The ego is controlled by the reality principle, which delays gratification of your instinctual urges until a more appropriate time.

Freud described 10 psychological defenses. Other ego psychologists, including his daughter, Anna Freud, followed his lead and added several others. There may be over 30 defenses, but I'm going to limit this discussion to the nine most common.

Your ego employs psychological defenses to process unconscious mental conflict. These are the desires of the id that your superego finds unacceptable. Picture an iceberg with a small part above the surface of the water that's visible, then a much larger part beneath the surface. These unacceptable conflicts lie beneath the surface of your conscious thought. Some examples of these conflicts are fears, traumatic experiences, violent motives, immoral urges, irrational wishes, selfish needs, unacceptable sexual desires, and shameful experiences.

What Lies Beneath

Conflict	Example
Fears	Fearing dying alone and no one missing you
Traumatic experiences	Watching your father beat your mother
Violent motives	Wanting to kill your father
Immoral urges	A desire to cheat on your taxes and keep all the money you rightfully earned
Irrational wishes	Wishing that your father would spontaneously combust so that he no longer exists and you don't have to kill him
Selfish needs	Regretting that you got bogged down with three children who keep you from pursuing your dreams
Unacceptable sexual desires	Fantasizing about sexual intimacy with your sibling's spouse who hits the gym every day, unlike your spouse
Shameful experiences	Feeling unlovable, like the "piece of crap" your father said you are

These conflicts are buried deep in your mind and hidden from you so that you don't have to deal with the torment they cause. But the anxiety they generate bubbles up into your conscious in disguised ways. Your ego recognizes the disguised versions and uses defenses to ward them off.

Psychological defenses are divided into three categories: primitive, neurotic, and mature. These psychological defenses are automatic, and sometimes we can get stuck using the old immature defenses to deal with adult problems. These behaviors can make you feel better at first, but in the long run, they cause more problems and hold you back from consciously managing negative emotions.

Psychological Defense Mechanisms

Primitive	Neurotic	Mature
Denial	Projection	Humor
Dissociation	Reaction formation	Sublimation
Acting out	Intellectualization	Suppression

Primitive Defenses

Primitive defenses are immature and childlike. They're normal responses in childhood, but we're supposed to adopt more of the mature defenses as we grow up. Some of the primitive defenses are denial, dissociation, and acting out.

Denial

Denial is where you refuse to accept the reality that is apparent to everyone else. A typical example of this is denial about having an addiction. You may recognize that you overconsume a substance (alcohol, food, etc.) or overindulge in certain behaviors (sex, spending, etc.). Still, you tell yourself that you can stop whenever you want.

A more subtle example of denial is when you ignore unmistakable signs that reveal something you don't want to accept. You don't have to say aloud, "I refuse to believe my partner is having an affair." But you can ignore glaring signs, like your partner never being home at night or getting lots of text messages that they quickly delete.

Dissociation

Dissociation is where you mentally block out distressing memories or experiences. This is a common defense mechanism in people who have suffered trauma. Your mind escapes to another place while you experience the trauma, or your mind hides the memory from you so that you can't recall it. The trauma doesn't have to be an experience like being assaulted. I've talked to people who can't remember most of their childhood. They remember experiencing emotional abuse and the way it made them feel. But they don't remember milestones like the first days of school or what they did during the summers. Their life feels like one big blur.

Like most primitive defenses, dissociation may help you feel better in the short term, but it's very destructive in the long term. It's never an effective defense because it numbs you emotionally. Some people can get so used to using this defense that they spend a lot of their time checked out and absent from the moment. It can also be very distressing to have gaps in memory and feel disconnected from your reality.

Acting Out

Acting out is when you get upset and have tantrums or engage in self-harm. You can see this in children if they miss their afternoon nap. If you're a parent, you're probably very familiar with the five o'clock meltdown. The child isn't aware of why they're upset; they just don't feel good and need to let it out. Similarly, as an adult, you aren't always aware of the trigger driving your reaction. You may feel suddenly very emotional or have a surge of anger and don't recognize the trigger. Sometimes, people use self-harm to relieve the tension of emotions they don't feel equipped to express.

Neurotic Defenses

Neurotic defenses are more helpful than primitive ones but less helpful than mature defenses. With the neurotic defenses, you dodge the unpleasant feelings without processing them into a more acceptable form. The behavior negatively affects your functioning or how you interact with others. Examples of neurotic defenses are projection, reaction formation, and intellectualization.

Projection

Projection is where you have feelings that are unacceptable to you, and instead of owning them, you assign them to someone else. This involves a lot of inaccurate mind-reading.

Here's an example. Tina has always lived in the shadow of her sister, who was always prettier, smarter, and more successful. Tina married her college sweetheart right after graduation and almost immediately became a stay-at-home wife and mom.

One night, while she and her husband watch television, a story about her sister appears on the news. Her sister was promoted to CFO of a technology company. Tina's husband says, "Wow, your sister is amazing." Tina feels hurt by his comment and says, "I bet you regret marrying me. I've never been good enough for you." Her husband is not surprised by her comment, because she frequently accuses him of having an affair with a "better" woman. Even though her husband feels she's let herself go since she had the kids, he still loves her, and he's sick of her accusing him of wanting other women.

What's really behind this is that Tina doesn't like herself. She loves her kids but feels like her stay-at-home life has kept her from blossoming into the best version of herself. Seeing her sister's accomplishments makes her feel even more insecure. Tina recognizes her insecurity, but what she doesn't recognize on a conscious level is her regret that she married and had children so young. Since her youngest child is nine, she feels trapped for the next 10 years in a life of denying her needs for the sake of others. Tina projects this unacceptable thought onto her husband by insisting that *he's* the one who regrets getting married.

Reaction Formation

With reaction formation, you moderate your undesirable thought by assuming a view opposite to how you really feel. In some cases, homophobia is reaction formation. Consider a person who feels attracted to people of the same sex but whose family would never accept this. Eventually, they defend against the attraction by taking on an overly harsh attitude toward homosexuality. That attitude affirms their heterosexual orientation: "If I hate it, then I'm not it. Right?"

Intellectualization

Intellectualization is where you think about unpleasant emotions abstractly to avoid experiencing your feelings. An example of this is finding out that a loved one has cancer and has less than 6 months to live. To avoid feeling the pain of losing your loved one, you think about how death is part of the normal life cycle. You focus on how to get their affairs in order and other such logistical concerns, instead of your impending grief.

There is some value in taking on this type of planning instead of lying in bed all day, ruminating about how horrible your life will be when you lose this person. But with intellectualization, you don't genuinely experience the pain, because you skipped over it with all this abstract thinking. You behave as if you're not part of the experience. The intellectual activity is excessive, and it doesn't advance you toward acceptance.

Mature Defenses

Mature defenses help you cope with anxiety by transforming distressing thoughts and emotions into more acceptable forms. You deal with the distress by managing it rather than escaping it. Examples of mature defenses are humor, sublimation, and suppression.

Humor

You may have heard of people using humor to diffuse tension in a room. Humor serves the same purpose for mental tension. Finding irony in a situation or identifying a funny aspect of it can change how you see it. Sometimes, you can use this too much to escape reality, or you can appear as a jokester who doesn't take things seriously. But used carefully and at appropriate times, humor can help you accept difficult emotions.

Sublimation

Sublimation is when you channel unacceptable impulses into more acceptable ones. Engaging in sports activities is a common way people redirect their unacceptable desires. Mothers Against Drunk Drivers (MADD) is an organization founded on the back of a tragedy. On May 30, 1980, 13-year-old Cari Lightner was hit and killed by a repeat drunk driver as she walked to a church carnival. Her mother, Candace Lightner, started a crusade to change California driving laws to increase the penalties for repeat offenders.

Candace has spoken publicly about her anger toward the driver and the system that allowed him to continue driving and hit other victims even *after* killing her daughter. No doubt Candace has permanent scars from this experience, but instead of becoming emotionally incapacitated, she channeled her emotions into effecting change. Through MADD's effort, hundreds of thousands of lives have been saved.

Suppression

Suppression is where you choose to move unsettling thoughts out of your awareness. We do this all the time when we suffer a loss. Suppose you're grieving after a break-up. You may wake up each morning and think about the loss, but you know you can't spend every waking hour thinking about it. So you decide not to think about it and purposely involve yourself with something to keep the topic out of your mind.

How do you change an unconscious, automatic process? Change starts with being aware of the behaviors. The unconscious part of this process is the impulse behind the behavior or the conflicts beneath the surface. If you use a lot of defenses in your everyday, you may need a therapist to help you uncover your conflicts.

But in the absence of a therapist, do some self-reflection. Have you engaged in some of these behaviors? Can you identify thoughts or feelings that may have triggered the behavior? Are you grappling with any moral issues or thoughts other people would find unacceptable, like wanting to harm someone who made you angry? How did you respond to that insult? You probably didn't sit with the emotion and let it pass. The usual thing to do is find a way to make the emotion go away.

Psychological defenses are the ways we separate ourselves from being fully aware of unpleasant thoughts and feelings. Being mindful of what you're experiencing at the moment helps you not automatically engage in these defenses. Instead, you use coping skills to manage your emotions. Most defense mechanisms are unconscious, but some of the mature ones can be made conscious and used as a coping skill. Coping skills are the things you consciously do to deal with distressing emotions.

At this point, you've learned about the many reasons you can feel anxious. Some of your anxiety can result from a disorder, or it can be part of your nature or personality. You may have daily, unmanageable anxiety, or it may pop up only in certain circumstances. In the second part of this book, we will look more closely at coping skills and other tools you can use to manage your anxiety.

PART 2

What to Do About Your Anxiety

CHAPTER 5

Prescription Medications

The Right Tool for the Task

When I was undertaking my psychiatry training, I lived in a tiny, 400-square-foot studio apartment in Manhattan. My miniscule kitchenette housed a small cooktop and a half-size refrigerator. Cabinet space was so tight that I had to store my pots and pans in the oven. Whenever I cooked, I used an ironing board as makeshift countertop space.

That was my life in the city, and after a while, I got used to it. But in the last few months of my training, I started to fantasize about living in a spacious apartment when I moved to Atlanta. I would daydream about my full kitchen with real countertop space. I prepared for my move by watching cooking shows on the Food Network. It had been so long since I'd cooked "real" meals that I needed to relearn the techniques—for myself, but also for the man I was going to find.

I began to notice that the TV chefs all used exquisite knives, and they had a different kind of knife for each task. This insight helped me plan for the knife set I would have to use in my gourmet kitchen. It would sit prominently on my countertop in a hand-crafted woodblock. After moving to Atlanta, I followed through with my plan and purchased an expensive semiprofessional knife set. It was a pleasure chopping and slicing with those knives, and they served me well for many years.

Then one day I went to the knife block to retrieve my carving knife, and I noticed that the tip was bent. My beautiful stainless steel knife had been compromised, and I knew exactly how it happened. I could picture it: the careless culprit using my knife to pry open the lid of a jar. I set aside my anger and returned to the knife block to retrieve a different knife. Adding insult to injury, I saw that the tip of the second knife was also completely broken off. The culprit hadn't learned from his first mistake. Now *two knives* were ruined because he'd used the wrong tool for the task.

Clients often ask me, "What can I do to get rid of my anxiety?" Usually, they're looking for just one thing that will permanently fix their problems. If only there were such a solution. Anxiety is multifaceted, and it takes a multilayered approach to manage it.

It's like having a full knife set. A paring knife can help you peel and segment an orange, but you'd need a serrated knife to slice through a baguette. Even if the paring knife works on the bread, it's not very efficient; the serrated knife is a tool that was designed for that purpose. (And neither knife should be used to open a stubborn jar.)

Similarly, there are many tools you can use to manage your anxiety. The tool you choose will depend on the type of anxiety you're experiencing (mental, physical, or behavioral), which interventions you respond to, and what is easy and convenient for you to execute.

In Part 1 of this book, I talked about the many reasons you might feel anxious. Part 2 aims to equip you with a multitude of tools to keep on hand for when you need them.

In this chapter, we'll explore interventions that involve taking prescription medications. In Chapter 6, we'll discuss some complementary and alternative treatments for anxiety, most of which you can administer yourself, without the help of a professional. Chapter 7 will look at a few different psychotherapies to treat anxiety symptoms. In Chapters 8 through 10, you'll learn about mind, body, and behavioral tools that you can use individually or as a group to help your anxiety.

Prescription Medication for Anxiety Disorders

How do you know if you should take medication for your anxiety? We usually prescribe medication for anxiety disorders that cause significant trouble for you in your day-to-day activities. Clinically, we call this kind of trouble "functional impairment."

Determining how your anxiety affects your functioning is a little more than guesswork. Clinicians use scales such as the global assessment of functioning (GAF), developed by the American Psychiatric Association, and the World Health Organization Disability Assessment Schedule. The publishers of the DSM removed the GAF from the fifth edition. However, many clinicians, insurance agencies, and disability companies still use it to quantify how much someone's psychiatric problems impact their lives.

To determine impairment, we look at your functioning in three realms: social, occupational, and personal. Your social functioning includes how well you relate to people and how engaged you are with your environment. Occupational functioning includes your school and work performance. Personal functioning refers to how well you're taking care of yourself—your hygiene, sleep, eating habits, etc. Personal functioning also incorporates how well you keep up with personal responsibilities, like paying bills.

We can group functioning into five categories: superior functioning, mild impairment, moderate impairment, severe impairment, and profound impairment.

Medications and Their FDA Anxiety Indications (Brand Names in Parentheses)

Generalized Anxiety Disorder	Social Anxiety Disorder	Panic Disorder
escitalopram (Lexapro)	sertraline (Zoloft)	sertraline (Zoloft)
paroxetine (Paxil)	paroxetine (Paxil)	paroxetine (Paxil)
venlafaxine (Effexor XR)	venlafaxine (Effexor XR)	venlafaxine (Effexor XR)
duloxetine (Cymbalta)		fluoxetine (Prozac)
alprazolam (Xanax)		alprazolam (Xanax)
buspirone (Buspar)		clonazepam (Klonopin)
diazepam (Valium)		
lorazepam (Ativan)		

How Anxious Are You?

Functioning Level	Example Symptoms
Superior	Stressors need to be extraordinary to generate anxiety.
	Anxiety is short-lived and not unmanageable.
	Your reactions reflect how the average person would react.
Mild impairment	Transient anxiety related to performance activities like taking an exam or giving a talk.
	Excessive worry over finances or life problems.
	Concentration problems after having a conflict.
Moderate impairment	Disrupted sleep (trouble falling asleep or fitful).
	Wake up with intrusive thoughts about problems.
	Motivation or focus problems that interfere with meeting personal, work, or school responsibilities.
	Panic attacks once a week or a few times a month.
	Many relationship conflicts.

Functioning Level	Example Symptoms
Severe impairment	Wake each morning vomiting.
	Miss days of work or school.
	Many physical symptoms like chest pain or trouble breathing.
	Severe insomnia such as less than 5 hours of sleep several nights a week.
	Intense obsessions or extensive rituals.
	Unable to keep a job or have meaningful relationships.
Profound impairment	Delusional beliefs.
	Persistent suicidal thoughts and possibly an attempt.
	Poor hygiene.
	Violence toward others.

With superior functioning, you have very little anxiety unless faced with an extraordinary stressor. Also, your anxiety reaction is short-lived and doesn't become unmanageable. Your reactions reflect how the average person would react. (Note that an "average person" is subject to one's personal observations of how other people behave. These categorizations are generalizations and not absolute standards.)

With mild dysfunction, you may experience transient anxiety related to an upcoming performance activity, like taking an exam or giving a talk. You may spend too much time worrying about your finances. Another example is having trouble concentrating after you have a conflict with someone.

With moderate dysfunction, you may see changes in your sleep. You can have trouble falling asleep because you feel on edge or experience broken sleep. You may even wake up early thinking about your problems. Another negative impact is that your anxiety may interfere with your motivation, focus, or concentration to the extent that you have trouble meeting personal or work responsibilities. At this level of dysfunction, you may have occasional panic attacks you experience once a week or a few times a month. For your social functioning, moderate impairment may cause you to have conflicts with coworkers or negatively impact your personal relationships.

With severe dysfunction, your anxiety is so intense you may not be able to work or attend school. You may wake up every morning and throw up. You may have other intense physical symptoms, like chest pain or trouble taking deep breaths. The anxiety disrupts your sleep so that you only get 2 to 3 hours per night. Because of the sleep deprivation and anxiety, your irritability is off the charts, causing even more serious relationship problems. If you have obsessive-compulsive tendencies, you may perform extensive rituals that keep you trapped in the house, or you may experience disturbing obsessions that make you suicidal. The net outcome from severe dysfunction is being unable to keep a job or have meaningful relationships because your anxiety is so severe that it interferes with these functions.

Profound impairment results in the most extreme adverse outcomes. You may become delusional, neglect your hygiene, become violent, or attempt suicide.

Let's get back to the question of when you should consider taking medication for your anxiety. We usually consider medication when anxiety causes moderate-to-severe impairment. Profound impairment usually requires hospital admission to stabilize your symptoms. Mild impairment can entail everyday anxiety that isn't necessarily due to a psychiatric disorder. Even if you have an anxiety disorder, there may be times when you have mild symptoms and can manage them without medications. Then at other times, your symptoms become unmanageable and cause moderate or severe impairment. At that level, you may decide to take medication to get your symptoms under control.

Notice that there is a difference between moderate-to-severe symptoms and impairment. You can have a few days of severe anxiety attacks or intense worry and physical symptoms but still go to work and take care of yourself. Even if the intense symptoms cause you to have a few tough days, these eventually pass. Here, your moderate-to-severe anxiety symptoms did not alter your level of functioning. It's usually persistent anxiety that lasts for weeks or more that causes you to fall behind on your daily responsibilities. If this happens, you may consider taking medication. Some people can't get by without taking medication, because they have intense daily anxiety, which causes many problems for them.

Medications for Anxiety

In this section, we'll dive into each of the main types of medications used for anxiety:

- Antidepressants
- Benzodiazepines
- Buspirone
- Propranolol
- Pregabalin and gabapentin
- Hydroxyzine and cyproheptadine

Antidepressants

Serotonin-enhancing antidepressants are a mainstay among the medications used to treat anxiety disorders. Yes, even if you're not depressed, we use some of the same medications for anxiety that we use for depression.

Examples are the serotonin reuptake inhibitors sertraline, fluoxetine, and escitalopram, and the serotonin-norepinephrine reuptake inhibitors venlafaxine and duloxetine. If you take these, daily doses are required.

When your doctor prescribes one of these medications, they'll start with a low dose and move up slowly to a higher dose. The dose that works is called the "therapeutic dose." This dose is often a few steps up from the starting dose, depending on the medication. The final dose you need to treat your anxiety is usually higher than the doses needed for depression.

For example, a therapeutic dose of sertraline for depression is 50mg to 100mg, but for anxiety it's 150mg to 200mg. Your doctor may start you at 25mg to 50mg and gradually increase your dose as needed. This process is tailored to your response. Even though the target anxiety dose for this medication is 150mg, you may only require 100mg (or even less) to treat your anxiety.

You may not realize if you've never taken these medications before that they don't work immediately. It can take 1 to 2 weeks for you to see an initial effect, then up to 6 weeks to see the maximum effect. The reason for this delay is that the drug has to reach a steady-state level in your bloodstream before it delivers a consistent effect. When you take a medication, the drug level rises, peaks, and then drops. How fast the medication concentration drops depends on the half-life of the drug, or the time it takes it to reach half of its initial dose. Most antidepressants have a half-life of one day (24 hours).

When you take your second dose, the concentration of the drug rises again and overlaps with the previous dose. In your bloodstream, you have medication leftover from yesterday mixed with medication you take today. It takes five half-lives to reach a steady-state level that your body sees as its daily allotment. Therefore, if your medication has a half-life of 24 hours, it will take 5 days to reach a steady-state level. It then takes several more days for your mind to respond to this steady-state level of medication.

I usually start patients on a small dose of medication and instruct them to increase to the next dose in 2 weeks. I tell them that they may see a tiny improvement after a week or two, but since they're starting on the smaller dose, they'll need to wait a full month before judging how well the antidepressant is working. At the one-month mark, they will have taken the higher dose for 2 weeks. At that point, they may feel better than they did when they first started the medication, and they can continue to improve over the next 4 weeks, even if their dose remains at the second step.

Antidepressant Side Effects

Like any medications, antidepressants can have side effects.

Increased Anxiety

It's normal for people with anxiety to feel worse when they start taking antidepressants. Some researchers believe that this is because serotonin activates your amygdala, which we know from Chapter 1 is the center of our instinctive anxiety reflex. To address this issue, doctors will usually start with a smaller dose of the medication than they would if you had depression. For example, the usual starting dose of escitalopram for depression is 10mg. But for people with anxiety, I usually start escitalopram at 5mg. This small dose still may aggravate your anxiety, but less so than the 10mg dose.

Your anxiety may increase every time you increase the dose. This transient worsening doesn't happen to everyone, but when it does, it usually only lasts for a few days before it settles down. The downside of this slower taper is that it lengthens the onboarding process. The antianxiety dose range of escitalopram is 30mg to 40mg (and some people respond well enough to less). If you need 30mg, it will take several weeks for you to reach this dose.

You might be wondering: "If the antidepressant increases anxiety, why would I take it?" Despite the short-term anxiety increase, these medications are still better for treating daily anxiety in the long term. There is also a chance that you may not experience this worsening effect if you start at a low dose and increase slowly. To help with this, doctors will often prescribe a benzodiazepine to dampen your anxiety as you wait to reach the steady-state effect. I discuss benzodiazepines in the next section.

Gastrointestinal Symptoms

If you're a Star Trek fan, you know that only officers are allowed onto the ship's bridge. The bridge is the command center where the captain and other officers navigate the ship. Nonofficers must be invited onto the bridge. You can think of your brain as your command center: it only allows authorized chemicals to leave your blood vessels and enter its chambers. This protective filter is called the *blood-brain barrier.*

The rest of your body doesn't have such a filter. The agents you ingest can affect any part of the body from the neck down that recognizes the agent and has a use for it. (And in fact, you have more serotonin receptors in your gut than in your brain.) Your gut is one continuous tube that spans your entire body. Think of it as a one-way railroad track that starts at your mouth and ends at your anus but makes several stops along the way. Since the entire track is lined with serotonin receptors, your medication can affect any part of your body along the track.

Common side effects include dry mouth, nausea, diarrhea, and constipation. Diarrhea and constipation typically resolve after a few days. You can often ease or prevent nausea by taking the medication with food. But unfortunately, dry mouth symptoms tend to only improve if you reduce your medication dose.

A NOTE ABOUT DIARRHEA

The consistency of your stool is more important than the frequency when classifying your stool as diarrhea. People vary in how often they produce stool. If your bowels move too slowly, your stool may become hard and difficult to pass. If your bowels move too fast, your intestines don't have enough time to absorb liquid from food, and your stool becomes soft or fluid. However, if you have a balanced diet with even minimal fiber, you will have solid stool. Usually, diarrhea that results from medication withdrawal produces stool that ranges from solid but mushy to a liquid consistency.

If you started eating a raw vegan diet and consumed a lot of green leafy vegetables, you might go from having one bowel movement day to two or three. But chances are all of them will be solid because of the increased roughage in your diet. In this instance, several solid stools a day would not be considered diarrhea.

Sexual Dysfunction

The serotonin effect can cause erection problems, decreased genital sensation, delayed climax, and decreased sexual desire (libido). Usually, these effects are dose dependent, which means that the higher the dose, the greater the response. It's possible for you to not experience these effects when you first start your medication, but then start to lose some sexual function after taking a higher dose.

Some people choose to stay on the medication despite these side effects because of the improvement in their anxiety symptoms. Sometimes, decreasing the dose a little may give you enough anxiety relief and restore your sexual functioning. If it doesn't, you may want to try a different antidepressant.

Weight Gain

All the serotonin-enhancing antidepressants can cause weight gain. We don't know exactly why, but one proposed mechanism is that it increases cravings for carbohydrate-rich foods, like bread and sweets. Another possibility is that it restores appetite in people who had been too anxious to eat enough before they started the medication.

Some antidepressants cause more weight gain than others. A 2003 study that examined several antidepressants concluded that the selective serotonin reuptake inhibitors are less likely to cause weight gain if you use them for less than 6 months. The exception was paroxetine (brand name Paxil), which was more likely to cause weight gain even in those who didn't take it for very long. I have had this experience using paroxetine with patients. It's a sedating antidepressant and can work well for people whose anxiety causes sleeping problems. But a common saying associated with paroxetine is "Paxil packs on weight." I've had numerous patients who didn't gain weight on Paxil, but when I inform people of this possibility, many will ask me to pick another medication.

Emotional Blunting

Sometimes, antidepressant medications can make you feel emotionally numb or dulled. People who experience this will say they don't feel like they experience their full range of emotions. Some feel unmotivated or apathetic. Some people can believe that they're becoming depressed. This problem is common and thought to affect 30% to 50% of people taking serotonin-enhancing antidepressants.

There is still some debate about exactly why the emotional blunting happens. One theory is that the extra serotonin works on a feedback loop that decreases dopamine in certain parts of your brain. This decreased dopamine causes blunting and apathy. It's as though the medicine causes an overshoot of serotonin levels that spill over and dampen your dopamine production. One solution to this problem is to pull back on the antidepressant by decreasing the dose just a little. If doing this increases your anxiety, you may not be able to take this medication, because the side effects limit how much you can take.

If any of these side effects don't improve with time or after reducing your dose, your doctor may need to prescribe a different one. Side effects that happen with one medication may not happen with another. For example, you might have sexual side effects with escitalopram but not with fluoxetine.

The symptoms above are ones you can experience when you take antidepressants. Medication withdrawal, also called *discontinuation syndrome*, is a separate set of symptoms you can experience if you suddenly stop taking the antidepressants. Not everyone experiences withdrawal symptoms if they stop taking the medications they had been taking for months to years; if you don't, you're one of the lucky ones.

Withdrawal happens because your brain and body receptors adapt to the medication and change how they function. Picture a group of people working as a team to build a structure. The group only has access to basic tools, like buckets and hammers. You arrive with power tools and motorized transport tools. To make operations more efficient, the team leader fires several unnecessary workers and discards the old tools. Your equipment and technology significantly advance the process, obviating the need for the old equipment and some workers.

Things move along at a good pace until you decide you don't want to help anymore. In a flash, you disappear with all your advanced equipment and technology. Your exit brings production to a screeching halt. The team must now scramble to find tools and more workers to resume operations. The interruption in the workflow has a damaging impact on the entire project.

In this analogy, the advanced equipment is the help you get from the medication. When your brain "sees" the help, it changes your neurochemistry and receptors to incorporate it. This adaptation makes you physically dependent on the medication, because it has been integrated into your brain and body functions. If you gradually remove the help (medication), your brain and body have the opportunity to rearrange the resources necessary to carry on daily functions without the help.

How long does it take to become physically dependent? There is no exact answer to this, as it depends on the drug and your body's physiology. But a broad range is 1 to 3 months of continuous use, after which you would experience withdrawal symptoms if you abruptly stopped taking the medication. To avoid having withdrawal symptoms, you would have your doctor taper you off the medication so that your body can adjust to being without it.

An easy way to remember the withdrawal symptoms is to use the mnemonic **FINISH**.

"F" is for flulike symptoms. You can feel you're coming down with the flu, with achiness, sweating, headache, and fatigue. It's not necessarily intuitive that these symptoms result from stopping your medication, so you might be tempted to get tested for COVID or take cold and flu medication to get through it.

"I" is for insomnia. If you suddenly stop your medication, you can have trouble falling or staying asleep and have very vivid dreams. The dreams are not necessarily nightmares, but they can still be disturbing. Their vivid nature makes them feel very real; you could be left questioning if your experience really was a dream. Having trouble knowing what's real and what's a dream can be very unsettling for some people.

"N" is for nausea. You can experience nausea as a persistent, nagging queasiness, or it can progress to vomiting. Even though it doesn't start with an "N," I would also include diarrhea in this category.

"I" is for imbalance. You may experience dizziness or vertigo. Dizziness is a different experience from vertigo. Dizziness makes you feel lightheaded, as if you might pass out or fall if you don't sit down. It may also seem like someone is dimming the lights.

On the other hand, with vertigo, you feel like your environment is spinning. Have you ever played the game where you turn around like a spinning top, then stop? If you do that (and I don't suggest that you do!), you'll continue to see the room spin until your inner ear adjusts to your new position. When this happens, you know the spinning came from the turns. But with medication withdrawal, you can have a sudden attack while you're sitting down. As you can probably imagine, this experience can be very alarming for people.

"S" is for sensory disturbances. The most common of these are burning and tingling sensations, usually in the arms or legs. You can also feel burning sensations that are more like hot flashes.

Another disconcerting sensory sensation is what some people refer to as "brain shocks" or "brain zaps." This sensory disturbance was discussed at length in Chapter 1. The sensation isn't painful, but it can cause a lot of distress. Some people notice that they get the zaps if they suddenly shift their eyes or change their head position.

Why do brain shocks happen? One theory is that they might be related to the sudden depletion of serotonin and norepinephrine in the nerve cells. When discontinuing the drug, you get a rebound effect that makes the nerves hyperactive. This hyperactivity of the norepinephrine in your brain causes a shocklike feeling.

"H" is for hyperarousal. Hyperarousal can include mental symptoms like anxiety, irritability, or aggression. It can also entail physical symptoms, like limb jerking or being easily startled.

These are the symptoms you can experience if you stop taking your medication suddenly, especially if your dose is higher than the starting dose. Even if you're diligent about taking your prescriptions, it's not that hard to miss doses here and there. You can go on vacation and leave your pills at home, or you can take your last pill and then forget to call the pharmacy for refills.

Withdrawal is less likely to happen at smaller doses and with medications that have a long half-life, like fluoxetine. The half-life of fluoxetine is about 4 days, and it takes a month to leave your system. With a half-life this long, it practically tapers itself. Because of this long half-life, some doctors will use fluoxetine to help you transition off a medication that has a short half-life, like duloxetine and paroxetine.

You can experience discontinuation symptoms within 1 to 4 days after taking your last dose. The symptoms can last from a day to about 2 weeks, on average. Some people have reported that the sensory symptoms, like brain zaps, last a year. I have seen some patients whose symptoms lasted longer than a week but did not occur daily. They may have symptoms for several days, then experience several months of sporadic recurrence.

What can you do about it? The first and obvious step is to always wean off your medication under your doctor's supervision. Suppose you go on vacation and leave your medication behind. In that case, you may want to get your doctor to send a temporary supply to a pharmacy near you. But if you can't do that or you're only away for a few days, know that once you return home and resume the medication, the symptoms should resolve quickly.

Benzodiazepines

As I noted in the previous section, it can take a few weeks to see a therapeutic effect from antidepressants and even longer if your doctor employs a slow taper. Even with the slow taper, you can have an initial increase in anxiety. Doctors sometimes address both the therapeutic delay and the anxiety increase problems by prescribing a benzodiazepine concurrent with the antidepressant. Benzodiazepines, or "benzos" for short, is the class of drugs that act on the GABA receptors in your brain to produce a relaxing or sedating effect.

Psychiatrists use benzodiazepines to treat short-term anxiety and sleep problems. But benzos have other uses. For example, they're often prescribed to relax people before a procedure like a colonoscopy. Diazepam, marketed under the brand name Valium, is commonly prescribed as a muscle relaxer to treat muscle strains. Lorazepam, marketed under the brand name Ativan, is used to stop a seizure and before a procedure. The common benzos used for anxiety are lorazepam, clonazepam, alprazolam, and diazepam.

Suppose that your anxiety is linked to disruptive symptoms, like panic attacks or insomnia. In this case, your doctor will likely prescribe a benzo to give you some relief until the antidepressant becomes effective. These medications provide an effect similar to pain medications. When you have pain, you take pain medication, and within an hour, your pain disappears or lessens. You feel better for several hours until the medication wears off, and then your pain returns. This immediate action is the same way benzodiazepines work. If you feel anxious, with either mental or physical symptoms, you can take lorazepam and feel calmer within 30 minutes to an hour. Some formulations, like those you place under your tongue, can work within minutes.

You can stay on the benzodiazepine for 2 or 3 months until your anxiety symptoms resolve, then your doctor will taper you off the benzodiazepine while you remain on the antidepressant. If you still have occasional intense anxiety attacks, you may decide to keep the benzodiazepine around to take as needed.

You might be wondering, "If these medications work so quickly, why would I bother using antidepressants?" The issue is that benzodiazepines are habit forming, especially if you take them daily. Your body develops a tolerance to benzodiazepines. Tolerance means that your current dose stops being effective, and you must increase the dose to get the same effect you had on the lower dose. After your doctor increases your dose, that dose becomes your new requirement, until that dose stops working, too.

Some people can quickly reach maximum doses of the medication, while others experience a slower tolerance progression. I have had some patients take the same dose for years without needing to increase. Generally, benzodiazepines are not the best choice for daily anxiety because of tolerance and dependence issues.

Most psychiatric medications are not addictive. Taking any of them every day causes physical dependence, but addiction involves developing a psychological dependence in addition to experiencing physical tolerance. You may wonder, "If anxiety is psychological, and I take the medication as prescribed, does that mean I'm addicted?" The answer to this is "not necessarily." Let's look at an example.

Phil has anxiety, and he sees his primary care doctor because he's not sleeping well. He has a lot going on at work and can't afford to go without sleep. He tells his doctor he can't get his brain to shut down at night, and he's been having some panic attacks in his office. His doctor prescribes fluoxetine and alprazolam and instructs Phil to take the alprazolam as needed. Phil takes the alprazolam and notices that he falls asleep as soon as his head hits the pillow. Then he takes it at work and doesn't feel anxiety for several hours. Fortunately, the alprazolam doesn't make him sleepy during the day, and he's able to get a lot more work done, because now he can calmly focus.

It feels like magic.

The directions on the bottle state that he should take the medication up to four times a day as needed for anxiety. It says this because alprazolam is a very short-acting benzodiazepine. It works quickly and doesn't stay in the body for very long. But a huge downside is that when it wears off, there can be rebound anxiety. With rebound anxiety, people feel worse than they did before they took the medication. So what happens? They take more to make that rebound anxiety go away.

Eventually, this is what happens to Phil. He and his wife aren't getting along very well, and whenever he gets home, she criticizes him. Phil takes another alprazolam soon after getting home to help him stay calm in his interactions with her. When Phil's doctor first prescribed alprazolam, Phil took it twice a day, but now he's progressed to taking it four times a day. A month later, he tells his doctor things are much better, but he needs a refill on the alprazolam. His doctor refills the alprazolam but tells Phil that the fluoxetine should be doing most of the work to control his anxiety by now, so he should need less alprazolam.

Phil feels reassured he has made it past the first month on the medication and has every intention to use less alprazolam. But then he has a very tough month at work and needs a little extra to help him through. When he asks for another refill, his doctor tells him to see a psychiatrist.

Phil comes to me, and I switch him to clonazepam, a longer-acting benzodiazepine. The longer-acting medication will make it easier to wean him off daily use, with a lower risk of rebound symptoms.

There are two things happening here. First, Phil is physically dependent, because he needs to take the benzodiazepine around the clock to control his anxiety. Second, he's psychologically dependent on using the medication to cope with stressful situations and wipe away all anxiety symptoms. Needing to escape or avoid the anxiety experience is central to developing an addiction to benzodiazepines.

A realistic goal for any anxiety treatment is that it reduces your anxiety but doesn't fully eliminate it. You will always have some degree of situational anxiety, because manageable situational anxiety is normal. If you have a bad day at work, you might feel tense at the end of the day. That's a normal response. You can use healthy coping skills that we will talk about in later chapters to manage this level of anxiety.

But for some people, benzodiazepines mute the response to everyday anxiety to the point where even minimal symptoms become intolerable. Instant relief can feel very good, especially if you've been suffering from intense anxiety for a long time. It can also be very tempting to use benzodiazepines to keep you free from all anxiety. But even people without an anxiety disorder are not anxiety-free. Therefore, benzodiazepines can give you a false sense of security by putting you in an unnatural state (having zero or minimal anxiety response).

Phil runs out of his month's supply of clonazepam, necessitating an early follow-up appointment. He says that he had a lot more anxiety last month because it was his year end at work. Because of the increased stress, Phil takes clonazepam every 2 to 3 hours. Sometimes, he only takes half of the pill, because he notices that it feels a little stronger than the alprazolam.

It so happens that clonazepam lasts much longer than 2 hours. Phil should not need to take it that frequently. The recommended frequency for clonazepam is two to three times a day. But Phil wasn't taking the pill because he needed it for unmanageable anxiety. He was relying on the pill to deal with any kind of emotional distress. When he experienced something unnerving, his reaction was to take a pill. And that's where he shifted from taking the medication to treat anxiety to using it to remove any negative experience. Using the pills to block out any distress is an addictive behavior, because it makes you psychologically dependent on the pill to cope with negative emotions. Another example of this mindset is requesting a benzodiazepine in advance of an event that you expect to be difficult.

So, what happened to Phil? He said he just wanted to get through the busy period at work, and that afterward, he would stop taking the clonazepam. He promised that he would not take it multiple times a day. After things at work slowed down, he and his wife went on an extended weekend trip. Phil forgot to pack his clonazepam but figured that this would be the time he stopped taking it anyway. On day two of the trip, he woke up in a panic and spent the entire day feeling like his whole body was shaking. He tried to tough it out, thinking that maybe he was just reacting to something he drank the night before. On the third day, his wife found him on the floor, unconscious and jerking. She called 911, and he was treated at the hospital for benzodiazepine withdrawal.

Most medication withdrawals are not life-threatening. The typical withdrawal symptoms from benzodiazepines are increased anxiety, tremors, poor sleep, irritability, sweating, elevated blood pressure, and a rapid heart rate. But benzodiazepines can also cause seizures, an extreme and dangerous withdrawal symptom. This is what Phil experienced.

Things are a little different if you don't take it every day. Some people get a bottle of 30 pills that lasts them 6 months or more because they take one only when they fly on an airplane, for example. Another example of irregular use is taking it once or twice every couple of weeks. I consider regular but infrequent use to be "weekly" and believe that twice a week is on the cusp of becoming frequent. In my experience, once a person starts taking benzos three times a week, three becomes four, and four becomes daily.

Daily long-term benzodiazepine use is associated with cognitive changes like a decline in mental sharpness. It can create balance problems in some people, where they don't feel quite solid on their feet. Imbalance can be a big problem for older adults and increase their risk of falls.

If you've been on the medication for more than 3 months and you're taking it daily, you need to have your doctor taper you off slowly when you decide to discontinue it. You don't want to stop taking it suddenly. Benzodiazepines require close tracking. It's not a good idea to run out because you're leaving town and notice that you only have two pills left. If you travel a lot or just have a hectic life, these medications tether you to your pharmacy, which can feel very confining.

The longer you've been taking benzos daily, the slower your taper should be. There's no set protocol for a taper length, and your doctor will use their clinical judgment on a case-by-case basis. How long it takes to taper also depends on how high a dose you're taking. I've had patients take a couple of years to wean off slowly. We just kept chipping away at the pill size over the years. It's like tricking your body into not noticing that it is getting less medication.

One way I help patients avoid this problem is by telling them to think of the medication as a "break-the-glass pill" only to be taken in extreme and unusual cases (like mistaking an anxiety symptom for a heart attack and heading to the ER). It should not be something they use to take the edge off a bad day.

Is it ever appropriate to take benzodiazepines as the only medication for anxiety? Yes, there are situations where benzodiazepines are the more optimal treatment. Benzodiazepines can be a better solution for performance anxiety to stave off a panic attack in performance situations. If you only need to use the medication infrequently, like a few times a month, it keeps you from dealing with taking something every day, and you can avoid the side effects of antidepressants. Another situation is specific phobias, like flying. If you have to fly for your job, but you only fly a few times a year, that infrequent use of the benzodiazepines rarely causes the long-term problems of addiction, dependence, or cognitive slowing.

Antidepressants and benzodiazepines are the most used medications for anxiety. But some people can't tolerate the antidepressants due to side effects, or they may not work well enough. We use this next group of medications as secondary options.

Buspirone (Buspar)

Buspirone is a serotonin-enhancing medication that works a little differently from antidepressants, and it's approved by the U.S. Food and Drug Administration (FDA) for generalized anxiety disorder. Like antidepressants, you need to take the medication daily, and it takes about 1 to 2 weeks to see improvement in your anxiety. Even though it increases serotonin in your brain, it achieves this through a different mechanism and doesn't have as many side effects as antidepressants.

Propranolol

The FDA approves medications that have been shown in research to be effective for a particular condition. Pharmaceutical companies will spend years developing a drug and testing it to see if it works as intended for that condition. These studies are called *clinical trials*. Usually, the drug manufacturer will seek approval for one condition to get the drug to the market. Once it's approved for one condition, like generalized anxiety disorder, the company may or may not invest the time and money it takes to get the drug approved for another related disorder, like panic disorder.

The upshot of this is that doctors will use medications that have been shown through research and experience to be helpful for a condition even if it doesn't have the official FDA approval for that condition. For example, your doctor could use buspirone to treat social anxiety, even though the drug isn't approved for this condition. Using a drug for a non-FDA-approved indication is called *off-label use* and is a common medical practice.

Propranolol is a beta-blocker medication mainly used to treat physical conditions, including high blood pressure, heart conditions, and migraine headaches. Psychiatrists prescribe it off-label to treat performance anxiety and tremors that you can get from medications like lithium. The medication works to slow your heart rate, and it's most effective for people who become anxious with physical symptoms whenever they need to perform. Recall from our discussion of social anxiety that "perform" can refer to any activity you need to do in front of people.

Whenever I prescribe this medication, I tell patients that it will reduce their physical anxiety symptoms, but it won't do much for the worry. This medication is best for people whose anxiety intensifies when they have physical symptoms like a rapid heartbeat. If the medication dampens those physical signs, they can push through the event and perform. This medication is not as effective for the worry symptoms you get with generalized anxiety disorder or obsessions of obsessive-compulsive disorder.

Gabapentin (Neurontin) and Pregabalin (Lyrica)

Neither of these medications is FDA approved for anxiety. They're both commonly used for seizures and nerve pain. Pregabalin is also prescribed for fibromyalgia. They work on the GABA system in the brain, which is also where benzodiazepines exert their action.

Neither drug produces a robust antianxiety response, but they may help reduce anxiety. In recent years, pregabalin has gained traction, with research showing it to be effective for anxiety. As such, clinicians are starting to favor it over gabapentin.

Hydroxyzine and Cyproheptadine

Both medications are antihistamines, similar to diphenhydramine, also known as Benadryl. Antihistamines are primarily used to treat allergic reactions, but doctors will use them off-label for other purposes. Antihistamines are sedating and can make you feel drowsy and calm. For some people, hydroxyzine works well to help them sleep, and improved sleep helps their daytime anxiety.

Doctors prescribe cyproheptadine for some gastrointestinal problems. There is a strong connection between your gut and your brain that we will discuss in a later chapter. An anxious mind leads to a nervous gut. In my experience, I find the people who respond best to cyproheptadine are those with health anxiety and those who have a lot of gastrointestinal symptoms with their anxiety.

Even though you can buy some antihistamines over the counter, it doesn't mean these medications come without side effects. Common side effects are feeling tired during the day, slowed thinking, dry mouth, and urinary retention (which feels like you can't fully empty your bladder). A few minutes after urinating, you have the sensation to go again, and you produce a little more urine that failed to exit on the first attempt. A more serious side effect is a slight risk of QTc prolongation, a heart conduction problem that causes your heart to have an abnormal rhythm. People with heart problems, especially heart rhythm problems, should avoid using hydroxyzine.

Dry mouth, also called *xerostomia*, is more than a simple nuisance. Sometimes your mouth is just a little dry, making you want to drink more. But sometimes, the dryness is severe enough to interfere with your speaking. Some people call it "cottonmouth" because your lips stick to your gums and you can't speak. You need an adequate amount of saliva to neutralize acids and wash away dead cells from your cheeks, tongue, and gums. Therefore, a more problematic outcome is bad breath, gum disease, and cavities. In more severe cases, the yeast in your mouth grows out of control, and you can get white patches on your tongue and cheeks, called *thrush*.

Prescription medications can make a world of difference for your anxiety, but they aren't for everyone. Many people take them without having side effects, or if they have side effects, they are mild or don't last very long. You need to be evaluated by a doctor to take them, but you can use this chapter as a guide for what to expect.

In the next chapter, we'll explore supplements and aromatherapy for anxiety, neither of which require a prescription.

CHAPTER 6

Complementary and Alternative Treatments

What is CAM?

Complementary and alternative medicine (CAM) is a treatment approach that deviates from conventional treatments, like prescription medication and psychotherapy. Complementary medicine is used alongside conventional treatment, and alternative treatment is used instead of conventional treatment. There are many CAM options, but I limit this chapter to widely available options with the most research support. We'll look at natural supplements, aromatherapy, acupuncture, hypnotherapy, and energy work. (Certain CAM interventions, like yoga and exercise, will be discussed in later chapters as self-help mind-body tools.)

Unfortunately, there is a lot of controversy over the use of CAM. On the one hand, opponents of CAM discount it because they believe there is inadequate research showing its effectiveness. Doctors may fear being sued for advising their patients to use something that is not "standard of care." Standard of care protocols are treatments that have been researched using controlled studies with many participants and have become a generally accepted practice among physicians. CAM treatments *have* been studied, but many studies are small or show mixed results. Therefore, rather than believing CAM has any value, opponents will see these mixed results as a reason to exclude these interventions entirely.

On the other side, proponents of CAM sometimes dismiss the concerns of traditional medical science and conclude that the field is too nuanced to apply traditional standards to measuring outcomes. Some will even promote CAM as the only treatment approach to consider if you want to avoid the dangerous side effects of traditional medicine. Indeed, traditional medicine has its limitations; in the previous chapter, you saw how prescription medications can lead to very negative outcomes. However, it's important to appreciate that just because something is derived from a "natural" source doesn't mean it can't have adverse effects. Anything that has a chemical effect can be considered a drug.

Somewhere in between these extreme views is the recognition that some of these options have benefits regardless of whether that benefit has been consistently proven in multiple, large, randomized controlled studies. Also, in examining the evidence for complementary treatments and anxiety, the usual standard for research trials was to examine the effectiveness of an intervention for someone with a disorder. Researchers haven't explored CAM's effect on anxiety symptoms in someone without a disorder.

Anxiety symptoms are called *state anxiety*, which is the situation of feeling anxious. *Trait anxiety* is having the predisposition toward being anxious, even though you may not always feel anxious. Anyone can feel anxious, but feeling anxious doesn't always mean having an anxiety disorder that causes functional impairment.

In this chapter, where applicable, I'll comment on which interventions have sound research evidence for use with a disorder. However, even if the intervention hasn't been shown to treat a disorder, it doesn't mean that it won't be helpful for situational state anxiety.

The cost of these interventions is another consideration when using CAM. Many supplements are expensive, and like prescription medications, it can take a few months for you to see an effect. Since medical insurance does not cover the cost of over-the-counter supplements, you could spend quite a bit of money before knowing if it's an intervention you want to continue.

Supplements

In this section, I examine some of the supplement options for anxiety. All of the clinical trials I reviewed tested adults and excluded pregnant women and those under 18 years. At the end of each description, I give my opinion about the treatment. None of my comments will apply to children or pregnant women. If you're pregnant, it's essential to consult your doctor before taking any chemically active substance, even if it's derived from a natural source.

Magnesium

There is substantial evidence that magnesium improves anxiety symptoms. Of all the natural supplements, it has the fewest side effects. It's also easy to get from your diet without needing to take it as a supplement.

Magnesium is one of the essential minerals that are involved in over 300 different body processes. It helps keep your heart beating and maintains the electrical stability of your nervous system. The body also uses magnesium to help regulate serotonin and other neurotransmitters. Research has shown that low magnesium levels are associated with depression and anxiety.

There are two mechanisms through which magnesium might ease anxiety: decreasing glutamate and increasing gamma-aminobutyric acid (GABA). Glutamate and GABA are neurotransmitters that have opposing functions. Glutamate activates cells, and GABA inhibits or slows cell activity. In other words, glutamate presses on the gas, and GABA pumps the breaks. You need both for optimal brain function.

N-methyl-D-aspartate (NMDA) is a glutamate receptor, and magnesium works by blocking this receptor, which blocks glutamate activity. You have NMDA receptors in your amygdala, and those receptors turn on the gas for fear conditioning and avoidance behaviors. Avoidance behavior keeps your phobias active. Blocking the NMDA receptors in the amygdala and the rest of your limbic system decreases your fear response and avoidance behavior, which reduces your anxiety.

Blocking NMDA also increases a brain chemical called *BDNF*, which stands for "brain-derived neurotrophic factor." *Neuro* refers to the brain, and *trophic* is Greek for "feeding." BDNF is one of the chemicals responsible for cell regrowth and neuroplasticity. Neuroplasticity is the ability to improve nerve connections by destroying damaged nerves and growing new ones. In this way, BDNF acts as a fertilizer for your brain.

Magnesium Sources

According to the National Institutes of Health (NIH), 68% of the population doesn't consume enough magnesium through their diet. The recommended daily amount for men is 400mg to 420mg, and for women, it's 310mg to 320mg.

Even if you consume enough magnesium, stress and anxiety increase cortisol, and cortisol depletes your body's magnesium supply. To investigate this phenomenon, A 2015 study from Gendle and colleagues studied a group of college students before and during their final exams. They found that the students had normal magnesium levels before the exams but became deficient during exam week. The stress had depleted their magnesium stores.

It's always best to get your vitamins and minerals from nutrient-dense food, such as dark, leafy greens, nuts, seeds, and avocados. Roasted pumpkin seeds have the highest magnesium concentration, delivering 156mg per ounce.

Supplements are good to take if you can't eat enough through your food or have persistent anxiety or digestive problems. As we get older, we have less stomach acid, which can lessen how much magnesium we absorb. The more you absorb, the more bioavailable the compound becomes. *Bioavailability* refers to how much of a compound your body is able to use.

If you take supplements, the recommended amount is 200mg to a maximum of 350mg. Several compounds are used to combine with the magnesium to form the supplement. Your body absorbs some combinations better than others. Common supplement forms, in order of least to most bioavailable, are carbonate, oxide, chloride gluconate, citrate, lactate, and aspartate. Some claim that magnesium L-threonate is better absorbed by the brain, but this research is still very new. Magnesium citrate is a popular formulation with good bio-availability. You'll want to avoid magnesium oxide, because it's poorly absorbed and can cause diarrhea. Sometimes it's paired with calcium as a combination tablet, because calcium is constipating.

Diarrhea and stomach upset are the most common side effects, but magnesium can also have a sedative effect, which you can exploit by taking it at bedtime. Sometimes, magnesium can interfere with the absorption of other things you're taking, such as zinc, some antibiotics like doxycycline and ciprofloxacin, and medications used to treat osteoporosis, like Fosamax and Boniva. If you take any of these medications, you should space your magnesium and other medication 6 hours apart from one another.

My Take on Magnesium

I think this is an easy intervention to implement. If you aren't consistently anxious, look to increase your dietary intake. If you have daily anxiety, you can adjust your diet in combination with supplements to give you an extra supply of magnesium, since your body wastes it under stress.

Inositol

Inositol is a sugar that's found in fruits, grains, nuts, and beans. The brain also makes it. The most common form of inositol that you will see among the supplements is myoinositol. Some people refer to inositol as "vitamin B8" because it's similar in some ways to B vitamins, but it's not a vitamin.

A few small studies have shown that inositol reduces the number of panic attacks per week in people with panic disorder. On average, panic attacks dropped by four to seven attacks per week. It's not a complete resolution, but for someone who has debilitating daily panic attacks, every panic attack they don't have can be a blessing.

Two studies showed that inositol improves symptoms of OCD. More studies are needed to show that inositol is helpful for general anxiety. The recommended dose is 14g to 18g per day for the powder formulation. The soft-gel formulation is more concentrated, and of this you take 4.2g to 5.4g per day. Note that you're more susceptible to gastrointestinal side effects like nausea, gas, bloating, and diarrhea at higher doses.

My Take on Inositol

It looks like inositol is only helpful for panic and OCD symptoms. Taking the soft gel may be an easy intervention, but we don't yet know if it does much for general anxiety symptoms.

Zinc

Zinc is an essential mineral that is considered a trace element because we have minimal concentrations in our bodies. You don't need a lot of the trace elements, but if you're deficient in them, you can run into serious problems. Zinc plays a role in critical body functions like DNA synthesis, gene expression, and tissue repair. Like magnesium, zinc decreases glutamate by inhibiting the function of the NMDA receptors.

You can get enough zinc from eating shellfish, meat, whole grains, legumes, nuts, and seeds. In addition, many commercial cereals are fortified with zinc. The recommended daily allowance of zinc is 8mg to 11mg per day for adults. Mild zinc deficiencies have been linked to anxiety, and some research has shown that zinc benefits OCD and panic disorder.

It's not too hard to consume enough zinc, but certain conditions can make you prone to becoming mildly deficient. Some medications for high blood pressure, such as ACE inhibitors, thiazide diuretics, and stomach acid blockers, like Pepcid, can reduce zinc levels. People with hypothyroidism and vegetarians can have low zinc levels, because the phytates in legumes and grains can block zinc absorption. If you don't have one of these situations, you probably won't see much difference in how you feel by supplementing with zinc, because you can get an adequate amount from your diet.

The maximum amount recommended for adults is 40mg per day. In the OCD study, researchers used 220mg of zinc added to fluoxetine to see mild improvement in OCD symptoms. The 220mg is considered a high dose, and taking high doses of zinc over time can lower levels of copper in your body, compromise your immune system, and even cause nerve damage.

My Take on Zinc

If you're not deficient in zinc, I think it's best to get it from food. The subtle improvement in OCD symptoms is probably not worth the risks associated with taking too much zinc.

Gamma-Aminobutyric Acid (GABA)

We've talked about how GABA is a neurotransmitter made by nerve cells and that its job is to slow down cell activity. Many of the supplements that reduce anxiety do so through the GABA system. So instead of using something else to trigger GABA production, why not just take more GABA? It sounds like the perfect drug to manufacture.

But what looks good on paper doesn't always work out in real life. We haven't been able to produce an oral form of GABA that acts the same way as our native GABA. The fundamental problem is that synthetic GABA has trouble crossing the blood-brain barrier. It's hard to take a high enough dose to get enough drug to cross this threshold and activate the GABA receptors. The recommended dose is 3,000mg to 5,000mg a day, but there's not much evidence that the supplement is effective. There are also many side effects; the most common are stomach upset, diarrhea, headache, and dizziness.

My Take on GABA

There's not much positive to say about taking synthetic GABA for anxiety. It's a great idea, but it just doesn't work well. Even if you experience some improvement, the side effects might not be worth it.

Herbs and Plant Extracts

Lavender (*Lavandula angustifolia*)

Lavender is an aromatic flowering plant in the mint family. The plant's oil has medicinal properties, and it has been used in aromatherapy for years. The active ingredients in lavender are linalool and linalyl acetate, which are organic chemicals called *terpenes;* these are responsible for the aroma of the oil.

In 2002, Schwabe Pharmaceuticals developed a proprietary lavender extract called Silexan. There have been numerous clinical trials testing

Silexan in people with either GAD or mild anxiety symptoms. Silexan has a powerful effect on anxiety that rivals prescription medications and even outperformed paroxetine in one large study from 2014 by Kasper et al. Silexan works on the GABA system (foot on the brake) and blocks NMDA receptors, which decreases glutamate (foot off the gas).

Silexan typically starts working after 2 weeks, and the effect increases over the subsequent 3 months. Silexan is not a sedative, but it improves sleep quality. The recommended dose is 80mg to 160mg. In the trials, more people did well on the 160mg dose, but as with prescription medications, it's always best to start at the lower dose and increase it after 1 to 2 weeks if you don't see enough improvement.

As for side effects, the most common are lavender-flavored burps and sedation. It does weakly increase estrogen levels, which can mean early breast development in boys and girls. So, it's generally not recommended for people under 18 years. If you have an estrogen-responsive tumor, check with your doctor before taking Silexan.

My Take on Silexan

I think Silexan is the best natural approach for treating general anxiety, given the strength of the research trials. It can either complement traditional medicine or act as a standalone alternative. I haven't seen any warnings about combining it with other medications. If you're taking an antidepressant and having a negative experience, you might add this supplement to see if it works better than your antidepressant. Of course, you should always consult with your doctor before adding to or discontinuing medications.

Passionflower (*Passiflora incarnata* L.)

This is a flower that grows in the southeastern region of the United States and Central and South Americas. It's an exotic perennial vine that produces a purple or yellow fruit high in fiber and other nutrients, and it has medicinal qualities. Historically, Native Americans used the sedative properties of the flower to help with sleep and restlessness.

There have been several trials in the past 20 years showing that passionflower improves anxiety. A 2001 study by Akhondzadeh et al. showed that people with GAD who took 45 drops a day for one month had the same reduction in their anxiety as those who took 30mg of the benzodiazepine oxazepam (Serax). But the participants taking passionflower didn't have the slowed cognitive functioning that the people who took oxazepam experienced. A few more trials followed; these tested passionflower as a premedication for surgical or dental procedures. The participants didn't have an anxiety disorder, but preparing for surgery is a situation that tends to generate high anxiety levels. The studies showed that passionflower reduced presurgical anxiety as effectively as oxazepam or midazolam (Versed).

It can be prepared as a capsule, tablet, liquid extract, or tea. Doses used in the studies were 45 drops of a liquid extract or 400mg to 700mg in a pill or syrup. Passionflower side effects aren't common but can include drowsiness, sedation, nausea, vomiting, and dizziness. Because of its sedating effects, you shouldn't take it with other sedating medications.

Passionflower has been combined with other agents to increase the effects. Euphytose is a combination capsule that contains passionflower, valerian, magnesium, and other ingredients.

My Take on Passionflower

I'm impressed that passionflower produced anti-anxiety effects similar to benzodiazepines. I'm not sure what to make of the fact that most of the studies are from outside of the United States. Often, traditional American medical science discounts international studies. But politics influences study interest and funding, and that could be a reason for the limited American studies. Excluding that confounder, passionflower may be very helpful for transient anxiety or as-needed anxiety relief. Seeing that it decreases anxiety presurgery makes me think that it might also be helpful for performance anxiety.

Even though it helped people with GAD who took it daily for a month, this was only one study, and we don't have enough information on how long the effects last. Also, because the studies used different protocols, you're winging it with how much to take and for how long.

Kava Kava (*Piper methysticum*)

Kava kava, or "kava" for short, is a plant found in the South Pacific and used for years in religious and cultural ceremonies. It's the national drink of Fiji, known as *yaqona* or *grog*. If you visit Fiji, you can take part in a ceremony that involves drinking the kava out of coconut bowls. People report feeling euphoric after drinking kava, along with some numbness in the mouth and throat.

Kava is commonly consumed as a tea but can also be taken as a pill. The typical dose for insomnia is 125mg to 250mg, taken at bedtime. We don't know exactly how kava works in the brain, but it's been proposed that the kavalactone found in the plant works on the GABA system and acts as a reuptake inhibitor of norepinephrine and dopamine. The antidepressant bupropion (Wellbutrin) works via this same mechanism.

Several controlled trials have shown that kava improves anxiety, promotes sleep, and gives a general sense of well-being. Because it affects GABA, it can have a similar relaxing effect as benzodiazepines.

The downside is that there have been several case reports of liver toxicity attributed to using kava, mostly outside of the United States. Liver injuries included hepatitis (inflammation), cirrhosis (liver hardening), and liver failure. Incidents of toxicity are low enough to be considered rare. Still, the FDA has issued warnings about the possibility and has urged people with pre-existing liver problems to consult their physician before taking any products containing kava. Canada and some European countries have banned the use of kava entirely.

Another precaution is that kava has many drug interactions, which can negatively affect other medications you take. Some people who have taken kava for 4 months or more have noticed a slight yellowing of the skin or a scaly skin rash. The yellow skin disappears once you stop taking the kava.

My Take on Kava

There is strong research support for kava's effectiveness for anxiety and sleep problems. However, the concerns about liver toxicity make me apprehensive about seeing it as a go-to remedy. Some believe that the liver toxicity results from people using it with other medications, or it could be related to how the formulation was prepared. If the toxicity lies in the preparation, that could explain why the people of Fiji continue to embrace it as their national drink. But the preparation explanation doesn't help you, the consumer, know what form is safe to use and for how long.

When in doubt, I err on the side of caution and avoid products that have questionable safety profiles.

Chamomile (*Matricaria recutita*)

Chamomile is a plant from the daisy family. Chamomile's sedating effect helps with anxiety and sleep. It also has an antispasmodic effect that people use to manage abdominal discomfort. You can consume chamomile as a pill, drink it as a tea, or inhale it as an essential oil.

To date, there have only been two randomized trials testing chamomile's effect on general anxiety symptoms. In one trial from 2009, participants who took 1,100mg of a chamomile extract had a modest improvement in their anxiety symptoms. The second trial, from 2016, evaluated the effects of 1,500mg doses over 6 months. Participants in both studies improved with the chamomile, but their symptoms returned at the same rate as those who didn't take it. Clinical trials haven't shown us how long the anti-anxiety effects last. Still, these studies and other nonrandomized trials have shown that chamomile has a relaxation effect.

If you prefer to drink chamomile tea, you'll probably need to have several cups spread out over the day to see a significant effect. There isn't a good way to know how much chamomile you're getting in a cup of tea. It's reasonable to assume that you're not getting as concentrated a dose as you would if you took 500mg pills three times a day.

Despite being well-tolerated, chamomile comes from the same plant family as ragweed and chrysanthemums. These plants can cause allergic reactions in people who are sensitive to environmental allergens. If you're prone to allergies, you should be cautious, because chamomile could trigger similar allergic reactions, such as wheezing, chest tightness, and hives.

Another issue with chamomile is that it contains coumarin, a naturally occurring blood-thinning agent. Coumarin differs from Coumadin, which is the brand name for a synthetically produced blood-thinning agent made from coumarin and other agents. The generic name for Coumadin is *warfarin*, which people take to treat blood clotting disorders. It's not expected that regular doses of chamomile would cause bleeding. Still, those who take blood-thinning agents such as Coumadin, aspirin, or even high doses of vitamin E should avoid chamomile supplements, as the combination could cause internal bleeding.

My Take on Chamomile

It's difficult to remember to take a pill three times a day. It's not clear if spreading it out over the day is necessary or if you can take the entire dose at once. It may be worth the trouble if you have moderate daily anxiety and don't want to take a prescription medication. Otherwise, you can drink the tea occasionally and pass on the supplements.

Valerian Root (*Valeriana officinalis*)

Valerian is a plant that is native to Europe and South Africa. It can be prepared as a powder, tea, tincture, essential oil, or capsule. The dietary supplement is made from the root of the plant. Valerian is thought to work by boosting GABA signaling.

Unfortunately, research into using valerian for anxiety is extremely limited, and studies have found no benefit over placebo. It's still widely used, and some participants in the studies reported improved sleep. The recommended dose for the capsule supplement is 500mg to 1,000mg a day, either at night for sleep or taken twice a day for anxiety. The common side effects are headache, diarrhea, drowsiness, and dizziness.

My Take on Valerian

I don't have a lot of confidence in this supplement for anxiety. It may be a nuisance to take it multiple times a day. Valerian has sedating properties, and it's likely best used as a sleep aid. If it works well enough to relax you for sleep, that extra sleep is always helpful for daytime anxiety.

Ashwagandha (*Withania somnifera*)

Ashwagandha is an evergreen herb in the nightshade family that grows in India, the Middle East, and Africa. The powder from the root has been used as a medicinal herb in Indian Ayurvedic medicine for centuries. It's thought to impart intellectual power, long life, and vigor. Its mental health application is for nervous exhaustion and insomnia.

The research evidence has been growing for the anxiety-reducing effects of ashwagandha. What's interesting about the trials is that ashwagandha seems to be more effective for chronic stress and anxiety symptoms than for anxiety disorders. Many of the studies are what researchers would consider low quality because the studies used a small number of participants or had flaws in their study designs. The data we have so far doesn't give enough information about an effective dose, but doses in some studies ranged from 250mg to 600mg a day. It's best taken in the morning, because it can interfere with your sleep if you take it at night. We haven't identified many side effects at the low doses, but in higher doses, usually over 1,000mg, people have experienced gastrointestinal problems like nausea, vomiting, and diarrhea. There have also been some reports of liver injury, possibly because of the herb.

My Take on Ashwagandha

I feel that ashwagandha shows promise, especially for ordinary, stress-related anxiety in the absence of a disorder. I included it because I think it's gaining popularity in its use for other problems, like hypothyroidism and weight loss, but we still have a long way to go before we know how to take it for anxiety and stress.

Cannabis

Cannabaceae is a family of flowering plants that contains 170 species, and cannabis is one of 11 genera within this family. This genus contains three species: *sativa*, *indica*, and *ruderalis*.

Cannabis is the botanical term for what is commonly called "marijuana." Some people believe that *sativa* is more energizing and *indica* is more relaxing, but research hasn't shown this to be a consistent pattern. Here's why the effects of cannabis are more complicated than examining the differences between plant species: cannabis, the plant, contains over 500 chemical substances that include over 100 cannabinoids, over 100 aromatic terpenes, and several flavonoids.

The two most studied compounds are the cannabinoids Δ9-tetrahydrocannabinol (THC) and cannabidiol (CBD). THC is a psychoactive compound that can produce psychotic symptoms and increase anxiety. CBD doesn't have these effects, and it can potentially decrease anxiety and psychosis. If you recall from our discussion of lavender, its active ingredient, linalool, is a terpene compound that is thought to decrease anxiety. By contrast, we know little about the terpenes in cannabis and what psychological effect they confer. So there may be terpenes in cannabis that have medicinal properties that expand beyond what we know about THC and CBD.

Naturally occurring cannabis that hasn't been altered contains a concentration of about 2% each of THC and CBD in a 1:1 ratio. But over the years, selective breeding has produced cannabis that is predominantly THC or CBD. With medical marijuana, the dispensaries offer the cannabis plant in varying ratios of THC to CBD.

Traditional medicine has created pharmaceutical products that are synthetic versions of THC or CBD. Dronabinol (Marinol) and nabilone (Cesamet) are synthetic THC prescribed for chemotherapy-induced nausea and vomiting. Dronabinol is also used for AIDS-associated loss of appetite and weight loss. Cannabidiol (Epidiolex) is synthetically produced CBD used to treat seizures in people with Lennox-Gastaut syndrome, Dravet syndrome, or tuberous sclerosis complex.

These three medications are all we currently have for using cannabis therapeutically, but many clinical trials on THC and CBD are underway. To date, the only conditions for which cannabis has been shown to be beneficial are chemotherapy-induced nausea and vomiting, chronic pain, and muscle spasticity from multiple sclerosis. There is no scientific data that supports the use of cannabis to treat any psychiatric condition. However, there might be potential for schizophrenia and PTSD; these conditions are the current focus of most research in this area.

My Take on Cannabis

I believe that cannabis has medicinal properties similar to other aromatic plants, like lavender. But the science just isn't advanced enough to detail the medically beneficial ingredients and how much of them we need to get the therapeutic benefit. CBD gummies are very popular, and it's hard not to want to try them. Using CBD for pain management is probably your best bet, but you still have the obstacle of finding a commercial product that works.

Aromatherapy

I've been a fan of essential oils for years. My family calls me the "potions master" because I like to whip up oil concoctions for almost any purpose, including sleep, bug bites, burns, and muscle soreness.

I think that essential oils can be very effective for calming mild anxiety, but how strong an effect you get and how long it lasts depends on several variables. These include the quality of the oil, the length of time you're exposed to it, the route of exposure (inhalation vs. skin absorption), and how often you use it. I'll address some of these issues in this section.

Let me begin by explaining how aromatherapy works. Aromatherapy is the practice of using essential oils for therapeutic purposes, like reducing anxiety and promoting relaxation. Essential oils are extracted from plants using a distillation process. You can use many plant parts, including flowers, leaves, stalks, bark, rind, and roots. The term *essential* doesn't mean that these oils are required for physiological functions, like essential nutrients. They're called this because they contain the essential elements, or essence, of a plant.

The oil is volatile, which means that it can become a vapor at room temperature and be inhaled. You can mix the oil with another substance, such as a carrier oil, alcohol, or lotion. You can then apply the oil mixture to your skin or spray it into the air. You can also put the oil in a diffuser that creates a continuous scented mist. Aromatherapy is commonly used in a therapeutic massage.

It's generally not recommended to consume essential oils orally because of their high concentration of organic compounds. Silexan (lavender) is an exception, because it's specially formulated for oral ingestion.

Many oils have a relaxing and sedating effect, but some are stimulating. They can also have other effects, like relieving pain or killing potentially dangerous microbes. For this discussion, we'll focus on the relaxing effects of the oils.

The main chemical constituents of the essential oils that have a therapeutic effect are the terpene compounds. We discussed earlier how lavender contains the terpenes linalool and linalyl acetate. There are terpenes in other oils, such as limene, geraniol, and citronellol, to name just a few. These chemical compounds give the oil its scent.

There are scores of scientific papers demonstrating the therapeutic benefits of essential oils. Much of this research was performed with animals, but there are enough human controlled trials to make aromatherapy a legitimate alternative approach to anxiety.

Here's how inhaling the oil affects your brain. Smell is one of your five senses, and it's controlled by the olfactory nerve. The olfactory nerve pathway starts in the upper part of your nasal cavity, penetrates the floor of your skull, and once on the other side of your skull, travels directly to the hippocampus and amygdala (among other areas). Your hippocampus and amygdala control emotional memory and reactions.

Back to the Star Trek analogy, inhaling chemical agents is like beaming straight to the ship's bridge. There's a direct pathway from your nose to your brain, and this is why inhaling gases and fumes is a big deal. However, not everything you inhale contains molecules that have a pharmacological effect. I don't want you to worry about everything you smell. But inhaling something is a faster route of absorption into your system than ingesting it, because the chemical gets straight to the brain and bypasses your digestive system.

Many essential oils have relaxing properties. Here are my top nine personal favorites.

Lavender (*Lavandula angustifolia*)

Lavender is extracted from the flowers and stalk of the plant by steam distillation. It has a sweet, floral aroma and is the most widely used and studied oil. The scent blends well with other oils. The key constituents are linalool and linalyl acetate.

Sandalwood (*Santalum album* L.)

Sandalwood is extracted from the bark of the Indian sandalwood, an evergreen tree. Because it comes from the woody stalk, it has a sweet, woodsy aroma. The key constituents are alpha-santalol and beta-santalol. Sandalwood is a premium essential oil and costs much more than the popular lavender.

Neroli (*Citrus aurantium* var. *amara*)

Neroli oil is distilled from the citrus blossoms of the bitter orange tree. It has a floral, citrus scent similar to orange oil. The key constituents are linalool, limonene, and beta-pinene. Neroli is also very pricey, because it takes a lot of blossoms to produce the oil. Fortunately, the aroma is potent, so you don't need much of it.

Vetiver (*Vetiveria zizanioides*)

Vetiver is a grass, and the oil is distilled from its roots. Its aroma is often described as smoky and woodsy. The key constituents are sovalencenol, khusimol and beta-vetivone. Most of the root oils have a heavy scent that lingers much longer than the floral scents. These long-lasting scents are called *base notes*. The lighter oils made from the flowers of the plants are called *top notes* and *middle notes*; these aromas fade faster than the base notes.

Roman chamomile (*Chamaemelum nobile*)

In the section on herbal supplements, you learned that chamomile petals can be dried and steeped as a tea. The flowers can also be steam distilled to make the essential oil. I include this as one of my favorites because it's much more effective than the tea for relaxation. The key constituents are angelate and pinocarveol.

Spikenard (*Nardostachys jatamansi*)

Spikenard is another oil I include among my favorites, even though I'm not a fan of the smell. Spikenard is a flowering plant in the honeysuckle family, which also includes valarian. The oil is steam distilled from the plant's roots, which gives it a woodsy, musty aroma. Its constituents are jatamansone, beta-gurjunene, and valeranone.

Some people find the aroma grounding, but I had the misfortune of spilling it on the tile in my bathroom. The oil penetrated the tile, and the aroma lingered for weeks. Although my husband and I found the aroma overwhelming, it made me feel like a loose noodle at bedtime.

A fun fact that drew me to spikenard is that it was the oil that Mary of Bethany used to anoint Jesus' feet.

Patchouli (*Pogostemon cablin*)

Patchouli is a flowering herb in the mint family. The oil is distilled from the leaves and stems, which gives it a woodsy, earthy aroma. The key constituents are patchoulol, bulnesene and alpha-guaiene. Patchouli became a popular fragrance in body oils in the 1960s and was associated with "hippie" culture.

Frankincense (*Boswellia carterii*)

Frankincense oil is distilled from the resin of *Boswellia carterii* trees in Northern Africa and is another oil with ancient and biblical references. Frankincense was one gift the wise men presented to Jesus after his birth. It was also used in religious ceremonies by the ancient Egyptians. Because it's distilled from the resin of the tree, it has a woodsy aroma. The key constituents are alpha-pinene, limonene, and alpha-thujene.

Valerian (*Valeriana officinalis*)

Valarian is a flowering plant also in the honeysuckle family. The oil is distilled from the plant's roots. The key constituents are bornyl acetate, camphene, and beta-pinene. The spikenard aroma eventually grew on me (maybe because I was forced to adjust to it in my bedroom until the scent wore off). But I still haven't learned to like the intense, musky odor of valerian root oil. Luckily, a little goes a long way, and if you combine it with more floral scents, you can create a very pleasant-smelling combination.

Ylang-Ylang (*Cananga odorata*)

Ylang-ylang is a tree that grows in tropical regions. The oil is distilled from the flowers of the tree and has a sweet, exotic aroma. The key compounds are germacrene D and alpha-farnesene. This oil can cause skin irritation or sensitization in people who are prone to develop allergic reactions.

And an honorable mention…

Bergamot (*Citrus bergamia*)

Bergamot is one of the citrus oils made from the rind of the bergamot orange. It's responsible for the distinctive taste of Earl Grey tea. This oil has a sweet, uplifting aroma. The key constituents are limonene and linalyl acetate.

Bergamot doesn't make the main list because it's phototoxic if you apply it to your skin. A phototoxic reaction occurs when you take a particular medication or apply phototoxic agents to your skin and then go into the sun. You can get a sunburn, skin irritation, or blistering from sun exposure. If you apply it to your skin, you should wait 18 hours before going out in the sun. (This warning doesn't apply to inhaling the oil.)

Aromatherapy Delivery Methods

One way to use essential oils is to put a few drops into a diffuser that creates a vapor scented by the oil. This method has the advantage of scenting an entire room, but it has two disadvantages. If you're in a large room, you may not be exposed to a large enough concentration of the oil's constituents. A second disadvantage is that other people exposed to the aroma might find it objectionable or react negatively to it.

Options that offer better control over your exposure are using single inhalers, mixing with a carrier oil and applying to your skin, applying drops to an absorbent accessory that you carry with you throughout the day, or adding to a bath.

Single Inhalers

You can buy aromatherapy inhalers that are tubes with an opening for a cotton wick that absorbs the oil. The tip of the tube has holes that allow you to smell the oil. It also comes with a cover to keep the oil and scent in the tube. The Vicks company makes a portable inhaler called the Vapoinhaler that uses the same principle. To make your own inhaler, you add 10–15 drops of your favorite oil, or you can make a blend of a few oils (for a total of 10–15 drops) and use the inhaler as needed throughout the day. If you keep the top on, these inhalers can last up to 6 months.

Skin Application

The essential oil can work through inhalation (the fastest route) and skin absorption. In most circumstances, you should not apply essential oils directly to your skin. There are some exceptions, like applying a few drops of lavender to a burn. The essential oils are very concentrated and can irritate your skin. To prevent this from happening, you dilute the essential oil with a carrier oil. Carrier oils are nonvolatile oils that are safe to apply to your skin. Some examples of carrier oils are sunflower oil, jojoba, avocado, fractionated coconut, and shea butter, just to name a few. Aloe vera gel makes an excellent carrier and is used more for hand gels and facial applications.

General dilutions guidelines are to use either 1% for a gentle concentration of oil, 2% for mild concentration, 3% for moderate concentration, or 5% for a strong concentration. Here is how to calculate the concentration: 1 milliliter is equal to about 20 drops of essential oil. If you start with 30 milliliters (1 ounce) of the carrier, five to six drops of essential oil will create a 1% dilution of the oil. For a 2% dilution, add 10 to 12 drops of essential oil to the carrier. Fifteen to eighteen drops will give you a 3% concentration; 25 to 30 drops will give you a 5% dilution.

Essential Oil Dilution	
1% for children, use in the bath, on the face, on sensitive skin, with the elderly, or during pregnancy (if the oil is safe in pregnancy)	5 to 6 drops of essential oil in 1oz (30ml) of carrier
2% for general long-term use, healthy adults	10 to 12 drops of essential oil in 1oz (30ml) of carrier
3% for short-term use like 3 to 4 weeks for an acute problem and in a concentrated area	15 to 18 drops of essential oil in 1oz (30ml) of carrier
5% for very short-term use (1-2 weeks) on a specific body area (no whole-body massage)	

For anxiety, stress, or sleep, stick to the 2% dilution to use it in a roll-on applicator or spray bottle. Essential oil bottles are usually sold with a top that allows you to dispense one drop at a time. Bigger bottles may have a dropper inside the top, but if they don't, you can buy droppers to extract the oil.

As for skin sensitivities, you should always test a small amount of the diluted oil on a small area to see if you react. Many oils are safe for the skin if diluted, but some oils are more irritating than others. Also, you can develop a sensitivity to an essential oil if you use it for a long time. This sensitivity is more likely to happen if you regularly use the concentrated oil directly on your skin without diluting it. Using it this way is referred to as using it "neat."

Essential oils most likely to cause skin irritation or sensitization:

- Bergamot oil
- Cinnamon bark oil
- Cinnamon leaf oil
- Clove oil
- Jasmine absolute
- Lemon leaf oil
- Lemongrass oil
- Melissa oil
- Myrtle oil
- Oregano oil
- Tea-tree oil (lemon-scented variety)
- Ylang-ylang oil

Essential oils known to be phototoxic:

- Angelica root oil
- Bergamot oil
- Cumin oil
- Grapefruit oil
- Lemon oil
- Lime oil
- Mandarin leaf oil
- Orange oil
- Rue oil

These lists are not all inclusive. (For a complete list, see Tisserand et al., 2014.)

Once you decide how you want to apply the oil, here are some ways you can use it to relax:

- Give yourself a foot massage with the oil in the evening.
- Apply a few drops to your pillowcase before bed.
- Keep the inhaler at hand and take a few whiffs during a stressful day.
- Put a few drops on the shower wall or door, or on a washcloth on your shower caddy.
- Mix a 1–2% dilution of the oil and add to Epsom or sea salt, then add the salt to a bath.*
- Put some oil in a roll-on applicator and rub on your wrists with it.
- Use an inhaler or diffuser to enhance your meditation.
- Apply some Peaceful Sleep Oil to your neck before bed (see recipe in the appendix).

> (*If you want to use the oil in a bath without the salt, you will need to mix the oil with a fixative to allow it to mix with water. You should not put drops directly in the bathwater, or it will float undiluted in the water and come in contact with your skin at full strength. Instead, you can use vegetable glycerin as a carrier to mix with your oil, then pour some of the solution into your bathwater. You should make a 1% dilution with the vegetable glycerin to use in the bath.)

Aromatherapy is a very versatile complementary approach to managing anxiety. I think it's very underutilized in traditional medicine, but it requires intention. Unlike a daily pill, it requires preparation and ongoing insight into the ebb and flow of your emotions. If you get yourself set up with easy access like inhalers and roll-ons with your favorite scents, it's something you can have at your fingertips to use whenever you want it. It's safe to use alongside the other tools I'll discuss in later chapters.

Acupuncture

Acupuncture has been a component of Chinese medicine for thousands of years. Western culture first adopted it in the 1800s. It rose in popularity in the 1970s, when Pulitzer prize-winning journalist James Preston traveled with then–Secretary of State Henry Kissinger to cover a presidential event. Mr. Preston developed acute appendicitis, requiring urgent surgery. The surgery was successful, but days after the surgery,

Mr. Preston experienced debilitating pain. He was treated with acupuncture, and his pain resolved. Mr. Preston wrote an article published in the New York Times on July 26, 1971, praising the "needle and herbal medicine."

Acupuncture is often used to treat pain, but there have been several studies showing benefits for state anxiety, generalized anxiety, and PTSD. The procedure is performed by someone trained in acupuncture medicine. The treatment is based on predetermined energy points in the body. According to Chinese medicine, there is an energy flow (Qi) that is aligned along meridian paths in the body. These paths need to be in alignment for optimal health, and disruption in the energy paths creates disease. Acupuncture uses needles inserted in specific points along the body to rebalance the energy flow between the opposing forces of yin and yang.

Chinese medicine incorporates spirituality and energy healing into the process. Western culture explains acupuncture as the stimulation of nerves with needles, pressure (e.g., acupressure), objects such as beads or seeds, or an electrical current. Scientists propose that stimulating sensory nerves activates endorphins, serotonin, and norepinephrine, and these chemicals are responsible for the clinical effect.

Traditional acupuncture and acupressure involve stimulating points along the body that correspond to the problem you want to treat. These points are mapped out along the meridian energy paths. Some of the anxiety studies have limited the paths to the ear, called *auricular stimulation*. The sessions usually last from 20 minutes to 1 hour. As with most complementary and alternative treatments, there isn't an established protocol for how many treatments are needed or how long the effects should last. Participants only had a few sessions in some studies, while others involved several sessions over 2 to 3 months.

Hypnosis

When I think about hypnosis, I imagine someone sitting in front of a hypnotist who is holding a swinging pocket watch. The hypnotist instructs the person to keep their eyes on the watch while they begin to feel sleepy. The person falls asleep and into a state where they can be easily manipulated with verbal commands. If the hypnotist says, "bark like a dog," they do it. When the hypnotist snaps his fingers, the person awakens from the sleep state and can't remember anything they did while asleep. This depiction is the television version of hypnosis and not the way it really works, at least not in a therapeutic setting.

Hypnosis developed from the work of German physician Franz Anton Mesmer in the late 1700s. He believed that people were affected by an invisible fluid in their bodies that was controlled by gravitational force. He termed this force "animal magnetism." He believed that the fluid's behavior had an impact on physical health and that a trained person could manipulate the force to heal clinical conditions.

Many in the medical community felt his Jedi Master force manipulation was not scientifically supported. But his methods became a popular movement called *mesmerism*. Mesmerism is where we get the term "mesmerized," which means to be intensely captivated.

Mesmerism was the humble beginnings of hypnosis, but in 1843, Scottish surgeon James Braid introduced the term *hypnosis* to refer to a trancelike state. Modern hypnosis is an altered state of awareness that results from profound physical and mental relaxation. You become selectively focused in a way that blocks out unconscious resistance that inhibits emotional processing. It's like taking down your defenses.

Hypnosis is usually conducted by someone trained in hypnotherapy. There are certification programs that require a minimum of a bachelor's degree in a health-related field. You can learn to induce a hypnotic state yourself, but you'll get better results if you have a few sessions with a hypnotherapist who can help you identify goals and develop scripts that fit those goals. You can also use prerecorded hypnotherapy audios to help you enter a hypnotic state and incorporate suggestions.

The Process of Hypnosis

There's the induction stage and the suggestion phase. The induction stage is about directing your focus using your senses. It can be visual, auditory, kinaesthetic, or imaginal.

With visual induction, you fix your gaze on something in the room, like a wall clock. For auditory induction, you can focus your hearing on music or other sounds, like tapping. Kinesthetic induction involves using movement such as progressive muscle relaxation. With this method, you start at one end of your body, either your head or your feet, and contract and then relax muscle groups. You continue to contract and relax muscles as you move to the other end of your body. Imaginal induction uses mental imagery: you immerse yourself in a past experience as if you were daydreaming about it.

The next part of the process involves hypnotic suggestions. One example is for your therapist to tell you to imagine that your limbs are heavy. Your limbs might then start to feel heavy. You could also use the postural sway technique to pretend that you're holding heavy suitcases with wind blowing against you. If you respond to this suggestion, you'll move ever so slightly, as if you're swaying back and forth with the wind.

It takes practice to let yourself relax and yield to these suggestions. Once you reach the trance state, the work begins. In this state, your mind is open and receptive to change. You're still aware of your surroundings, but you're detached from the external world and selectively focused on your thoughts and emotions. It's like having extreme tunnel vision or tunnel awareness. Because you have reduced awareness of your environment, you've entered a controlled, dissociative state.

Some people are more suggestible than others. The more suggestible you are, the more hypnotizable you are. There are questionnaires that might be able to measure your suggestibility or susceptibility, but some researchers feel that hypnosis hasn't been studied enough to allow us to reliably quantify suggestibility. In general, people with active imaginations who "zone out" or daydream frequently have the highest levels of hypnotic suggestibility.

There are different goals for hypnosis. Suppose you're addressing anxiety symptoms that resulted from trauma. In this case, hypnosis can allow you to revisit the trauma in a less threatening way so that you can process your painful emotions around it. Let's say that the experience was so devastating that you can't remember parts of it. This means you're not consciously aware of everything that happened, but your mind hasn't forgotten; it stays on threat-awareness duty, watching for things that might be similar to what happened. These similar events can trigger intense anxiety. But since the memories are unconscious, you won't necessarily connect the anxiety to the trigger.

Here, you could use hypnosis to reach a state of focused awareness of the event to recover memories and manage the emotions related to them.

Why would you want to recover the memories? Because stuffing them away and trying to forget about them doesn't heal you of the trauma. Instead, these unprocessed memories fester in your mind, randomly come to your attention, and create anxiety. Therefore, hypnosis can be a way to address repressed emotions and memories while your mind is open to exploring the event and you can handle the emotions.

Hypnotherapy can also help you overcome anxiety related to phobias. Once you reach the hypnotic state, a goal could be to help you understand the root cause of your phobia. Another goal could be to learn how to eliminate your aversion to the feared object or situation.

The length of a hypnotherapy session varies depending on the problem being addressed, but typical session times are between 30 minutes and one hour. You may find that you get sleepy if you spend too long in the relaxed trance state. After you've processed suggestions related to your issue, the last phase is to come out of the trance and return to full awareness. During this transition, the therapist or audio recording may give you a post hypnotic suggestion that applies to the issues you addressed. For example, if you'd had a traumatic experience that was accompanied by the sound of a whistle, a post hypnotic suggestion could be that you'll know you're safe the next time you hear a whistle. If this session and suggestion are effective, when you next hear a whistle, you still may feel unsettled, but you won't have a panic attack.

Extensive research establishes the benefits of hypnotherapy, but many studies are criticized for being of inferior quality. The absence of high-quality studies prevents experts from establishing clear protocols for using hypnotherapy. But in practice, people have used hypnotherapy as a standalone treatment for many problems, including pain, anxiety, depression, and to break habits like nail-biting. Hypnotherapy can also be used in combination with traditional therapy treatments, like cognitive behavioral therapy (CBT). If you want to try hypnotherapy on your own, there are scores of books, audio, and videos that provide guided inductions and scripts.

Reiki

Reiki is a type of energy healing that originated in Japan in the mid-nineteenth century. The process involves a healer placing their hands on or just above your body. With this movement, the healer manipulates your internal energy and transfers energy from their body to yours.

This requires a healer who is trained to use the technique. There are three levels of training: first degree, second degree, and master/teacher. A first-degree practitioner has the power to heal themselves and others with face-to-face contact. A second-degree practitioner has reached the first degree and can heal someone remotely, without face-to-face contact. A master has reached the first and second degrees and can train others.

Reiki is a spiritual experience, but it's not religious. The spiritual aspect of using symbols to advance the healing process makes some people uncomfortable receiving the treatment. Supporters of the Reiki technique say that you don't have to subscribe to beliefs to benefit from the process.

There is some limited research evidence that Reiki helps reduce anxiety symptoms, but none of the studies to date evaluated people with anxiety disorders. Whether or not you believe in the principles behind the healing, it can be a meditative practice that promotes relaxation. In general, relaxing experiences help with anxiety symptoms.

In the next chapter, we'll look at psychotherapy and a nerve-stimulation treatment.

CHAPTER 7

Psychotherapies

What is Psychotherapy?

Psychotherapy, also known as "talk therapy," is any form of treatment involving a dialogue between a patient and therapist to explore and resolve emotional issues. Psychotherapy facilitates change by increasing self-awareness and improving coping skills.

There are many available forms of psychotherapy to address various problems. Some therapies address specific issues, like trauma, while others focus on broader issues, like modifying your personality. The more focused therapies are usually brief, with weekly sessions lasting from 12 to 16 weeks.

Psychoanalysis and Psychodynamic Therapies

These are longer-term treatments that can last for years. Psychoanalysis, which was developed by Sigmund Freud, is one of the earliest forms of psychotherapy. The treatment aimed to make unconscious thoughts and behaviors conscious so that they could be changed and made more adaptive. (Psychological defense mechanisms are examples of maladaptive behaviors driven by unconscious motivations.)

Traditional psychoanalysis, which is still alive and well today, involves one to five sessions per week. In some cases, the patient lies on a couch facing away from the analyst; in others, they sit face to face. This type of therapy focuses on resolving unconscious conflicts that often originate in early childhood. The process can involve free association, where you talk about whatever comes to mind with minimal prompts from the analyst or censoring from yourself. It also incorporates dream interpretation, analyzing transference (projecting feelings you had for authority figures onto your therapist), and recognizing resistance (attempts to stay distant or uninvolved).

In each session, you do most of the talking, with only occasional input from the analyst. Since the process can take years to complete, over time, the analyst helps you become more aware of your unconscious fears and fantasies to allow you to gain control over them.

Because of the time and financial investment required, psychoanalysis is not the predominant form of psychotherapy today. It's also difficult to find practicing psychoanalysts in smaller cities and rural areas. As a result, a less intensive form of this therapy was developed, called psychodynamic psychotherapy. Practitioners may or may not be trained in psychoanalysis, but psychoanalytic theory is the lens through which they view mental health and the therapeutic relationship. The frequency of this therapy can be as often as one or two times per week or as infrequently as once every 2 to 4 weeks. The therapist is also more involved in prompting you on what to talk about and giving you direct feedback on your interpersonal conflicts.

Psychodynamic psychotherapy still aims to help you understand unconscious fears and motivations; it can also help with anxiety. But both therapies are more directed at changing personality styles, improving relationships, and addressing personal issues like low self-esteem. These therapies are not as effective for addressing phobias, panic attacks, obsessive-compulsive symptoms, or trauma. For these symptoms, you might need a therapy that has a more specific focus on treating anxiety.

Cognitive Behavior Therapy (CBT)

This is the grandaddy of psychotherapies. It has the most evidence behind it as a standalone treatment for anxiety and depression. CBT is effective for treating all anxiety disorders, OCD, and PTSD. It's a combination approach that has two parts: cognitive and behavioral. Your therapy can focus on one or both. With a cognitive focus, you examine your thinking style and how it contributes to your behavior or your beliefs about yourself. With a behavioral focus, you engage in activities that break the cycle of your maladaptive, conditioned behaviors and reinforce new, adaptive behaviors.

Unlike psychoanalysis and psychodynamic therapy, CBT focuses on the here-and-now and doesn't necessarily explore your early experiences with your caregivers. You can think of CBT as an *approach* to therapy, because there are many types of CBT.

Here are some therapies that incorporate CBT:

- Rational emotive behavior therapy
- Cognitive restructuring
- Graduated exposure with response prevention
- Dialectical behavior therapy
- Systematic desensitization
- Relaxation therapy
- Behavioral activation
- Cognitive processing therapy

These therapies are very focused and specific, often involving homework assignments. I've had some patients who love getting homework, because it makes them feel actively involved in their treatment and holds them accountable. I've had patients who loathe assignments and would rather keep the work of their therapy to the session time. Once they leave my office, they don't want to feel bogged down with things to do for next time.

All these therapies require specialized training, and most of them are manualized, meaning there is a specific protocol for the therapist to follow. Any licensed provider can be trained in these therapies, and often Master's-level therapists and psychologists have several of these therapies in their repertoire.

In your search for a cognitive behavior therapist, your psychiatrist options will probably be limited. This is because psychiatry training programs vary in what therapies they teach residents. Additionally, economic factors like low insurance reimbursement for therapy often drive psychiatrists to focus more on medication management over therapy.

In later chapters, we'll look at tools to address your anxiety symptoms, many of which are based on CBT principles.

Acceptance and Commitment Therapy (ACT)

This is a relatively new therapy model with some cognitive behavior elements. ACT teaches psychologically flexibility, which is the ability to adapt to emotionally distressing experiences without the need to escape or control them. You learn to face difficult circumstances by reframing them around your values. To put it another way, psychological flexibility allows you to continue to pursue your goals even in the face of adversity.

As you learned in our discussion of phobias, the more we avoid things, the more threatening they can become. ACT teaches you to use mindfulness skills to appreciate and observe your distressing thoughts and feelings without judgment. Facing your fears with openness and acceptance helps you defuse the negativity associated with the fear, making it less distressing.

Facing distress doesn't mean you have to *enjoy* feeling anxious. Imagine that social anxiety makes you fear being embarrassed to the extent that you refuse your friends' invitations to social gatherings. The more you avoid engaging with groups of people, the harder it becomes. Eventually, your fear around going to a happy hour grows so large that you experience intense chest pain at just the thought of going. But your fear and anxiety response didn't start that intensely. It began with uneasiness around people, and through avoidance, this uneasiness grew into a physical symptom.

In this example, ACT could help you sit with your fear of embarrassment and see it as an emotional reaction you create in your mind. It's not a fact that you are stupid; it's your negative assessment of yourself that makes you conclude this and keeps you isolated from others. Since having close friendships is important to you, nurturing these relationships becomes the priority when considering your friends' invitations. Your relationship values prompt you to override your resistance to go out with your friends.

ACT has been shown in some cases to be more effective than more traditional therapies like CBT. The mindfulness component of ACT helps you focus on the present rather than dwelling on the past or future. Past regrets and future worries are prominent themes in anxiety.

Trauma Treatments

Trauma causes very complex reactions, including anxiety. It requires a targeted therapy to address the complex symptoms. We talked in Chapter 3 about the anxiety that comes with post-traumatic stress disorder (PTSD). PTSD results from a sudden acute event, but you can also experience the effects of trauma from chronic exposure to traumatic events, like bullying or childhood abuse. Adverse childhood events like the death of a parent or witnessing a difficult divorce can also produce a traumatic response that is best handled by a trained trauma specialist.

A person who markets themselves as a trauma specialist usually spends most—if not all—of their working hours treating trauma patients. Their training might include working in a facility with a trauma unit, such as a veterans hospital. To sufficiently address trauma, your therapy must include more than improving your coping skills. Focusing on your coping skills can be helpful, but it's insufficient to address the full scope of your trauma symptoms.

Currently, there are three evidence-based therapies for trauma:

1. Eye movement desensitization and reprocessing (EMDR)

2. Cognitive processing therapy (CPT)

3. Prolonged exposure therapy (PET)

Let's look at an example that might lead you to seek out one of these therapies.

The Gas Station Hold-Up

You pull into a gas station to fill up your car. After putting the hose in the tank, you sit in your car while the tank fills with gas. As you look down at your phone, someone holds a gun to your head and tells you to get out of the car. You have two children in the back seat and don't want the attacker to drive away with your children. You don't know what to do, so you freeze. The attacker then aims the gun at your whimpering children and tells them to "shut the F$%** up!" You stick your wallet through the window in front of the gun, hoping that it will satisfy the attacker and block any gunshots. Your throat is closing. Unable to scream, you barely whisper, "Please, don't." The attacker takes your wallet and aims the gun back at you. If he shoots you, he can still take your children. You want to drive away, but he may shoot as you restart your car. As you contemplate your options, another car pulls up, and the attacker runs away with your wallet.

The police arrive and get your account of what happened. You can't give the police a physical description of the attacker, because he covered his face with a ski mask. You remember his eyes but can't recall what he was wearing or describe his build. How can the police expect you to notice his clothing while he's pointing a gun at your sweet, helpless children? The police interrogate you about why you didn't call for help, as the gas station attendant was only 20 feet away. They also want to know why you gave the attacker your wallet, which contained your driver's license and home address. By the end of the interview, you feel like a reckless, poor excuse for a parent who has put their entire family in danger.

You spend weeks afraid that the attacker will track you down at your home. You stop sleeping at night so you can watch your security cameras. You have dreams about your children being bound and executed by a firing squad. You have intrusive waking thoughts of seeing the barrel of the gun in your face. You ruminate about various scenarios that could have played out if you'd let him take your car. You have panic attacks as you wait in the carpool line to drop off your children at school.

Here's how these issues might be resolved with EMDR, CPT, and PET.

EMDR

EMDR works on the theory that traumatic memories are stored differently in the brain than nontraumatic memories. It's as though the intense negative emotions around the experience block your ability to process the memory fully. With incomplete processing, you selectively associate memories of the experience with negative cognitions. For example, when you think about the gas station, you focus on how you failed your children and acted ineptly with decision making, like not screaming to alert others or giving away your wallet and identifying information. Your memories of the event are predominantly negative and self-critical. These unprocessed memories replay in your mind and cause you a lot of distress.

You don't think about how all your actions revolved around protecting your children. Instead, you blame yourself, and anything positive about the experience (like being saved by the other customer's arrival) is forgotten. Also, as is typical for traumatic memories, your recall of the event feels like it is happening in real time. You feel the same level of fear you felt that day, as if you are currently in danger. You can't tell the difference between your level of safety then and today.

EMDR works by desensitizing your traumatic memories, restructuring negative beliefs around the memories, and reducing the physical and mental arousal you feel when reminded of the event. With the standard procedure, you focus on the emotionally charged memories and associated emotions. While you think about the memories, your therapist uses a process to activate both sides of your brain. This brain stimulation can happen visually, using your eyes to follow your therapist's finger left to right or following a light on the wall that moves side to side. Some therapists use auditory stimulation, like a tone or a tapping sound, that plays on your left and right sides. Bilateral brain stimulation is theorized to enhance emotional processing and allows you to develop complete memories that include positive associations.

With EMDR, there is a preparation phase and a processing phase. In the preparation phase, your therapist will help you think of troubling memories from the event and identify your negative beliefs. Your negative thoughts focus on how you feel about yourself (being defective or inept), your level of responsibility (self-blame), your current level of safety, and your level of control.

Let's say your worst memory from the event is seeing the man turn the gun toward your children. You see it as if it happened in slow motion. To identify your associated negative thoughts, you can ask yourself, "What's the worst thing this memory says about me?" Your answer could be that you think you failed to protect your children. You also believe that you too easily collapse under pressure, and because of this weakness, you can't be trusted with your children's safety.

The discovery process also helps you recognize the emotions and bodily sensations you experience when you visualize the scene. In your case, you feel shame, embarrassment, self-hatred, nausea, and chest tightness.

During the processing phase, you imagine the distressing scene and think about your negative beliefs while moving your eyes from left to right or listening to sounds from alternating sides. Your distressing scene is the gun being pointed at your children while you sit frozen, unable to move or cry out for help. Then, you let yourself think about whatever else comes into your mind.

Part of the processing phase includes integrating positive thoughts into the memory. To do this, the therapist may ask you, "When you picture the gun and think about how you couldn't stop the robbery, what would you prefer to believe about yourself today?" Your answer might be, "I did the best I could in the split second I had to react. I put my children's needs first."

The therapist would ask other questions about how much you believe your statement and use a body scan exercise to process nausea, chest tightness, and other negative body sensations. The length of the sessions varies, but they average 90 minutes. The number of sessions you require depends on how many memories and negative thoughts you need to process.

EMDR can also be used for multiple traumatic exposures. Each of those experiences may be associated with unique memories and negative thoughts. Therefore, having a history of multiple traumatic experiences will probably require more sessions.

EMDR is a very targeted treatment that can produce improvement in symptoms in just a few sessions. Studies have looked at the number of sessions required to eliminate PTSD symptoms. Those results show that 90% of people with one trauma experienced a resolution of their symptoms after three sessions, 77% of people with multiple traumas recovered after six sessions, and 77% of combat veterans recovered from PTSD after 12 sessions.

EMDR has been validated to work for PTSD, but more studies show improvement with general anxiety symptoms that are not rooted in trauma.

CPT

Cognitive processing therapy is a type of CBT that helps you change unhelpful thoughts and beliefs about the trauma you experienced. It's based on the premise that people who experience traumatic events develop faulty thinking that reinforces their traumatic symptoms. CPT is used by the United States Department of Veterans Affairs as a primary treatment for PTSD.

The therapy is very structured, and practitioners use a manual to guide them through 12 weekly sessions. It starts with a homework assignment: you write an impact statement that details the event and how it made you feel. You then read your impact statement to the therapist, who will help you identify your "stuck points": the thoughts and beliefs that stifle your recovery from the trauma. Stuck points center on five trauma themes:

- Safety
- Trust
- Power or control
- Self-esteem
- Intimacy

From your gas station experience, some of your stuck points are the beliefs that you're never safe (safety), you never know when this will happen again (control), you can't be trusted to make smart decisions in an emergency (self-esteem), and you're a failure as a parent (self-esteem). These beliefs keep you in a state of panic and tank your self-esteem.

The next step is to challenge these thoughts using the ABC Worksheet: The "A" stands for activating event. "B" is for belief or stuck point. "C" is for consequence or feeling that stems from your belief. To complete the worksheet, you describe an event that activates your emotions and describe what you think about the event and how it makes you feel. You then examine whether your thoughts are realistic, and if not, how you'd think differently if the situation arose in the future. In addition to focusing on triggering events, you spend several sessions exploring your beliefs across the five trauma themes.

With this therapeutic approach, you perform a deep analysis of your faulty thinking and how it shows itself in different situations. You learn to stop letting automatic negative thoughts dominate your behavior. This approach differs from EMDR, which works to lessen the intensity of your negative thoughts and emotions by activating both sides of your brain while you relive the experience.

In some ways, CPT and general cognitive therapy give you more longstanding mental tools you can apply to other life situations. Because EMDR has you relive the experience by talking about it, it is more like exposure therapy.

PET

Prolonged exposure therapy is a behavioral therapy that addresses the avoidance symptoms of PTSD. As I previously mentioned, avoiding unpleasant things lets your fears take a stronger foothold and intensifies their negative impact. With PTSD, you avoid memories of the event or things that remind you of it. By exposing yourself to the things you're avoiding, you become desensitized to their anxiety-provoking effects.

PET involves having you face the unpleasant experiences and teaches you how to manage the anxiety that accompanies the experience. In this way, you gradually gain control over how the event or memories affect you.

There are two kinds of exposure techniques: in vivo and imaginal exposure. In vivo exposure entails exposing yourself to a real-life situation; imaginal exposure is doing this in your imagination. The in vivo exposures are homework assignments you complete in between sessions, and you engage in imaginal exercises in the therapy sessions. PET is less structured than CPT regarding the number of sessions and how the therapist conducts each session. But generally, PET is completed over 12 to 16 weekly sessions.

If you receive PET for your gas station experience, your therapist will talk to you about the experience and determine what things you're avoiding because of it. After the first session, you might realize that you've avoided all gas stations since the event. To protect you from feeling retraumatized, your spouse has taken over the responsibility of filling up the cars with gas.

You used to avoid driving, but you couldn't get out of your children's carpool duty. You tolerate driving your children to school, but you wait until the last minute to pull up so that you don't have to sit in the car very long. You're not always successful in coordinating this timing, so your children are now late to school at least once a week. You also manage to drive to the grocery store and other places within a 3-mile radius. But you've postponed important doctors' appointments because those offices are further away and have parking decks that remind you of the tight space of the gas station.

For your in vivo exposure, your homework might be to arrive earlier in the carpool line and wait in line with the other cars. To manage your anxiety, you're instructed to practice controlled breathing while you tolerate being uncomfortable. Over time, the situation will trigger less anxiety. After you master the carpool line, your next assignment is to drive to your doctor's office or any other office with a parking deck. The last step involves driving to gas stations.

To engage in imaginal exposure, you repeatedly talk about memories of the experience in the session. Your therapist may also have you record yourself talking about it and listen to the recordings at home.

As you can see with this therapy, you're not addressing any of your thoughts about the trauma, but learning how to re-experience the event in real life and in your mind with less fear and trepidation. Gaining control over how the experience makes you feel dissipates the negative thinking about the trauma. Changing your behavior around the trauma to lessen your symptoms has more in common with EMDR than CPT.

All three therapies have been shown to work effectively in treating trauma reactions. Which one you choose depends on your therapy preferences and what would be a good fit for you. CPT and PET involve homework assignments. The CPT worksheets are analytical and require attention to daily triggers and your corresponding emotions. If you dislike being this reflective, you may prefer the behavioral exercises or EMDR. On the other hand, some people find EMDR too abstract with its intensive processing of memories and emotions. In that case, you may prefer to measure your progress with the structured exercises of CPT or PET.

Neuromodulation

In the last part of this chapter, I want to discuss a nonmedication treatment used for moderate to severe cases of obsessive-compulsive disorder: deep transcranial magnetic therapy (dTMS).

Severe cases of OCD often don't improve enough with medication alone. The preferred therapy is exposure and response prevention. With this therapy, patients are gradually exposed to situations that involve their obsession, and then they're kept from performing the compulsion that mitigates the anxiety. Here's a simple example: a person with a germ phobia may be asked to stick their hand in a trashcan and not wash it for 20 minutes.

This kind of behavior therapy may not be workable for those whose obsessions keep them locked in their home or prevent them from speaking to a therapist. Severe avoidance is better addressed with brain stimulation.

Deep TMS uses magnetic fields to stimulate nerves in the medial prefrontal cortex and anterior cingulate cortex. Researchers believe the electrical circuits in this part of the brain misfire, causing an unregulated fear that you can't extinguish on your own. The magnetic stimulation serves as a "reset button" to unscramble the nerve signals, which optimizes communication pathways. The process is similar to getting a

brain scan using magnetic resonance imaging (MRI). TMS was first
approved for treatment-resistant depression, but now there is a protocol
for OCD called *high frequency deep TMS*.

During a session, you wear a helmet with a built-in magnetic coil.
The sessions last about 20 minutes, and you remain awake for the entire
procedure. A standard course of treatment is five treatments a week for
6 weeks. You can combine TMS with other treatments, like medication or
psychotherapy.

The procedure is safe, and because it doesn't require anesthesia, you're
not at risk for confusion or memory loss. The magnet coil tapping in
the helmet can cause some people to experience temporary scalp pain or
headaches after the procedure. But after a few sessions, your scalp becomes
less sensitive to the tapping, and the side effects become less pronounced.
The most serious possible adverse effect is a risk of a seizure after the
procedure. These are rare and tend to be a one-off occurrence after the
session and not the start of a permanent seizure disorder.

Clinical trials show that dTMS reduces OCD symptoms about as well
as antidepressant medications. But dTMS has the advantage of a faster
therapeutic response without the medication side effects. An added benefit
to this treatment is that clinical trials showed people continue to improve
weeks after the treatment ends. Therefore, once you finish your session,
there's still room for more improvement with time.

That's a wrap for psychotherapies and treatments that require
intervention from a trained professional. In the next chapters, we'll look
at mind, body, and behavioral tools you can use on your own to improve
your anxiety.

CHAPTER 8

Mind Tools

People cope with anxiety and distress in different ways. Sometimes your response will be adaptive, meaning helpful to you. Other times, your response will be maladaptive or problematic.

In the next three chapters, we'll look at various tools you can use to manage your anxiety. Remember that no single tool will resolve all aspects of your anxiety. With a natural approach, you'll want to use multiple tools to reduce or eliminate your target symptoms (those that are causing distress).

Recognizing Your Target Symptoms

First, let's consider how you might identify your target symptoms. Suppose you have significant social anxiety that causes you to miss important work-related gatherings and prevents you from speaking up in meetings. When forced to participate, you experience shortness of breath, a racing heart, and nausea. Your anxiety causes you to sleep poorly the night before a scheduled meeting. After the meeting, you spend hours ruminating about what others thought of you and how you were "such an idiot."

For this example, here are the target symptoms you'd want to reduce or eliminate:

- Avoidance of social gatherings.
- Momentary autonomic arousal in the form of a racing heart, shortness of breath, or nausea.
- Insomnia when anticipating an event or encounter.
- Worry about your performance.
- Ruminations about what others think of you.

There probably is not a single intervention that will eliminate all of these symptoms. And certain tools will work better for some people than for others. It's important to recognize your different target symptoms so that you can address them individually. If you lump everything together—these symptoms are all "anxiety," after all—you can end up using the wrong tool for the job.

The behavioral tools can help with specific situations or help turn down the dial on your general anxiety. Worry and anxiety related to distorted thinking typically respond better to the mind tools. On the other hand, physical symptoms and sleeping problems respond better to the body tools.

Here are some tools you could use for the target symptoms listed above:

- **Avoidance:** journaling and reframing, graded exposure, interoceptive exposure, self-hypnosis, affective labeling

- **Autonomic arousal:** applied relaxation, deep breathing, vagal maneuvers, grounding, yoga, weighted blanket
- **Insomnia:** applied relaxation, supplements (magnesium, lavender), aromatherapy, scheduled worry time, meditation, ASMR, music, weighted blanket
- **Worry:** journaling with reframing, affirmations, affective labeling
- **Ruminations:** journaling with reframing and affirmations, meditation, scheduled worry time

As you can see, there are a lot of different tools. This is just an example to illustrate how you might take a layered approach to natural solutions for your mental health. If you expect one thing to erase all your symptoms, you'll be left believing that nothing works. Layering interventions takes discipline and patience.

Now, let's look at the mind tools you could use to reduce the mental angst and negative thoughts that drive your anxiety. You can think of mental anxiety as having two components: (1) selectively focusing on threats and fears, and (2) acting on negative assumptions. Mind tools teach you how to shift your focus of attention away from worry and fear and change your negative thoughts.

Here's how these tools break down:

Attention Tools
Mindfulness
Meditation
Grounding

Thought Content Tools
Journaling
Gratitude
Affective labeling
Affirmations
Worry time
Reframing

Mindfulness

There is a misconception that mindfulness is a structured meditation practice. But the term *mindfulness* refers to a practiced mindset with which you experience the world. Mindfulness is attending to your present experience in a way that is open and nonjudgmental.

It takes effort to be in the present moment because, whether or not you realize it, we're always thinking about the past or the future. For example, while you're at work, you might look forward to the end of the day or plan for your weekend. You may spend time regretting something you said in the past and worry about how it will affect your reputation. This type of thought process is automatic for many. Mindfulness allows you to center yourself in the present and not place yourself in the past or future. Through this mechanism, you can reduce self-critical thoughts.

Experiencing a moment differs from thinking about it. We spend more time thinking and processing thoughts than we do experiencing them. Thoughts can be your friend when they're creative or they help you make plans or solve a problem. Thoughts can be your enemy when they make you worry, ruminate, or weave negative stories about yourself.

To be clear, there are benefits to reflecting on the past and future. It's important to enjoy pleasant memories and plan effectively for future events. But worry makes you spend most of your time in the future, and rumination makes you spend most of your time in the past. Practicing mindfulness can expand how much time you spend fully experiencing the present.

Jon Kabat-Zinn, Professor of Medicine Emeritus at University of Massachusetts Medical Center, brought mindfulness to mainstream medicine in the United States through his Mindfulness-Based Stress Reduction (MBSR) program. Mindfulness is now integrated into other therapies, such as mindfulness-based cognitive therapy, acceptance and commitment therapy, dialectical behavior therapy, and mindfulness-based eating awareness training.

The following components of mindfulness can help you better understand how it works:

Attention. Mindfulness starts when you pay attention to something in the moment. This can be a situation, like a conversation, or a task, like washing dishes. You want to be aware of both internal and external sensations. Tune into your thoughts, emotions, and physical sensations to accomplish this.

Awareness. Awareness involves observing things without judgment. You simply see them as existing and present without labeling them as good or bad. This is not to say that you should never have an opinion, because you will. But with mindfulness, even your opinion is something to observe with passive curiosity.

Acceptance. This is accepting the current situation as it is without wanting or striving to change it. For example, if you feel sad, you don't struggle to change your emotion or suppress it. You accept that you're experiencing sadness as one of many possible emotions.

Detachment. With detachment, you learn to appreciate that you are not defined by your emotions or experience. If you notice that you feel angry, you can recognize the feeling without reducing yourself to it (e.g., "I'm just an angry person."). Identifying with the anger primes you to act on it, usually impulsively. When you stop identifying with your thoughts, you can see how your thoughts are not fact. Distorted, anxious thinking makes it difficult to see individual thoughts as subjective and temporary.

Conscious reaction. By pausing and observing your thoughts and emotions, you delay your reaction. This delay breaks the rhythm of automatic (mindless) responses and reduces impulsive reactions.

It's very easy to engage in activities mindlessly. Multitasking is a common way we act without focusing intently on the present experience. Other examples of acting mindlessly include …

- Forgetting someone's name a few minutes after they introduce themselves.
- Walking past a place and not remembering it later.
- Eating a bag of chips while you're watching television and not realizing the bag is empty.
- Breaking things out of carelessness.

There are several ways you can practice mindfulness. One informal way is to become mindful of daily activities like washing dishes, brushing your teeth, eating, pumping gas, or grocery shopping. Mindful eating is a weight-loss strategy because it helps people eat less food and pay more attention to the quality of the food they consume.

Using an Anchor to Control Your Thoughts

Mindfulness trains you to focus even when you're surrounded by distractions, like television or phone notifications. Unless you close yourself in a vault, you will always be subject to these distractions. The aim of mindfulness is to learn how to take back control over your attention.

Even in the absence of distracting stimuli, it's natural for your thoughts to drift back to the past or present. When this happens, one way to redirect your attention is to focus on an object or experience that becomes your anchor. This anchor can be your breathing, an item, or something sensory, like a smell or sound.

Let's look at how this could play out if you were worrying about something while washing the dishes. Since this task entails a lot of physical movement, you might pick an anchor that remains constant, like your breathing pattern. Then, use your senses to observe the activity. Notice the temperature of the water, the texture of soap bubbles, or the slickness of the plates. Notice the sound the plate makes when you set it down to dry. These are all tiny details that you probably miss most of the time. If you find your mind wandering back to the phone call you need to make when you finish or the presentation you have to give tomorrow, simply redirect your thoughts back to your anchor, then go back to observing all other aspects of your current process. If you spend 15 minutes washing the dishes, you've just engaged in a 15-minute mindfulness exercise.

Conscious Listening

Another way to incorporate mindfulness into ordinary activities is to engage in conscious listening. This entails listening intently while someone is speaking to you. Listen as though you must repeat what the person says to someone who is not in the room or as if you'll be quizzed on this information later. If you don't talk to many people, you can watch someone talk on television or listen to a podcast.

While you're listening, resist the urge to think ahead to anticipate the punchline. You may find that this activity is more challenging than it appears because your mind processes words much faster than we speak them. So if you listen to a slow talker (like myself), it may be hard to stay in the conversation and not wonder what color eyeshadow the person is wearing. Just as with any other mindful exercise, your mind will inevitably wander away from your intended focus. When that happens, bring your focus back to the conversation. There's no judgment with this process, and there is no perfect way to do it. With practice, you can gain better control over your mental process.

Grounding

Grounding differs slightly from mindfulness because you do more than observe whatever comes to your mind without judgment. Instead, with grounding, you selectively focus on things that help you feel safe in the present moment. Put another way, mindfulness is an attitude of present awareness, and grounding is a mechanism you can use to remain present.

You can use grounding to calm yourself from a panic attack or reduce fear triggered by traumatic memories. Another use for grounding is if you dissociate. Grounding helps pull you out of your detached state and brings you back to the moment. Grounding works by channeling your attention to a neutral object or activity in the present.

There are many exercises you can use as grounding techniques. Some involve constructing mental images, and others engage you in a relaxing activity. Here are a few examples. There are more for you in the appendix.

5-4-3-2-1

This exercise helps you use your senses to notice your environment.

5. Name *five* things you can *see*.

Scan the room and say the first five things you see. You can name them aloud or think them to yourself. Since your mind is usually very active when you're anxious, I think it's best to say them aloud for greater impact, even if you whisper them.

4. Name *four* things you can *feel*.

This can be something in your hand, the clothing on your skin, or the chair you're sitting on. It can also include body sensations like your heartbeat or your chest moving up and down as you breathe.

3. Name *three* things you can *hear*.

Some examples include the sound of a clock ticking, cars outside, or a television in the next room.

2. Name *two* things you can *smell*.

If the room you're in doesn't seem to have a smell, check yourself; Are you wearing a fragrance or scented deodorant? Do your clothes smell of laundry detergent or sweat? If you're outside, can you smell the soil or flowers?

1. Name *one* thing you can *taste*.

You don't need to taste something new. This can include your toothpaste or a lingering taste from the last thing you ate. Since it's not always easy to sense a distinctive taste, you can also name something you would like to taste. Some people eliminate the taste sensation and instead name one good quality about themselves.

Glitter Jar

A glitter jar is similar to a snow globe that you shake in order to watch the snow settle. The floating snow (or glitter, in this case) is a metaphor for how your scattered mind will eventually settle. When you feel anxious, you shake the jar to stir up the glitter. Then you remain still as the liquid clears up and the glitter falls back down.

Waiting intently for the glitter to stop falling can put you into a state of mindful awareness. Seeing the glitter fall to the bottom can also remind you how fast-moving thoughts impair your mental vision. To gain clarity, you need to remain still while your thoughts settle. The glitter on the bottom of the jar is analogous to how your anxious thoughts don't completely disappear; instead, they move aside to allow you to see through them.

Another way you can use the glitter jar is to use it as a timer for a mindful exercise. You can shake the jar and focus on your breaths until the glitter settles. Then, try to move on to your next task calmly, with greater clarity.

There are several ways to make a glitter jar, but here is one simple recipe.

Materials:

> 1 glass jar with a tight-fitting lid (or a plastic bottle, if used with children)
>
> Glitter (preferably of different shapes and sizes, so they fall at different rates)
>
> Clear glue or vegetable glycerin
>
> Water (preferably distilled)
>
> Food coloring (optional)

Instructions:

1. Use one part glue (or glycerin) to two parts water. One of the water parts should be warm, and the second part can be cool or room temperature. You can add more glue as you like, but be careful not to make the liquid too thick, or your glitter will float indefinitely.
2. Add the one-part warm water to your jar with the glue and mix. Using warm water will help prevent the glue or glycerin from remaining in a clump.
3. Add the remaining one-part water. Shake to mix thoroughly.
4. Add as much glitter as you like, a little at a time.
5. Optionally, add a few drops of food coloring, one drop at a time. Take care not to make it too dark to see the glitter.
6. If your mixture is too thick, you can thin it out by adding one or two drops of liquid soap.
7. Secure the lid, and it's ready for use.

Mental Challenges

These are exercises that require focus and problem solving, so they can distract you from your anxious thoughts. Here are a few examples:

- Name as many states as you can.
- Say the months of the year backward.
- Recite multiplication tables.
- Recite the lyrics to a song you like.

Reassurance Statements

Remind yourself that you are safe. Remind yourself that your anxiety will pass, as it always does. Remind yourself that your anxiety is your mind playing tricks on you, and it doesn't mean that something is physically wrong with you.

The best way for these grounding techniques to work is to practice them when you're calm and don't need them. Once you become accustomed to the flow of the exercise, it can become an automatic reflex when you're in distress.

Meditation

Meditation is a formal practice that involves focusing your attention and awareness on a specific object, thought, or activity to achieve mental clarity and emotional stability. Meditation has its roots in the contemplative practices of Hinduism and Buddhism. However, since the nineteenth century, the practice has spread to other parts of the world and has become a nonreligious mental exercise.

There are many ways to practice meditation, and the different methods can be grouped into three categories: attentional, constructive, and deconstructive. These fall on a spectrum from basic to advanced.

Attentional Meditations

The most basic kind of meditation, these focus on your awareness of your thoughts, behaviors, emotions, and perceptions. Two simple attentional meditations are breathing meditation and the body scan.

Breathing Meditation

Despite how simple it may seem, breathing meditation is a powerful way to exercise your attentional control. To do it, you just need to focus on your breathing. When your mind wanders, bring it back to your breaths. Notice the rise and fall of your abdomen and chest. Gauge how deeply you are breathing. Do your lungs fully expand? Can you hear the air moving in and out of your nostrils? Close your eyes so that you are not distracted by what you see in the room. Stay focused on your breathing for 5 to 10 minutes.

Body Scan

For this exercise, you bring awareness to each part of your body. Start from a relaxed position, like sitting or lying down, and then systematically focus on various parts of your body. You can start with your feet and move up to your head, or vice versa. For each body part, observe the physical sensations. For example, what is the temperature of your feet? Are they touching a hard surface like the floor or a shoe? Then, move up your body to the lower part of your legs and then your upper legs, and so on. If you're sitting in a chair, notice the feel of the floor against your shoes or the part of the chair on which your forearm is resting. Spend a minute or two on each part, just observing.

At first, it can be easy to get distracted. If you're thinking about your legs and your stomach gurgles, take notice of that body sensation, but then take your attention back to your legs. This exercise teaches you how to control your thoughts and remain intentionally focused rather than controlled by distractions.

These attentional exercises require you to be aware of mental distractions and actively change your focus back to the present moment. It takes discipline to deliberately focus on the nuances of your body functions and shut out all other unrelated thoughts. When you first start, you might notice your mind frequently straying. Or you might quickly pass over body parts without taking careful notice of all the sensations related to that body part. In other words, you'll be tempted to do a quick visual inspection in your mind, attaching no other sensory information to the visual image. When these things happen, simply direct your attention back to pick up where you left off. Over time, you'll notice your mind wandering less and you'll be able to sustain your attention for longer periods.

Earlier in the book, I introduced the default-mode network (DMN), an area of the brain that activates when your mind wanders. People who are prone to anxiety tend to lurk about in the DMN. You can think of it as a forbidden closet or the Room of Requirement (if you're a Harry Potter fan): a room that houses many negative thoughts that have the potential to consume you. When you enter the room, you get so bombarded with thoughts that your rational mind retreats. It knows that these thoughts aren't helpful.

As long as you stay actively focused on something, you can stay out of the room. This is what meditation enables. Meditation reduces the activity of the DMN. It also strengthens the frontoparietal network, a part of the brain that controls your executive function (i.e., high-level thought processes like planning, decision making, working memory, self-control, and mental flexibility). So besides reducing your anxiety, meditation also improves these high-level mental functions.

Constructive Meditation

Advancing to the next level in complexity is constructive meditation, which focuses on cultivating a more adaptive way of thinking. Rather than mainly turning your attention away from negative thinking, constructive meditation helps you change your thoughts to make them more positive. If you think of your brain as your central processing unit, this type of meditation refurbishes your processor.

Examples of this kind of meditation are loving-kindness, wellbeing therapy, and compassion-cultivation training. You probably haven't heard of some of these, because many of them require some training or help from a therapist. With loving-kindness meditation, you connect to feelings of love and compassion toward yourself and others. You can start by imagining something that would evoke these feelings, like a baby, a pet, someone who has been kind to you, or a place you see as safe and nurturing (your "happy place").

After you conjure the image in your mind, you repeat positive and kind statements about yourself that match the warm, fuzzy feelings you get from the mental image. For example, you might say, "May I be safe; may I be happy; may I be healthy." These statements stabilize the images and positive emotions.

Next, you would extend these positive feelings to someone else as if you were passing the baton of kindness to the next person. To do this, you would imagine a familiar person and say, "May you be safe, may you be happy, may you be healthy" while you keep an image of the person in your mind.

Once you become comfortable with these statements, you would imagine someone with whom you have a conflict or feel negatively. You would use their name and say, "May Joan be safe, may Joan be happy, and may Joan be healthy." And as you say it, you imagine and picture Joan experiencing these situations of safety, happiness, and health. If you don't have someone who comes to mind, you can apply this to the world at large. This process helps rid you of negative emotions by using compassion as an antidote to indifference and ill feelings, even if the antagonism is self-directed. Cleansing your mind with compassionate thoughts is good for your soul.

Deconstructive Meditation

Deconstructive meditation is an advanced practice that can help you unpack how your thoughts and emotions form your reality and how your reality shapes your thoughts and emotions. It's a way of improving your insight through self-inquiry.

Deconstructive mediation is not for your average meditator, but it is hugely impactful. Actual change starts with understanding how you think, what you do, what effect the things you do have on others, and what effect the things others do have on you. Once you see and understand these things, you can change yourself one detail at a time.

Deconstructive meditation usually requires some level of training, education, or therapy for you to ask yourself questions that promote this level of self-awareness independently. Some examples of this kind of meditation are mindfulness-based cognitive therapy and a Buddhist technique called *vipassana*.

Meditation is definitely the heavy lifter for restructuring your mindset and creating long-term benefits. Meditation is what you do when you're not intensely anxious. Think of it as mental strength training. Several mobile applications and audio recordings can guide you in developing a meditation practice.

How long should you meditate? In many of the research studies I reviewed, subjects meditated for 30 minutes to 1 hour at a time. I realize that 30 minutes or an hour a day is a lot, and you don't have to start with that. Even 5 to 10 minutes of mindfulness is helpful and can be the way you build up to a more regular practice.

Keep in mind that practicing mindfulness does not always involve sitting in a room with your eyes closed in quiet meditation. You can be in a mindful state in your day-to-day activities. A good place to start is 5 to 10 minutes, once a day. Advanced meditators can stay engaged for hours.

Journaling for Catharsis or Analysis

Another way to process anxiety is by writing out your thoughts and feelings in journaling exercises. Journaling is documenting your thoughts in written form for later self-reflection. Even if you don't later review your writings, the process of getting your thoughts out of your head and onto paper is therapeutic.

Have you ever experienced pent-up emotions that felt like they were eating you up inside or taking over your mind? Then when a friend asks about how you are doing, you spew out everything that's on your mind, and you feel so much better?

In the psychological world, we call this *catharsis*. Both catharsis and cathartic trace their origins to the Greek word *kathairein*, which means "to cleanse or purge." Catharsis entered the English language as a medical term for the process of getting rid of unwanted material from the body, particularly from the bowels. Eventually, people began using the terms metaphorically to refer to an emotional release and spiritual cleansing.

There are many approaches to journaling. I will focus on five ways you can journal to purge negative thoughts or analyze and reframe your thoughts. The five types are:

1. Gratitude
2. Affective labeling
3. Affirmations
4. Worry journal
5. Reframing automatic negative thoughts

Gratitude Journaling

Focusing on gratitude elevates your perception of happiness and life satisfaction. There are many things from which we benefit that we take for granted. If you think of anxiety as being preoccupied with negative thoughts, exploring and appreciating the things you are grateful for helps you balance the negative with the positive.

As an example, let's say you hate going to work each day. You don't like your coworkers, and you feel the organization has unrealistic expectations about how much work you can produce. Each morning, you wake up feeling tense and angry, as you expect to face another 8-hour shift of the same soul-sucking nonsense. You even worry about how you'll make it through the day without losing your dignity from an explosive meltdown.

First, with this intensity of emotions, you'll probably need to do more than journal. (We'll discuss some helpful body tools in the next chapter.) To address this with the mind tools, you could add a loving-kindness meditation as your first layer. You could set aside 10 minutes first thing in the morning to quiet your mind with meditation. You could focus on compassion toward yourself first, then extend that to compassion toward your workplace.

To help you feel authentic as you say the kindness statements, you can add a second layer by writing gratitude statements the night before. To establish a journaling practice, I suggest you dedicate a notebook especially for this purpose. Start by putting the date and type of journaling exercise at the top of the page. Each time you sit down to do another exercise, start on a new page.

For the gratitude exercise, focus on people, objects, or events for which you feel grateful or that you know bring something positive into your life. It may feel hard to think of things beyond the general, like being grateful for air to breathe or that you woke up this morning. But the more you practice, the more specific things will come to mind.

Start with things that are unrelated to the situation at work. For this example, you could spend 10 minutes every evening writing all the things that come to mind for which you are grateful. Be specific. Start your sentences with "I am grateful for ..." or "I am grateful that ..." Over time, you could start to incorporate things related to the anxiety-producing situation at work.

Here are a few journal prompts to get your mind thinking:

- Did I experience or receive something I expected?
- Did I learn something new?
- Did a person or situation make me smile?
- What was the best part of my day, and why?

And here are some example statements:

- I am grateful that I can wake up feeling rested even though I had trouble falling asleep.
- I am grateful that my car starts whenever I want to go somewhere.
- I am grateful that my friend feels comfortable talking with me about their gender identity.
- I am grateful that I have generous vacation leave time, and I get to take whatever days I want without negotiating around my coworkers' leave requests.

Whether you start with a prompt or a gratitude statement, be specific. It's better to go deep rather than have several superficial statements that don't mean very much to you, like "I am grateful I have air to breathe, food to eat, and that I don't live in a war zone."

These are good starter statements if nothing else comes to mind. You can still write them down and, during another session, expand on them. But it's also possible to take these general statements and make them more specific to your situation:

- *Air to breathe:* I am grateful that even though I can't stand my coworkers, they attend to their personal hygiene in a way that allows me to breathe the air in their presence comfortably.
- *Food to eat:* I am grateful that today I could digest my food without my stomach hurting.
- *War zone:* I am grateful that I live in a community where I do not worry about my home being bombed by enemy fire.

Gratitude journaling helps you see beyond your adversity and appreciate the positive things you might otherwise overlook. The practice of experiencing gratefulness amidst adversity increases your psychological flexibility.

It's similar to viewing things mindfully. With mindful awareness, you observe events or situations and detach from any emotions or judgments associated with those situations. With gratitude, you embrace the positive emotions around an object or event while you simultaneously experience adverse events. In other words, being thankful that you woke up this morning doesn't negate the fact that you don't like your work. But generating positive feelings about a negative object lessens the impact of the negative object and allows you to better tolerate the situation.

Although it's a good practice for many to journal daily, you may want to limit your gratitude journaling to a few times a week to keep your thoughts fresh.

Affective Labeling

In Chapter 1, we looked at how the amygdala lives in the lower part of your brain and when activated produces a fear response. Science has shown that we can control these instinctive and automatic emotions by using higher brain processes like rationalizing, reasoning, and labeling how we feel about something. Assigning words to your feelings is called *affective labeling*. Brain studies show that affective labeling reduces amygdala activation. Affective labeling is not limited to journaling; it can also be used in talk therapy and exposure therapy.

Some researchers have proposed that affective labeling regulates emotions through the process of self-reflection. Being aware of your experiences is a feature of mindfulness. Another proposed mechanism is that attaching a label to any emotion reduces uncertainty, which is often a source of distress. Low tolerance for uncertainty is a common feature of anxiety.

What if you have trouble naming your emotions? There's a lot of complexity behind feeling "bad." "Bad" can mean angry, disgusted, frustrated, deceived, exploited, aggrieved, shamed, embarrassed, and so on. All of those emotions are negative but tend to stem from very different situations. Journaling can help you get to know yourself better and, eventually, pinpoint what you feel with greater specificity.

Let's return to your work situation. In a project meeting, your coworker Jane presents your findings to the group in your absence. As a result, the group appoints Jane as the team leader, a position you feel you earned after all the hard work you put into the project. You don't understand how the group could promote Jane to this position over you—unless Jane spun the presentation in a way that allowed her to take credit. You realize that must be what happened, and you're furious. Jane says she presented the material just as you delivered it and has no idea why they chose her to lead. You feel angry toward Jane but feel even worse that you can't prove her wrongdoing. You distance yourself from your coworkers because you feel they should have known that Jane couldn't lead the team. Your "bad" feelings persist for weeks, causing you to distance yourself from your coworkers and wake up every morning feeling very sad about your life.

Here, this one incident has led to general negative feelings about your entire workplace and your future career. Being able to assign the correct emotions to specific situations can keep your emotions compartmentalized to the offending situation instead of bleeding into every aspect of your life.

For this situation, you would start on a new page in your journal to write about your emotions as specifically as possible. If you have let your negative feelings fester, you may not be able to think through the situation with enough clarity to pinpoint the origins of each emotion. Once you get the hang of journaling, you can jump in sooner and get more granular with how you feel about specific conversations or situations. But for now, let's start with the general "bad" feeling related to work.

Here are some prompts that can help get you started:

- What do I fear?
- What do I wish were different with my life?
- What do I think are the worst things that can happen to me?
- How will I feel if the worst outcomes come to pass?

While journaling, you can write about your situation in as much detail as you want. If you're short on time or don't enjoy writing, you can use bullet points just to remind yourself of the situation when you reflect on your feelings. The more salient part of the exercise is to write out your labeling statements.

Here is how you might respond to these prompts regarding the situation with Jane at work:

- I fear no one respects me at work or sees how good I am.
- I wish that this situation could be undone and I could get the recognition I deserve.
- The worst thing that can happen is I never get promoted and that idiot, Jane, becomes my supervisor.
- This would make me feel cheated by Jane, slighted by my coworkers, and unsupported by the management. I feel angry, mistrustful, disrespected, invisible, and unappreciated.

Writing about how you feel doesn't change the fact that Jane is the team lead. But research shows that accurately recognizing your emotions in any situation helps you better process the emotions and diminishes the power the emotions have over you.

You feel mistrustful, disrespected, invisible, and unappreciated, all of which illustrate how you feel your office overlooks your efforts and doesn't reward you for your hard work. Those injuries are the root cause of your distress and "bad" feelings. If you understand what you feel and why you feel that way, you can better tolerate the negative emotions and shore up your positive feelings with gratitude and loving-kindness. Then if you have more balance between the negative and positive emotions, you can work with less distress and keep your thoughts from spiraling into existential questions like "What's the point?" or "Why am I even doing this?"

Depending on how self-reflective you are, you probably won't immediately draw these sophisticated conclusions. It takes practice. If you have trouble identifying emotional labels, refer to the emotions chart in the appendix.

Affirmations

Affirmation journaling is a form of self-care that involves writing positive statements that challenge your negative self-talk. Negative self-talk has the power to convince you that what you think is fact. When you get consumed with negative thoughts, you can have trouble knowing what to say to counteract them. Positive affirmations give you a narrative to replace your negative thoughts with positive ones.

Research using functional MRI scans has shown that certain nerve pathways (in the ventromedial prefrontal cortex) are enhanced when you say affirming statements. Affirmations restore self-integrity and bolster self-worth. Affirmations decrease threat perception by narrowing your view of the threat and expanding your perspective of the entire situation.

Positive affirmations encourage optimism. However, it's also been shown that affirming statements work best for people who already have a healthy level of self-esteem and just need a course correction. For people with low self-esteem and self-loathing thoughts, positive statements about themselves only make them feel worse. This is probably because positive statements are most easily accepted if they are close to your baseline beliefs. If they are too far from what you believe, they only draw attention to the disparity between what you want and what you currently have.

If you have an unflattering view of yourself, it's natural to resist adopting an overly positive view. It's natural to want to maintain your current view of yourself. So when faced with negative thoughts, a better approach is to develop positive statements about the situation instead of yourself.

Imagine that you believe you deserved to be overlooked at work after that meeting. You resent being overlooked despite this belief. If you try to affirm yourself with statements like "I am the best person for the job" or "I am a natural leader," it will feel so fake that it has no effect. Those statements may even backfire by making you feel worse about yourself, because you know you're not leadership material. Or at least, that's what you believe, and your workplace appears to have confirmed it.

In this situation, instead of writing positive statements about your character, think of things you have accomplished or good things that you do. For example, "I'm good at what I do, which makes my job easy for me," or "My efficiency allows me to complete all of my work on time" are better statements than "I am an expert and more competent than anyone else on the team." Because of your negative view of yourself, you don't really believe you are more competent (at least, not yet). Therefore, focusing on how fast you get your work done or how easy it is for you to understand problems makes your statement more relatable and helps you get you to the point of believing you are a competent expert.

Therefore, for affirmations to have the best effect, they need to be realistic, believable, and applicable to you. For example, if you struggle with social anxiety, writing "I am relaxed and confident in social situations" won't be effective, because it's not true. These statements may reflect your goals, but they can make you more anxious by highlighting your failings if you're not there yet. Writing "I can handle whatever comes my way" or "I know more about this topic than the people I'm talking to" are more believable statements because they specifically address your insecurities.

Here's how to develop believable affirmations:

- **Be specific.** Specific statements are more believable and effective than general ones. Be as detailed as you can when you write affirmations. Instead of writing "I am wealthy," write "I have enough money to meet my needs." Instead of writing "I am successful," write "I have accomplished my goals."
- **Use the present tense.** You should write affirmations in the present tense, as if they're already true. For example, you should write "I am satisfied and content" instead of "I will be satisfied and content."
- **Use positive language.** You should frame your statement using positive words and avoid negative ones. For example, "I am generous with my friends" is better than "I'm not stingy."
- **Be realistic.** Affirmations should be realistic and relatable so that you will believe them. For example, if you struggle with weight loss, writing "I am thin and healthy" is not likely to be very effective. However, writing "I am working hard to lose weight and I am seeing results" is more believable and will likely produce better results.

- **Use your personal experience.** An affirmation can be something general like "Someone loves me," or it can be based on personal experiences, such as "My spouse loves me." You can also keep a list of important people in your life and journal things they have done for you to remind you of the loving acts. Then when you say "My friend loves me," you can visualize when your friend was the only person who remembered your birthday. Recalling these acts of kindness helps reinforce your affirmations and creates a mental database of positive experiences you can conjure at will when reviewing your list.

There are many different ways to create affirming statements. For example, you can start with a prompt where you fill in the blanks with something positive about yourself:

> I am …
>
> I have …
>
> I am capable of …
>
> I look forward to …
>
> I am hopeful that …
>
> I enjoy …
>
> I am free of …

After writing down the statements, say them aloud. Sometimes, it's more powerful to say it into the mirror, while looking back at yourself. It's like telling yourself these things and watching your reflection take it in. It might feel silly, but consider that you probably do this with negative thoughts already. If you're anxious, you probably tell yourself hundreds of negative things about your appearance, relationships, performance, future, and so on, every single day. So why are those thoughts more acceptable than the ones you'd like to believe because they make you feel good?

Here are some good general affirmations:

- I will focus on the things I can control.
- My confidence increases because I allow it to.

- My efforts yield incremental improvements in my life.
- I allow myself to be imperfect.
- I am not my mistakes. My mistakes are wrong choices I make that I have the power to change next time.
- My anxiety is unpleasant, but it does not control me.
- I have access to tools that I can use to calm myself.
- I don't have to let others determine my self-worth.
- I am strong because I tackle my anxiety every day.
- My breaths cleanse me of inner tension.
- I can always get through tough times one day at a time.
- I have the ability to find solutions when I need them.
- My faith grounds me and makes me feel secure.
- I can handle seeing my friends succeed before me because I believe my success will come in due time.

Worry Journal

Some amount of worry is helpful. Helpful worry includes thinking ahead, anticipating problems, and trying to solve them. Unhelpful worry is fretting about consequences you can't change or worrying about your worry. If you have general anxiety, you can worry about anything and everything.

One journaling intervention for worry is to set aside time to write out your worries. This is a way of compartmentalizing them. Often, if there is something we're worried about, we want to keep it top of mind so that we don't forget it. Setting aside worry time means giving yourself permission to pause thinking about your concerns, because you have set aside time to fully engage in your worrying.

Worry is intrusive, so it can take discipline to defer your worry until your worry appointment. When you have a worrying thought pop into your mind, make a note of it and tell yourself that you're going to save it for later. Then practice mindfulness to pull yourself away from that thought.

Chances are, when you defer a worry, it won't seem as critical or distressing at the worry appointment. It can also be reassuring to review your past worry entries and see how the things you worried about did not come to pass. Seeing your worry on paper may also reveal how your concerns are unrealistic. In this way, worry journaling serves to infuse some reality into your perspective.

Reframing Automatic Negative Thoughts

Anxiety generates negative thoughts in your mind that are often automatic, like a reflex. These automatic negative thoughts (ANTs) stem from your beliefs about yourself and the world. They can intrusively pop into your mind, or they can run in the background like a looping audiotape. Either way, they affect your behavior, emotions, and decisions, often without you realizing it.

For example, if you believe a panic attack can lead to a heart attack if it's severe enough, you might worry that your anxiety will shorten your life. You may avoid situations you suspect will increase your anxiety and trigger your final deadly panic attack. If you believe everyone will notice when you're anxious and lose respect for you, you will avoid speaking in group settings. You may even avoid being around people altogether.

Based on a cognitive-behavioral model, these thoughts are called *cognitive distortions*. Most times, you are unaware of your cognitive distortions and assume that they are facts. You can challenge these distorted thoughts and reframe them using cognitive therapy techniques. Once you challenge the thoughts, they become less automatic and less controlling.

Here is how you turn this into a journal exercise:

1. **Identify the thought.**

   Think of an anxiety-provoking situation and then ask yourself, "What thoughts went through my head?" When you're anxious, it's natural for your mind to draw negative conclusions about what could happen to you. Therefore, think about what you thought would happen.

   It's best to write the thought as a statement and not a question. Let's return to the work situation where Jane threw you under the bus and took your promotion. When you reflect on it, the thought that runs through your mind may be, "What if they never promote me?" For your journal exercise, you would write that as a statement: "They will never promote me."

If you can't think of a specific situation that triggered anxiety, you can also think of times you experienced negative emotions, even if you were alone. Think about what ran through your mind when you experienced this negative emotion. As an example, suppose you are lying in bed and unable to sleep. You don't feel tired and fear that you won't fall asleep for hours. There isn't anything you recognize that could have caused you to have trouble falling asleep, but now that it's been an hour since you got in bed, you feel your anxiety building.

If you think about what runs through your mind when you're in this situation, you may discover a cascade of spiraling negative thoughts. It may look something like this:

- I can't believe I can't fall asleep.
- I'm not going to be able to function tomorrow.
- I'm going to fail my exam because I won't be able to think or remember anything I studied.
- I won't be able to bring up my grade, and I will lose my scholarship.
- I'll have to withdraw for a semester and get a job to pay for school.
- Even if I return to school, I'll lose my friends because they'll move on without me.
- I'll get depressed.
- Why can't I be normal, like everyone else?

This thought spiral started with frustration over having trouble falling asleep and progressed to failing school and being a faulty, emotional outcast who will never be happy. Using this example, you would write out all these thoughts to challenge them later. You would change the last thought from a question to the statement: "Everyone is normal except me."

2. Recognize cognitive distortions.

In 1976, psychiatrist Aaron Beck wrote a groundbreaking book called *Cognitive Therapy and The Emotional Disorders*, which captured his research on cognitive therapy. In 1989, David Burns, MD expanded on this concept and established names for many of the cognitive distortions in his book, *Feeling Good*. Others have been added to the list of cognitive distortions, but I will limit my discussion to 10 of the distortions that commonly occur with anxiety.

These distortions form the mnemonic **SCALPED MOP.**

You can think of it this way: a scalped mop is useless. The scalping removes the absorbent cloth, which is the essence of the mop. You are then left with only a stick, which is useless for mopping.

Back in the day, when my grandmother took care of me while my parents worked, I had to use my imagination to keep myself occupied. I didn't have a friend to play with, and my grandmother spent much of her afternoons watching soap operas, which she called her "stories." I found the stories painfully boring and would sit miserably in one of the matching recliners wishing to be rescued. That was until I met my new friend, Melanie, the mop.

I found Melanie hidden away in the back of a utility closet, waiting for a friend like me. I liked Melanie because she had long, whitish-grey hair that swung back and forth when she moved. Her hair, made of a coarse yarn, formed thick ropes that were like my own ponytails. I twisted her hair and used rubber bands to pull it back into different styles. Melanie and I wiled away my afternoons singing and dancing together. One day, I went to the closet and did not see Melanie. I frantically searched the house to no avail. I asked my grandmother what happened to the mop, and she said, "That old thing? Your daddy got me a new one. The string started coming out after you kept putting those rubber bands around it." She proudly showed me her shiny new mop with a self-squeezing sponge head. I felt sick inside, thinking that my hairstyles made Melanie's hair fall out, leading to her demise. She had already been taken away by the trash collection, so I didn't have the chance to get one last look at her. It was probably best because it would have been very upsetting for me to see her without her lovely ropey hair. My hairstyling days were over, and I had to resume my place on the recliner.

Just as removing the absorbent portion of a mop renders it useless, cognitive distortions ruin your mental flexibility and ability to see a situation objectively.

Here are the **SCALPED MOP** cognitive distortions that can skew your view of yourself and your situation:

"S" stands for should statements. You think in terms of should, ought, and must. Using should statements is a way to hold yourself and others to an unrealistic standard. In the case of rumination, should statements presume you had access to knowledge and resources that would have allowed you to make a different, better decision. These statements foster impossible expectations, resulting in disappointment, resentment, and failure.

"C" stands for catastrophizing. You expect the worst possible outcome for any given scenario. To challenge this thinking, you must remember that there is more than one possible outcome, and most times, the worst one doesn't happen.

"A" stands for all-or-nothing thinking. Some people call this "black and white thinking." With this thinking, you see things as one extreme or another, such as all good or all bad. You may also frequently use words like "always" and "never." This is inflexible thinking. A way to address this distortion is to look for exceptions to your point of view.

"L" stands for labeling. With labeling, you attach a judgment to someone (or yourself) instead of recognizing the undesirable behavior. An example of this is calling yourself "a sucker" rather than someone who missed an opportunity.

"P" stands for premature conclusions. This is also called "jumping to conclusions." You quickly react to something without having much information on which to base your opinion. This distortion often involves other faulty thinking, like mind reading and fortune telling. For example, let's say you email someone asking for a favor. When you don't hear from them within a few hours, you assume the person doesn't want to help you but doesn't have the backbone to tell you directly. You assume they are ignoring you so they don't have to think of a way to say no. You didn't consider that maybe the email went to the person's junk mail folder, and they never saw it.

"E" stands for emotional reasoning. Emotional reasoning is a belief that what you feel is true because it feels true in your gut. An example is believing a disaster is looming because you feel anxious. If you feel guilty, it must mean you did something wrong, even if you can't identify a specific misdeed.

"D" stands for discounting the positive. By discounting the positive, you downplay the good things and attribute the positive event to someone or something other than yourself. For example, I find myself thinking this way when I get profuse compliments. I think, "Is what they say true, or are they just being nice?" Another example is if you practice affirmation journaling and have fewer panic attacks, you think your improved panic is a coincidence. You don't conclude that your journaling was effective at reducing your anxiety.

"M" stands for magnifying and minimizing. With magnifying and minimizing, you overfocus on your weakness and downplay your strengths. Magnifying is a little different from catastrophizing because you primarily focus on yourself. Whereas catastrophizing is how you see a *situation* exploding to catastrophic results. An example of this is feeling like an inept singer because your voice cracked on one of the high notes. Never mind that you sang a complex song and hit all other notes perfectly; that one mistake ruined your self-impression.

"O" stands for overgeneralizing. With overgeneralization, you believe something will always happen, even if it only happened once or twice. For example, you let your friend borrow your book and they lose it. Now you won't trust them with any of your belongings because you believe they are not capable of keeping up with anything. A way to recognize this kind of thinking is if you find yourself often saying "always," "never," "everything," and "no one."

"P" stands for personalization. Personalization is when you take responsibility for negative situations and blame yourself even if you had nothing to do with them. People who are victims of abuse will often blame themselves for their abuser's behavior—for example, "If I hadn't made him so mad, he wouldn't have hit me."

These are the **SCALPED MOP** thoughts. In step 2, you examine the thoughts you wrote in step 1 and see if any of the thoughts match these distortions. Are there any distortions that you use more than others?

It's helpful to see your thought patterns, because you will probably repeat them in other situations. Once you see the pattern and learn to analyze the distortions, you can catch yourself thinking this way and correct your thinking before you act on the irrational thoughts.

3. **Challenge the thought.**

In this step, you challenge your distorted thoughts with questions to identify their irrational aspects. This helps you adopt a different perspective.

Here are prompts to challenge your thoughts. Depending on the distortion, some prompts will be more helpful than others.

Evidence prompts:

- What is the evidence that what I believe is true? How reliable is that evidence?
- What is the evidence that what I believe is false? How reliable is that evidence?
- Is the evidence based on what someone said or did in this situation or is it based on inferences, hunches, or past experiences?
- What are other possibilities?

Evidence Test

More Reliable	Less Reliable
What someone said	Inference based on related statements
What someone did	Hunches based on your intuition
What someone wrote	Assumptions based on your experience with the person or past situation

Perspective prompts:

- What would I tell my friend if they said this to me?
- What would my friend say to me about what I think?
- What is the worst thing that could happen if what I believed were true? How does that consequence harm me?
- How would I cope with the negative outcome if what I believe is true?

Skewed-thinking prompts:

- Am I holding myself to an unreasonable standard that I don't expect from anyone else?
- Am I demanding too much from others?
- Is there another outcome that isn't as bad as what I'm expecting?
- Am I thinking in black or white extremes? What does the grey area look like?
- Am I labeling myself? If so, what's the behavior I'm labeling?
- Have I considered other possibilities before drawing these conclusions?
- Is what I feel logical? Is there possibly another outcome or conclusion that has nothing to do with how I feel?
- Am I dismissing the importance of something good that's happened or praise I received?
- Do I only identify with my shortcomings and minimize my attributes?
- Has there been a time when what I believed wasn't true or what I predicted didn't come to pass?

- Am I blaming myself for something that was out of my control?

Self-interest prompts:

- What positive outcome results from the thought?
- How will the thought help me reach my goals?
- Does the thought interfere with my day-to-day interactions (e.g., impact big decisions)?

Once you challenge your thoughts, move on to step 4.

4. Rewrite the thought.

In this step, rewrite the thought(s) in light of the challenges in step 3 to reflect a more realistic view with less negative bias. Now that you have a fresh understanding, what is a different statement that you might experience as less distressing?

5. Meditate on the new thought.

You want to marinate in your recomposed thoughts. Think about the situation, then think about your modified response. How do you feel while you're thinking about this? Does it feel like something you could apply to a similar situation from the past or future?

6. Bonus: Develop a positive affirmation.

Although focusing on affirmations is another journaling exercise, reframing your negative thoughts is an excellent opportunity to create a positive affirmation. Since affirmations work best when they are specific and personal, performing an autopsy of your negative thoughts provides an opportune time to add to your list of affirming thoughts.

Here's an example. Suppose I worry about having a panic attack in front of people. I conclude that I'm a loser socially because I'm always anxious and experiencing panic. After analyzing my thoughts, I realize they are based on the distortions of overgeneralization (I'm always anxious), labeling (I'm a loser), and discounting the positive (ignoring the days when I don't have a panic attack).

I reframe my statements to say that being anxious doesn't make me a loser; I am too hard on myself. I'm not always anxious, and I have gone two days without a panic attack. Then, I add in some affirming statements using the suggested affirmation prompts:

- *I am* good at making people feel comfortable when they talk to me.
- *I have* the skill of giving someone my full attention.
- *I am capable of* connecting with people individually.
- *I look forward to* developing the social asset of making someone feel heard.
- *I am hopeful that* I can continue to improve my social skills.
- *I enjoy* listening to other people tell their stories.
- *I am free of* self-criticism for having anxiety.

When creating your affirming statements, you don't have to use any prompts. You may find that your rewritten statement is sufficiently affirming.

In this chapter, we covered several techniques that you can use as tools to address your anxiety from a cognitive (thinking) perspective. You can think of mindfulness, meditation, and grounding as mental strengthening and calming exercises. These tools are helpful to use along with the body-focused tools we will discuss in the next chapter. We also discussed several ways you can journal your thoughts. Journaling is a more active coping strategy that helps you process your thoughts and feelings to reduce anxiety.

CHAPTER 9

Body Tools

In the last chapter, we looked at tools you can use to relieve anxiety through changing mindset and perspective. This chapter will focus on tools that relieve anxiety by manipulating your body. Some of these body-focused tools have been shown to decrease trait anxiety, which means that they can do more than relax you when you're in an anxious state. By decreasing trait anxiety, you can reduce the intensity of an anxious nature and establish long-term improvements.

Some people find body tools easier because they are more active than mind tools, which can take more work and discipline. Here is what the body tools work best for:

- Decreasing the effects of stress.
- Turning down the dial on tension.
- Reducing acute anxiety, panic attacks, and intense situational nervousness.

- Taking the edge off a bad day.
- Helping you relax for sleep.
- Deepening your sleep.
- Slowing the effects of stress-related aging.

This is good stuff, right? Let's jump in with the most fundamental of all the body tools: breathing.

Breathing

Focusing on your breath can be a part of other tools, like meditation, mindfulness, yoga, and aromatherapy. Since some types of meditation focus on breathing, those can be seen as both mind and body tools. This means breathing can be its own relaxation practice, and there are many ways you can breathe for relaxation.

I never used to like breathing exercises, because they always made me feel out of breath. I realize now that I wasn't doing them correctly. I followed a guided exercise that used a breathing technique that was too advanced for my level. I'll explain the different breathing patterns and how you can progress from beginner practices to advanced. But first, let's break down the anatomy of breathing.

Most of the time, breathing is a passive, automatic process that happens with no conscious effort on your part. The control center for your breathing is in your brain stem, the lower part of your brain that controls several critical, life-sustaining functions, like blood pressure. There is no problem solving or reasoning that happens in your brain stem. Those higher-order tasks occur in the upper parts of your brain and allow you to consciously override your automatic breathing process. It's kind of like the operations of a self-driving car: you can let the car drive itself, but you can also grab the steering wheel and take control of the driving yourself.

Breathing involves your diaphragm, a large muscle located under your rib cage that separates your chest from your abdomen. When you inhale, this muscle pulls downward, creating negative pressure inside your chest. This negative pressure makes the air you inhale through your nose and mouth inflate the airspaces of your lungs. When you exhale, your diaphragm pushes upward, pushing the air out of your lungs. The tiny air spaces of your lungs are where you get oxygen exchange between the air and your bloodstream. Your cells create carbon dioxide as a waste product from regular cell activity, which your body removes using your blood vessels. When your blood passes through your lungs, it takes oxygen from the airspace and dumps the carbon dioxide. You then release the carbon dioxide into the air when you exhale.

If you hyperventilate (such as during an anxiety attack), you overbreathe, causing your carbon dioxide levels to get too low. As a result, you can feel tingling in your limbs, nausea, dizziness, and sometimes even chest pain. When this happens, you can slow your breaths by breathing into a paper bag and re-inhaling the carbon dioxide you're exhaling, which raises your levels and restores normal breathing.

Anxiety, stress, inflammation, certain medications, and illnesses can all make your baseline breathing rate faster when you are at rest. Heart and breathing rate come together as a package unless you are taking medication to slow your heart rate. Otherwise, when your sympathetic system turns up the dial, your heart and breathing rates both increase. This means that if you're a daily coffee drinker or consume other stimulating agents that can increase your baseline resting heart rate, your resting breathing rate may also increase. On the other hand, regular, vigorous cardiovascular exercise can drop your resting heart and breathing rates. Your blood pressure is a lagging third wheel that increases slightly in response to an uptick in adrenaline.

Why does any of this matter? Because the intimate connection between your heart rate and breathing is how you can use breathing to slow down your entire system. You can't manipulate your heartbeat directly, but you can override and slow down your breathing, which in turn slows your heart rate, lowers your blood pressure, reduces inflammatory chemicals, and reduces anxiety. Controlling your breaths is like grabbing the steering wheel of the self-driving car.

Heart Rate Variability

Your heart does not keep perfect pace like the hand of a clock. It speeds up when you inhale and slows when you exhale, and the intervals between beats vary from beat to beat. This changing heart rate is called *heart rate variability* (HRV).

Mounting research evidence shows that the more varied your heart rate, the better your overall health, including emotional resilience. Yes, you read that correctly: heart rate variability reflects your emotional and physical health. The higher the variability, the better. And one way to increase your variability is through slowed, paced breathing.

Resonant Breathing

Your heart rate and breathing are synchronized, or in resonance, at a frequency of 0.1 Hz. This frequency corresponds to about six breaths a minute on average and is considered a resonance breathing rate. Your heart rate variability can be measured using biofeedback technology. Each person has an individual resonance frequency based on how much blood their heart pumps through the body, but most people fall between 4.5 to 7 breaths per minute. Research has shown that taller people and men generally have higher blood volumes and resonance frequencies lower than six breaths per minute.

The significance of the resonant frequency is that it is the respiratory rate that produces the best results when slowing your heart rate and increasing heart rate variability. So without having your rate measured, you can use six breaths per minute as a target for your paced breathing exercises. With practice, you can advance to slower breathing using complex rhythms. Some advanced yoga practitioners get their controlled breathing, also called *pranayama*, down to less than one breath per minute.

If you are new to breathing exercises, here is how you can start and advance your practice of slow, paced breathing. It's important to maintain a posture that will maximize airflow while you're breathing. You can do this by sitting upright without leaning over. You can also lie flat. For deeper breathing, you'll want to breathe from your abdomen and not your chest. You can tell how much you're breathing from your abdomen by putting one hand over your abdomen and one over your chest. As you breathe, see which hand moves more and adjust to favor the abdomen.

You should progress through rhythmic breathing in stages. The first stage involves even breathing, in and out, for a length of time that's comfortable for you. Resonant breathing at six breaths per minute means that each breath cycle takes 10 seconds. Using even breathing, you would inhale and exhale for 5 seconds each.

You may find it difficult to extend your breaths that long to start. A typical starting point is to set your inhale and exhale time to 3 or 4 seconds each. If you chose 3 seconds, one breathing cycle is 6 seconds, corresponding to 10 breaths per minute. If you chose 4 seconds, your breathing cycle is 8 minutes, corresponding to 7.5 breaths per minute. Both breathing rates are faster than the average resonant breathing rate of 6 breaths per minute, but still much slower than your normal resting breathing rate, which is likely 12 to 20 breaths per minute. At this rate, you're inhaling and exhaling for 2.5 to 1.5 seconds, respectively. That's pretty quick breathing, even though it's your automatic rate. Keep this automatic rate in mind as a reference when deciding what to use as your starting point.

Once you're comfortable with even breathing, try changing your rhythm to uneven breathing, where your exhale is longer than your inhale. A typical ratio to start with is to inhale for 4 seconds, then exhale for 6 seconds. The conventional way this ratio is noted is to write it as 4-6 or 1:1.5. Use dashes to denote the time and a colon to denote the ratio.

The next step in advancing your breathing pattern is to add a pause after you inhale and before you exhale. This pause is also called *breath retention*. A good starting ratio for this pattern is 1:0.5:1. So with your 4-second inhale at this next level, you would inhale for 4 seconds, pause for 2, then exhale for 4. The notation for this is 4-2-4. The next level up would be a ratio of 1:1:1. With this ratio, you inhale for 4 seconds, hold for 4 seconds, and exhale for 4 seconds. With this breathing cycle, you're getting 5 breaths per minute.

The last step in advancing the complexity of your breathing is to add a pause after the exhale, which gives your breathing four parts. This advanced pattern can start with a ratio of 1:2:2:1. This translates to an inhale of 4 seconds, a pause for 8 seconds, an exhale for 8 seconds, then a pause for 4 seconds (4-8-8-4). With this cycle, you're getting 2.5 breaths per minute, which is much lower than the average resonant breathing range. Most people do not progress to this breathing level without some formal training and supervision, usually from a yoga teacher or breath-work therapist.

Practice breathing twice a day for 10 minutes a day to increase your HRV.

Breathing Stages

Stage	Description	Breathing ratio	Breathing rate in seconds
One	Breathing without retention (pausing), start with even breaths, then progress to uneven	1:0:1, 1:0:1.5, 1:0:2	4-0-4, 4-0-6, 4-0-8
Two	Breathing with retention after the inhale	1:0.5:1, 1:1:1, 1:1:2	4-2-4, 4-4-4, 4-4-8
Three	Breathing with longer retention after the inhale	1:2:1, 1:2:2	4-8-4, 4-8-8
Four	Breathing with retention after the inhale and the exhale	1:2:2:1, 1:2:2:2	4-8-8-4, 4-8-8-8

There are more advanced stages of breathing that involve increasing the time you hold your breath at the top of the inhale and bottom of the exhale. Typically, the pause after the inhale is longer than after the exhale. You don't want to jump straight to this kind of breathing. That's the mistake I made that left me starving for air and dizzy. Having no prior experience with breathwork, I jumped right in with a guided meditation where I was told to breathe in for 5 seconds, hold, and then breathe out for 5 seconds. Then the narrator paused before priming me to breathe in again. So I had an unintentional hold at the end for probably several seconds, and I had no idea how long to hold the pause at the top of the inhale. I might have been doing something like 5-3-5-3. I know that each time I paused, I thought, "I will not last long holding my breath." Those numbers equal a breathing cycle of 16 seconds, which is 3.75 breaths per minute. As a beginner, I had no business slowing my breathing down that far.

Alternate-Nostril Breathing

Resonant, paced breathing is a good way to structure your breathing pattern, but there are variations. Two other methods to incorporate paced breathing are alternate-nostril or one-nostril breathing. Some research suggests that breathing in and out of one nostril at a time produces more relaxation. Left-nostril breathing produces a more calming effect, while right-nostril breathing is associated with an activated state. Nostrils are nostrils; how can one make a difference over another?

Two Brain Hemispheres, Two Experiences

Our two nostrils function differently in terms of how much airflow passes through them and what kinds of odors we smell through them. This asymmetrical functioning happens because the brain has a daily cycle of turning up the activity of one side of the brain while turning down the other side's activity. The brain switches the active sides every 1.5 to 3 hours.

To illustrate how this works, let's look at specific sides of the brain. When your left brain ramps up its activity, it increases adrenaline to the right nostril. This sympathetic input causes the blood vessels in the right nostril to constrict and shrink your nasal turbinates, which are the folded walls of your nasal passage. This vessel constriction decongests the nostril, and you get maximum airflow. Meanwhile, your parasympathetic system acts on the blood vessels of your left nostril, causing them to dilate. These dilated vessels engorge your left nasal turbinates, making them swell and congest. With this setup, your right nostril provides most of your airflow, but you still get some from your left nostril. Your nostrils remain this way from 25 minutes to 3 hours before they switch states.

This decongestion/congestion cycle all happens automatically, without you being aware of it. In the nondominant nostril, you get a usual level of congestion that differs from the pathological congestion that you get with a cold or sinus infection. With pathological congestion, your nasal passage can become so congested that you may not be able to breathe through your nose at all. Pathological congestion from a cold or allergies still follows this pattern of alternating nasal dominance, making your congestion worse. If you have this kind of congestion, it's best to wait until your passages are clear before using alternate- or single-nostril breathing.

You'll still need to maintain a posture that allows for unobstructed airflow for alternate- or single-nostril breathing. Close one nostril while you inhale and exhale from the same open nostril. You can continue to use one nostril for the duration of your breathing exercise or switch and breathe in and out of the other nostril on the next breath.

CAUTIONS ABOUT BREATHING EXERCISES

Breathing exercises are safe for most people, but there are some things for which you should be aware. As previously discussed, avoid deep breathing exercises if you have nasal congestion that impairs your normal breathing. If you're pregnant, avoid holding your breath or any kind of rapid breathing exercise. If you have panic disorder, you must be careful with breathing that becomes stimulating, such as right nostril breathing. Increased deep breathing can cause more anxiety and trigger hyperventilation. Also, if you have a cardiac or respiratory condition, such as obstructive pulmonary disease or emphysema, check with your doctor before engaging in the more advanced breathing exercises.

If you cannot tolerate the paced breathing exercises, you can practice awareness breathing. This is a mindfulness exercise where you notice your breathing without changing it. This exercise is like the body scan meditation, but instead of bringing your awareness to different parts of your body, you only pay attention to your breathing.

Yoga

For years, I didn't understand yoga. I knew people who raved about it, but I couldn't see how getting into certain poses made you feel better. I figured it must be because of the spiritual component that works magic on the mind, which led me to write it off as a religious experience for people who follow certain Eastern religious practices. As time passed, however, yoga continued to cross my radar as an acceptable complementary approach to addressing depression and anxiety. I started talking to patients about their experiences, and I concluded that the benefit must be similar to the positive feelings you get after exercise or a good stretch.

So I tried it. My gym offered a power yoga session, and I signed up. I thought the "power" just meant "good for you." I didn't know power related to the intensity of the yoga. That session kicked my butt, and I was stiff and sore for days afterward. I thought, "How is this relaxing? What's wrong with me that I can't see the benefit of this?" I did some reading and saw that there were different kinds of yoga (imagine that) and that power yoga was not for beginners or people wanting to relax.

I gave it another try, but my reading was not informative enough to help me choose the appropriate class. My next attempt was hot yoga, which was another miserable experience. It scared me away from yoga for several years. Even though I thought of myself as being in decent shape, I concluded that I did not have the constitution to endure yoga.

This was an unfortunate conclusion to draw from something that has such great mental and physical benefits. I continued to have this nagging suspicion that I was missing something and needed to give it another chance. When the pandemic hit, and we were all trapped inside our homes, I tried an online class called "Gentle Yoga." Finally, I saw the light. I fell in love with yoga.

The most common type of yoga in the United States is hatha yoga, which focuses on physical movements in addition to meditation and breathing. There are many styles of hatha yoga, such as Ashtanga, Iyengar, Kundalini, and Bikram. Some forms of yoga don't have a physical component at all and focus instead on mental wellbeing. For example, raja yoga is predominantly a meditative practice.

The magic of yoga is that it combines several components that each have individual benefits. It's like the sum of the parts magnifies the effect of the individual parts. There are many types and styles of yoga, but the basis of yoga's benefits can be reduced to three key components: physical postures (asanas), controlled breathing (pranayama), and meditation/relaxation techniques (dhyana). Some yoga styles may emphasize one of these components over the others. For example, in my power yoga class, the primary emphasis was striking poses to build strength and endurance. I don't remember much focus on breathing, perhaps because I struggled to keep up without hurting myself.

The poses (asanas) of yoga strengthen muscles, increase flexibility, and improve your balance and body awareness. When you assume poses that stretch tight muscles and release tight joints, you induce a relaxed state supported by breathing and meditation.

Controlled breathing (pranayama) is an integral part of yoga. Yoga uses your breath to move you into poses and create movement within a pose. For example, the lizard pose is a posture that stretches your hips. You start the position with both hands on the floor, as if you were doing a push-up. With your hands still on the floor, you bend one leg at the knee and place your foot on the floor. The second leg is extended straight behind you with the top of your foot face down on the floor. Your body weight pushes you into the pose, and your breathing relaxes your muscles and helps you sink deeper into the pose.

Most of the breathing in gentle yoga is slow and rhythmic, but more intense yoga practices engage activating breaths like the bellows breath and breath of fire. These are energizing breaths that involve forceful use of your diaphragm when inhaling and exhaling.

Alternate-nostril breathing is a calming yoga breath called *nada shondhana*, and left-nostril breathing is called *chandra nadi*. You can practice these breathing techniques as part of a breathing meditation or during your yoga practice. Another breath technique specific to yoga breathing is the lion's breath, also called *simhasana*. With this breath, you inhale deeply, then open your mouth wide and bring the tip of your tongue toward your chin as you exhale. Then you let yourself exhale loudly, making an "aah" sound. You can repeat this two or three times to release tension. Because you are engaging your vocal cords with this breath, the lion's breath directly activates your vagus nerve and can be one of the vagal maneuvers discussed in the next section.

The meditation/relaxation techniques (dhyana) can be a subtle part of the yoga practice. For example, you might be directed to notice how your body feels as you move through the poses. Bringing your awareness to your body is a mindfulness practice. Some yoga programs may include a guided visualization exercise toward the end of the session. You might also be instructed to contract and relax different muscle groups as a relaxation exercise.

How long should you engage in yoga? In many of the studies referenced for this book, participants practiced yoga for 90 to 120 minutes, once a week. That's a long time to dedicate to a single session if you're just starting out and trying to fit it into an already busy schedule. I suggest starting with a 20 to 30 minute session two to three times per week. With this schedule, you'll get the cumulative effect of practicing yoga for 40 to 90 minutes a week. If your session includes some meditative parts, then this time also counts for meditation time.

The Power of the Vagus Nerve

Chapter 1 explained how your sympathetic nervous system works automatically to detect threats and turn on your fight-or-flight response. In response to a threat, you get a surge of cortisol and adrenaline that speed up your heart rate and breathing. When the threat has passed, your body produces a parasympathetic response that slows things back down and brings you back to where you were before the threat. You can think of the sympathetic system as the accelerator and the parasympathetic system as the brakes that slow things back down to a resting state. Under stress or when you are anxious, you can remain in this revved-up state without an obvious threat or trigger.

The vagus nerve is the brake system that restores you to steady state by secreting acetylcholine. That is, your vagus nerve is the wizard behind the curtain that makes yoga and breathing exercises effective.

The vagus nerve is a long nerve that starts in your brain stem, at the base of your skull. It's called the "wandering nerve" because it stretches from your skull, through your neck, and into your chest cavity and abdomen. It provides nerve power to your internal organs, like your vocal cords, heart, lungs, and intestines. Therefore, your vagus nerve helps control your speech, heartbeat, breathing, and digestion. It also decreases anxiety by reducing inflammatory chemicals called cytokines.

In the previous section, you saw how slowing your breaths could slow your heart rate. This slowing action happens by activating the vagus nerve. There are other ways to activate your vagus nerve, which we call *vagal maneuvers*, including the following techniques.

Humming: Between where your vagus nerve leaves your head and enters your chest, it branches to your vocal cords. When you hum, your vocal cords vibrate and stimulate the nerve. Humming bee breath, called *bhraamari* in Sanskrit, is a yoga breathing technique that stimulates your vocal cords. Another way to vibrate your vocal cords is to make the "ohm" sound. Some yoga and meditation practices will instruct you to say this as part of the practice.

Splashing cold water on your face or taking a cold shower: The sudden change in skin temperature triggers a relaxing parasympathetic response. If you don't want to put water on your face (like you're at work and don't want to mess up your makeup), you can try putting a cold compress on the back of your neck.

Valsalva maneuver: Cardiologists may prescribe this for their patients when they need to slow their heart rate, so you must be cautious about using it if you have a heart problem or other serious medical illness, like increased pressure inside your head. If you have such a condition, check with your doctor before using this maneuver.

There are two forms of Valsava maneuver. The first one is to hold your nose and try to blow air forcefully out of your nose. You just do it for a second or two. This is the procedure people will recommend to unpop your ears after you've been on an airplane. This maneuver stimulates your vagus nerve by increasing the pressure in your head and is more aggressive than the breathing, humming, and cold water on your face. It's generally used when someone has a rapid heart rate.

The second type of Valsalva maneuver is to hold your breath, which increases the pressure in your chest. Holding your breath is not as aggressive as blowing into your nose and you may naturally hold your breath sometimes, like when you are underwater. You would also do this one just for a few seconds.

These vagal stimulation maneuvers work best for anxiety you feel physically, like heart racing, sweating, or feeling lightheaded. But you don't have to be in the throes of a panic attack to do it. You can also use them if you feel tense and want a reset. I find the *ohm* humming useful when I want to calm myself.

Probiotics and the Microbiome

The story of your vagus nerve doesn't end with breathing exercises and yoga. Arguably, the vagus nerve's greatest influence on your mental health is through its interaction with your gut bacteria.

Your gut is the barrier that separates the outside world from your internal organs. It processes food and creates waste for removal from the body. Imagine your gut as an internal garbage bag; you don't want a garbage bag full of rotten food to burst and spill all its contents on the ground, nor do you want the bag to leak and drip toxic waste all over your house. To prevent this from happening, you can buy extra strength garbage bags. Similarly, bacteria in your gut regulate the strength of your gut barrier.

Your intestinal barrier is a selectively permeable membrane made of tightly connected cells. Selectively permeable means that not everything can pass through the membrane. When you have a healthy gut, you have a diverse population of microorganisms that allow vitamins and minerals to pass through but block bacteria and toxins. Inflammation and autoimmune disorders create loose connections between your cells, allowing waste products to leak from your gut to your abdominal cavity.

About 10 to 100 trillion microorganisms live in your intestines. We call this collection of organisms the microbiome and it is dominated by bacteria, though viruses and fungi are also present. Collectively, your microbiome weighs about 3 pounds, which is also about the weight of your brain. The central nervous system comprises your brain and spinal cord. People often refer to the microbiome as your *enteric nervous system* or "second brain."

There are about a thousand different species in this bacterial ecosystem, some of which are helpful and others harmful. You need good bacteria to digest food, fight disease-causing bacteria, and maintain homeostasis throughout your body.

Good bacteria produce the neurotransmitters GABA, serotonin, and dopamine. The microorganisms send these chemicals to the brain through the vagus nerve, so the vagus nerve is the conduit that allows your microbiome direct access to your brain.

Not all bacteria are helpful. Harmful bacteria secrete inflammatory proteins that cause the intestinal cells to become loose and "leaky." This leakiness allows large proteins and bacteria to pass through the intestine and bloodstream. The leaky barrier also allows toxins to enter the body, leading to autoimmune disorders and mental disorders like anxiety and depression. This condition is what people refer to as a "leaky gut."

What Causes Harmful Bacteria?

Several things determine whether you have good or bad bacteria. Harmful bacteria thrive on foods high in processed ingredients, sugar, fried foods, alcohol, and red meat. Antibiotics kill off both good and bad bacteria, and some studies show that the effects of the changes to your microbiome can last for years with some antibiotics. Laxatives negatively affect your bacterial diversity because loose stools contain fewer bacterial strains. Other medications that negatively affect the microbiome include proton-pump inhibitors, which reduce stomach acid, like omeprazole (brand name Prilosec); lipid-lowering statins, like atorvastatin (brand name Lipitor); the diabetes medication metformin; beta-blockers; ACE inhibitors, a kind of blood pressure medication; and selective serotonin reuptake inhibitors (SSRIs).

Other factors that affect your microbiome are your age, sleep, and activity level. As you get older, your bacteria population becomes less diverse. Bacteria are sensitive to circadian rhythm changes, so poor sleep promotes harmful bacteria. Aerobic activity has a positive effect and improves the diversity of your microbiome. One effect worth mentioning is that of stress and anxiety. Just as your bacteria can send messages upstream via the vagus nerve, your brain can send messages downstream to your gut. Because of this, stress and anxiety can negatively affect the balance of good and bad bacteria.

Medications That Negatively Affect Your Microbiome

Class	Main use	Some examples
Proton-pump inhibitors	To reduce stomach acid	Omeprazole*, esomeprazole*, lansoprazole*, rabeprazole, pantoprazole, dexlansoprazole
Lipid-lowering statins	To lower cholesterol and triglyceride levels	Atorvastatin, fluvastatin, lovastatin, pitavastatin, pravastatin, rosuvastatin, simvastatin
ACE inhibitors	To lower blood pressure	Benazepril, captopril, enalapril, fosinopril, lisinopril
Beta-blockers	Used for blood pressure, heart disease, migraines, panic attacks	Metoprolol, pindolol, propranolol
Laxatives	Promote a bowel movement	Bisacodyl*, polyethylene glycol 3350*, senna glycoside*
Selective serotonin reuptake inhibitor	Treat depression and anxiety	Fluoxetine, paroxetine, sertraline, fluvoxamine, escitalopram, citalopram
Metformin	Lowers blood sugar levels in type II diabetes	Brand name Glucophage

*Available over the counter

Now that we know how vital microbiome diversity is for your physical and mental health, how do we keep our gut population filled with helpful bacteria? Some negative factors may be things you can't change, like your age, and you may not have much flexibility around medication choices. Instead, you can rely on diet and probiotics to grow your army of good microbes.

Four steps to improve your microbiome:

1. **Clean up your diet.**
   The first thing to do is eliminate or reduce processed food, sugar, and red meat. You can choose from many diet options, such as the Mediterranean, ketogenic, paleo, vegetarian, or vegan diets. The Mediterranean diet has been shown to reduce depression and can be an excellent choice to address anxiety. However, there is not one specific diet earmarked as helpful for anxiety. Your diet should be a personal decision based on your lifestyle and what's easiest to sustain. Regardless of which diet you gravitate towards, they all share two common factors: reducing sugar and processed food intake; and eating whole foods as close to their original form as possible, with no preservatives or hydrogenated fats.

2. **Consume probiotics.**
   The next step is to increase your bacterial population with probiotics. Probiotics are foods or supplements that contain the bacteria you want in your gut. Some examples of dietary probiotics are fermented foods like yogurt, sauerkraut, kimchee, pickles, and kombucha. Because these foods contain live bacteria, check with your doctor if you are severely immunocompromised.

   You can also increase your bacterial diversity by taking probiotic supplements. The probiotic capsules contain freeze-dried bacteria that reconstitute once they pass through your stomach and enter your gut. Because of these supplements' positive effects on mental health, some people refer to probiotics as "psychobiotics."

   If you've taken probiotics before, you might have noticed that they have different directions about when to take them. Some brands advise taking them 30 minutes before a meal, while others recommend taking them with your meal or just after eating.

The question of when to take the probiotic is related to how long the bacteria will survive passage through your stomach's abrasive environment.

Your stomach is a very acidic environment with a pH ranging from 1.5 to 3.5. The pH scale ranges from 0 to 14, with 7 representing neutrality. A substance with a pH of less than 7 is acidic, whereas one with a pH greater than 7 is classed as basic, or alkaline. The pH of your body fluid is around 6.5 to 7.5. The low pH of your stomach is necessary to break down proteins in your food, but it can also kill the live bacteria in your food or a probiotic supplement.

Some bacteria are resistant to stomach acid. The most common good bacterial strains are *Bifidobacteria* and *Lactobacilli*, which can survive the stomach acid if they're not exposed to the acid for too long. You may wonder, "What about food poisoning? How do those bacteria survive?" Certain bacteria, like *E. coli* and salmonella strains that cause food poisoning, survive the stomach acid and secrete a toxin that causes vomiting and diarrhea.

The research isn't conclusive on whether taking probiotics with food or without makes a difference, as some strains survive better than others. Nevertheless, there are a few ways to increase the survivability of good bacteria. First, meals that contain some amount of fat can serve as a buffer for the bacteria on its passage through the stomach. Second, movement through the stomach is fast when it's empty. When you eat a heavy meal, there's a backup while the food gets processed, like waiting in line to go through airport security. In that case, the bacteria can get killed off while they sit in the stomach. Therefore, taking the probiotics on an empty stomach or with a very light meal can increase their survivability. Third, if your supplements are enteric coated, they have a coating on them that protects them from your gastric acid.

3. **Feed your bacteria with prebiotics.**

Once you have more good strains of bacteria in your gut, you'll need to give them a healthy diet to thrive. Prebiotics are high-fiber foods that are not fully broken down by the stomach. Your stomach tries, but it's not entirely successful, and it passes on the prechewed food to the intestines. The partially digested fiber becomes an all-you-can-eat buffet for your gut microbes.

Examples of prebiotics are foods that are high in inulin, fruit sugars, polyphenols, and polyunsaturated fatty acids. Most plant-based foods, like vegetables, fruit, and whole grains, contain polyphenols. Some examples of prebiotics are onions, garlic, bananas, walnuts, wine, oily fish, and oats.

4. **Increase your activity level and sleep time.**

    The next thing you want to increase is your aerobic exercise. The Centers for Disease Control and Prevention (CDC) recommends 150 minutes of moderate or 75 minutes of vigorous exercise each week.

    With moderate intensity, you can talk, but not easily, and you can't sing because your breathing is too fast to hold the tune. If you're talking, you're likely huffing and feeling out of breath. Examples of moderate exercise are brisk walking at around 3 miles per hour, slow biking, dancing, or tennis. If you're walking your dog or gardening while humming a tune, you're not working hard enough.

    With vigorous intensity, you can't talk because you're breathing too hard. Examples of this are running or jogging at around 6 miles per hour (which would be a 10-minute mile), swimming laps, or an aerobic exercise class, depending on how hard they're working you.

    You can divide these times up however you want, but it's best to spread it out over the week, like walking 30 minutes on a treadmill five times a week for moderate exercise or taking a fast bike ride for 15 minutes, five times a week. I delve more into the benefits of exercise later in this chapter.

    To optimize your sleep, set a consistent bedtime that allows you to get 7 to 9 hours of sleep each night. Sleep should not be something that happens whenever you stop moving around or put away your phone. You also don't want to go to bed only when you feel sleepy, because watching a good movie can keep you awake past the time your body is capable of falling asleep.

Your body responds well to the circadian rhythms of light and temperature. You can train your body to fall asleep around the same time each night.

Start by setting a bedtime 1 hour before your sleep time as a wind-down period. Spend the first 30 minutes of the hour preparing for bed (brushing teeth, washing face, etc.) and the second 30 minutes in bed with the lights off, waiting to fall asleep. The average time it should take to fall asleep is between 10 and 30 minutes. What if you have trouble falling asleep? You can try relaxation exercises or use a weighted blanket, both of which I'll explain next.

Relaxation Exercises

Guided Imagery

Some people think of guided imagery as a type of meditation. I include it as a body tool because I think its greatest effect is to relax you rather than strengthen your mental control, but there is sufficient overlap to consider it both a meditation and relaxation exercise.

With guided imagery, you use all your senses to visualize a pleasant scene or situation. Typical visualizations include being on a beach or a mountain. Spend some time in the scene and soak in everything pleasant about it. Then once you feel relaxed, return to the present.

Whenever my husband takes his blood pressure, he sits in a recliner and closes his eyes as if he's meditating. One day, I asked him what he thinks about while the cuff was inflating. He said he takes himself back to our honeymoon and pictures the lovely afternoon we had sitting on a restaurant patio in Jamaica. That's his happy place. Whenever he does that visualization, his blood pressure is normal. If he takes a reading on the fly with his eyes open, his pressure is high.

The effect of the happy place doesn't last forever, but it can help overcome a temporary state of anxiety. For example, let's say you feel anxious just before taking a test. Instead of spending your pretest time drowning in dread, visualize yourself smoothly sailing through the test and understanding all the questions, feeling prepared and able to remember all the things you studied. You can then visualize yourself finished with the test and enjoying the rest of the day without worrying about the results. The visualization is not a way to trick yourself into believing that you will achieve something beyond your capabilities. Instead, this type of situational visualization distracts you from your anxious thoughts and allows you to start the test with a more positive mindset.

Progressive Muscle Relaxation

Progressive muscle relaxation (PMR) is a technique used to reduce muscle tension. As you constantly hunch over a computer or text or your smartphone, you gradually accumulate muscle tension throughout the day. Often, you're not aware of your tightening muscles, you may feel physically tired after very little physical exertion. Chronic tension still leaves your muscles tired.

When our muscles are tense, we tend to feel pain in them directly, such as a sore neck or back. However, tension in the scalp or facial muscles may manifest as headaches, anxiety, or irritability.

It's easier to relax a muscle if you first tense it. PMR is a simple process of systematically tensing muscle groups and then relaxing them. One way you can do this is to start from one end of your body and work your way to the other end. For example, you could start with your hands by clenching them for a few seconds, then releasing them. You then move to the next muscle group, perhaps your forearms, and do the same. How would you tense your forearms? The muscles in your forearm help move your wrist, so you could pull your hand or fist inward, hold for a few seconds, then release.

Here's a suggested sequence: hands, forearms, upper arms, shoulders, neck, jaw or cheeks, eyes, scalp and then chest, abdomen, buttocks, thighs, lower legs, and feet.

PMR is very safe, but tensing muscles could worsen certain medical conditions, such as muscle spasms or back problems. You should consult with your doctor before engaging in PMR if you have these kinds of medical conditions.

PMR is one of those things you can do in the 30 minutes before bed as part of your bedtime preparation. You can also do it in the middle of the day during your lunch hour to give yourself a recharge. Once you get the hang of it, it's something you can easily do at any time.

Applied Relaxation

Applied relaxation combines PMR with biofeedback from a monitoring device or a therapist. However, you can do a modified form of it on your own. With applied relaxation, you start by recognizing early anxiety triggers and then use relaxation techniques to manage the anxiety you usually feel in those situations. The idea behind applied relaxation is that, when we become emotionally anxious, the anxiety causes a domino effect due to a physiological stress response. If you reduce the physiological tension, you halt the anxiety response. We tend to avoid thinking about anxiety-provoking situations except when we worry about them. When you intentionally bring these unpleasant thoughts or situations into your mind and pair it with relaxation, you desensitize yourself to the threat.

The first thing you want to do with this approach is to select a clean journal page and write about situations that trigger anxiety. Practice recognizing things that negatively affect all four areas:

- **Thoughts:** things that make you worry.
- **Feelings:** situations that irritate you or leave you feeling overstimulated.
- **Body sensations:** chest tightness, heartburn, or headaches.
- **Behaviors:** overindulgence in substances or self-harm.

The next thing you want to do is get into a comfortable position, seated or lying down, then imagine one situation that makes you anxious and think back over it as if you are telling someone about it or making a movie about it. When and where did it happen? Who was there with you? What happened, and what about it made you uncomfortable? If it's something you fear will happen, what's the worst-case scenario? How will you react if that scenario comes to pass?

Tense and release the muscle groups as you walk through the scene in your mind. Pay attention to your breathing; it may be too complicated to perform a specific breathing pattern with the PMR, and you don't need to. But you want to ensure good airflow and not hold your breath while tensing your muscles. Once you become comfortable with the exercise, add the last step of repeating the word "relax" when you exhale. This practice of allowing anxious thoughts into your mind while you relax weakens the power of the anxiety trigger.

Deep Touch Pressure and Weighted Blankets

Deep touch pressure (DTP) is a form of tactile stimulation you experience from being held, stroked, swaddled, or firmly touched. It has been heavily studied as a treatment for autism, but it's also been shown to benefit anxiety.

Your skin has touch receptors that sense pressure even at a short distance from your skin. These receptors allow you to sense if someone is about to touch you or is very close to you. These pressure receptors in your skin feed back to your brain's limbic system (the insular cortex, to be exact), which processes emotional information about the touch. For example, your reaction to touching the skin of someone you care about will feel distinctly different and more pleasurable than your reaction to touching the rubber case on your phone.

DTP works by stimulating serotonin and dopamine in your brain and triggering a parasympathetic release through the vagus nerve. This dual mechanism of brain activation relaxes your heart rate and breathing and calms your emotions.

Weighted blankets exert their influence by providing DTP. Weighted blankets are more than just heavy blankets, they are filled with objects like glass beads or pellets, dispersed throughout the blanket to give them extra weight.

Weighted blankets come in different sizes and weights, but the general rule is to get one that weighs about 10% of your body weight, based on a single user for the blanket. For example, the standard sizes for weighted blankets are 10, 15, 20, 25, and 30 pounds. If you weigh 140 pounds, your ideal blanket weight would be 14 pounds. Since this weight falls between the usual sizes, you could choose the 10- or 15-pound blanket. You should pick a size that will cover you from chin to feet. If you want a blanket for you and your bed partner to use together, the 30-pound blanket may be a better option, because the weight of the blanket is distributed across the entire bed and not limited to only your body.

In my personal experience, the 15-pound blanket is reasonably heavy, even though it's the right weight for my body size. If my husband wanted to use one, I would prefer a second blanket. The advantage of two blankets for two people in one bed is that you get more of a swaddling or hugging experience from having the blanket wrapped around your body. You lose that effect if the blanket is stretched across two people with space between your bodies.

You can use your blanket to help you sleep, but you can also use it anytime you want to feel soothed from the pressure of the blanket. Some people will use it while engaging in deep breathing exercises or meditation. If you use it this way, you may want to try a lighter blanket, like 10 pounds, so that the weight of it doesn't feel constricting.

A variation on the weighted blanket is a weighted lap pad. These are smaller blankets designed to lie across your lap. It's recommended you get one that weighs about 5% of your body weight or less. Since they are smaller and lighter than the blankets, they are very portable and discreet. It can be a great option to use at work or in a setting that is not your home to help you feel calmer and focused.

Weighted blankets are not recommended for very young children or frail adults who cannot move the blanket independently, or for people with breathing, skin, or circulation problems.

Intermittent Fasting

In Chapter 6, when I talked about magnesium, I mentioned that it increases "brain-derived neurotrophic factor (BDNF)." BDNF stimulates the growth of nerve cells in your hippocampus and other brain regions. Those new nerve connections make you more adaptable to change. BDNF also increases serotonin. We know antidepressants increase serotonin to treat anxiety, and intermittent fasting also increases BDNF, which by extension increases serotonin levels.

There are many ways you can implement intermittent fasting. Some people choose to fast one day a week (with no food for 24 hours), while some will fast on alternate days. The more common way to practice intermittent fasting is to limit your eating window to 6 or 8 hours. Here's an example to illustrate how this can work.

Let's say you have a 9 a.m. to 5 p.m. job. You wake up at 7 a.m., have breakfast around 7:30, and leave for work at 8. Then you get home around 6 p.m. and have dinner around 7 p.m. With this schedule, if we assume you take 30 minutes to eat, your eating window is 7:30 a.m. to 7:30 p.m., which equals 12 hours. Your fasting window is also 12 hours.

If you sit on the couch and sip a glass of wine to wind down until 9:30 p.m., you've extended your eating window to 14 hours, which reduces your fasting window to 10 hours. Even though wine is not solid food, it contains carbohydrates that your body treats as food. Anything you eat or drink after dinner with calories extends your eating window. This long period of eating is probably the pattern for most people.

To get the effect of increased BDNF, limit your eating window to 6 to 8 hours. If you eat over 6 hours, you're fasting for 18 (18/6), and if you eat over 8 hours, you're fasting for 16 (16/8).

These are ideal windows, but you may need to build up to them. So the first step is to look at your schedule and establish your usual eating window. You can reduce your eating window by 1 to 2 hours at a comfortable frequency for you. In the previous example of the 12-hour eating window, it may be too drastic for you to switch immediately to eating for 8 hours. In that example, if you start with a 10-hour window, you could move back your breakfast to 2 hours to 9:00 a.m. and keep your dinner time the same. You would also eliminate any snacks or calorie-containing drinks after dinner. I specify "calorie-containing" to distinguish this kind of drink from water or unsweetened tea. A warm cup of chamomile tea may be a nice substitute for wine during your evening unwind.

Once you feel comfortable with the 10-hour window, you can reduce it further to 8, and so on. You may find that adjusting your meals becomes inconvenient when you need to work around your work schedule. For example, let's say you start working at 9 a.m. and it's not feasible for you to eat at work except for during a designated break, like lunch time. Here, you may only be able to delay your breakfast by 1 hour to 8 a.m., and even then, you may have to eat in the car to make this work (so much for mindful eating).

Let's say you want to do a 6-hour window. You move your first meal to 12:30 p.m., but you can't make it home in time to prepare and eat dinner before 6:30 p.m. Fasting can create a conundrum for people who have inflexible work schedules with baked-in break times that don't necessarily fit an ideal eating schedule. If this is the case, you can opt for the alternate fasting schedules of every other day or once a week. You can still benefit from intermittent fasting if you only apply it to a few days a week when you have more control over your schedule.

Intermittent fasting isn't for everyone. The level of attention it requires may not work well for the person with ADHD or OCD. Also, being meticulous about or limiting your eating may trigger unhealthy eating habits in someone with an eating disorder. Intermittent fasting is also not advisable for certain other people, including pregnant women, children under 18, and people with diabetes or hypoglycemia. Certain chronic illnesses may not be compatible with intermittent fasting. If you have a chronic illness, check with your doctor before starting an extended fasting schedule.

You want to be generous with drinking water when you're fasting. You can drink coffee and tea without sugar, but make sure you also drink water to offset the dehydrating effects.

It's important to recognize that intermittent fasting is not a diet but a schedule adjustment. You eat while you expend energy, stop and rest your body and mind, then break the fast and eat again. Establishing this eating and fasting window condenses the time you're eating so that you're not grazing on food throughout your waking hours.

You still need to make healthy choices with the food you eat during your window. Some people will try to go all-in with a very short eating window for what they think will produce maximum results. They may choose to regularly eat for only 2 to 3 hours a day. Then when their eating window arrives, they stuff down massive amounts of unhealthy food because they're starving and feel they've earned the right to eat whatever they want. If you do this, the inflammation created by the unhealthy food could offset any gains made from extended fasting.

Exercise

We all know that exercise is good for your body and brain, but why? How does exercise improve depression and anxiety?

You've probably heard of the term "runner's high," which describes a rare phenomenon where people experience euphoria and an overall sense of well-being after intense aerobic exercise like running. For years, it was hypothesized that this was because of the release of endorphins, your body's natural opiate. Opiates and their synthetic form, opioids, provide pain relief and make you feel good. Anyone can experience a relaxed feeling after moderately intense exercise, but science now concludes that the chemicals responsible for that feeling are not endorphins but endocannabinoids.

Endocannabinoids are cannabinoids that are produced naturally in the body. They activate cannabinoid receptors in a similar fashion as THC and CBD, which are cannabinoids produced outside of your body from the cannabis plant. The two most studied endocannabinoids are AEA and 2-AG and these homemade cannabinoids have mood-lifting and anxiety-reducing effects.

You do get some endorphin release with exercise that serves the purpose of lessening pain perception during and after intense activity. But those endorphins don't affect your brain or your mood because they don't make it across the blood-brain barrier. Endocannabinoids, however, do cross the blood-brain barrier.

But wait, it gets better! Yes, endocannabinoids give you an instant good feeling, but regular exercise has a broader-reaching effect on your mood and anxiety by triggering—can you guess?—BDNF. This means that regular exercise causes neurogenesis and repairs damaged nerve cells.

Researchers have seen that people who exercise regularly have bigger hippocampi. In the brain world, you want a big hippocampus and a small hippocampus is considered a hallmark of depression. If you recall from our brain anatomy discussion in Chapter 1, your hippocampus is in your temporal lobe and associated with memory and learning. It controls learning tasks, like problem solving, and your ability to process emotions and gain psychological insight. Researchers also believe that neurogenesis creates a downstream effect of increasing dopamine and serotonin, both of which we know to improve mood and anxiety.

What kind of exercise can give you this nice, big hippocampus? You can follow the same exercise recommendations from the CDC that I mentioned above when improving your gut microbiome. Although weight and resistance training are important aspects of physical exercise, it's the aerobic exercise that increases your heart rate and confers the beneficial effects of neurogenesis.

In the final chapter, we'll look at behavioral interventions that you can use to address your anxiety.

CHAPTER 10

Behavioral Tools

In the last two chapters, we looked at things you can do with your mind and body to reduce or manage your anxiety. In this last chapter, we'll dive into interventions that are considered "behavior modification." Some of these strategies are borne out of behavioral therapy and are best learned under the guidance of a therapist. That said, you can still benefit from doing a modified version of them on your own.

Your senses play a key role in modulating your mood and interpreting what is going on in the world. The cognitive areas of your brain process thoughts, but those thoughts are influenced by your brain's input about its surroundings. All five senses contribute to how you experience the world, and you can use them to your advantage to help you with your anxiety.

So far, you've seen how your sense of smell can affect your mood and emotions with aromatherapy. Your sense of touch kicks in with deep pressure touch stimulation, which includes weighted blankets. Your eyes play a role in guided visualizations and coloring, which we'll look at shortly. Even though you close your eyes when you engage in guided imagery, your visual cortex is active in replaying scenes in your mind. As you'll learn in this chapter, hearing and sound are very impactful at reducing anxiety.

Sound

You may realize intuitively that music affects your emotions. Some music can make you feel good, while some can make you feel sad. We embed music into our memories, such that music can remind us of a time from the past. The emotions that experience evoked in the past are the emotions you'll feel in the present.

Listening to music is an easy tool to use because it's portable and passive: all you have to do is listen. You can combine it with many other tools, like guided imagery, relaxation, breathing, meditation, and yoga.

Music therapy is an established treatment provided by trained professionals. They use music in creative ways to treat various mental and physical disorders. A music therapist will customize a program for you that may include passive and active ways to use music therapeutically. Even without a music therapist, you can use music for anxiety and improve your mental health.

Nature Sounds

Natural soundscapes have a similar calming effect to music. These are environmental sounds created by animals or other elements of nature. Some theorize that we instinctively find nature sounds relaxing because we perceive nature as a frictionless system that functions without human intervention. The sounds of human society—traffic, construction, yelling—remind us that life is complicated and mentally taxing.

A 2021 study from Buxton et al. demonstrated that nature sounds "improve health, increase positive affect, and lower stress and annoyance." The researchers found that water sounds had the most significant, positive impact on health and emotional responses, while bird sounds reduced stress and annoyance. The study did not specifically assess other natural sounds, like wind, but their conclusions can be generalized: it's likely that most reduce anxiety.

WHY DOES SOUND WORK?

There's a science behind why what you hear has an emotional affect. According to research, music triggers neuroplastic changes in the brain. The brain areas affected are structures involved in emotion, like your hippocampus and amygdala. Neurologic music therapy is a growing area of research that uses music to rehabilitate people with brain injuries, those who have had strokes, and people with speech and language problems. The rhythm and beats of music create a framework on which new information can be mapped and encoded.

You can think about this as analogous to how concrete is poured. I recently watched my neighbors get a beautiful new concrete driveway. I hadn't realized before this that a layer of wire mesh reinforces the concrete. The concrete is poured on top of this mesh foundation. In this analogy, the rhythm of music is the mesh onto which you can overlay new information (the concrete) that your brain encodes and makes accessible to you when you need the information. Have you ever noticed that it's easier to remember the lyrics of a catchy song than it is to memorize the lyrics without music? This is because the music provides a framework that allows you to group information to reduce your memory burden for easier retrieval later.

All this is to say that music is powerful.

How to Use Music to Soothe Anxiety

What kind of music should you choose? There are no songs that have been rigorously studied and determined to be the best for anxiety. Slower songs with consonant (vs. dissonant) harmonies work best, because they sound pleasing. Songs marketed as soothing may be so, but ultimately, you should choose something you enjoy. If you want a style change, you can try nature sounds like waterfalls, rain, wind, birds, or other animal sounds.

Start by sitting in a comfortable place or lying down. Take three deep breaths to clear your mind. Turn on your music and let it fill the room, or listen with headphones. Listen mindfully—that is, turn all your attention to the music. Notice the tone. Is it fast or slow? Does it have a repeating melody? How does it make you feel?

A variation of this exercise is to listen to music while visualizing a peaceful place. Choose music that fits the scenario. For example, if you want to visualize a beach scene, try listening to the sound of ocean waves to enhance the experience. You could also listen to island music. For extra relaxation help, practice progressive muscle relaxation, deep breathing, or a mindfulness exercise.

ASMR

Autonomous sensory meridian response (ASMR) is a newly defined sensory phenomenon that came to light in an online forum on steadyhealth.com. In the forum, people talked about unusual, pleasant sensations they had in response to certain sounds, sights, or experiences. In 2010, one of the forum participants Jennifer Allen created the term *ASMR* to give the experience more credibility and to generate interest from the scientific community. She also founded an ASMR Facebook group for people who shared this experience. Interest in the topic has steadily grown, and today, there are thousands of online videos and podcasts demonstrating ASMR triggers.

ASMR is a reflex response. The reflex is a tingling sensation that starts at the top of the head and moves down your spine and shoulders. ASMR is similar to frisson. Have you ever listened to someone speak or sing and felt so moved that you felt tingling or goosebumps on your skin? That's frisson. It's a physiological response to something you hear or see that is intensely pleasurable or exciting.

Over the past 10 years, there has been a growing body of research into ASMR. Some studies have shown that it can be calming and can slow the heart rate, similar to a vagal response.

There are many kinds of ASMR triggers, and what works for one person may not work for the next. Here are some of the reported triggers divided into four categories:

1. **Mouth sounds**
   Chewing
   Whispering

2. **Repetitive sounds**

Tapping

Scratching

Objects that crinkle, crumple, or crackle

Rain

3. **Watching an activity**

Watching someone paint or draw

Watching someone brush their hair or apply nail polish

Watching someone open a package

Watching someone cook

4. **Personal Attention and Simulation**

Getting a haircut

Getting an eye exam

Getting a facial

Slow body movements and smiling

As you can see, this is quite a variety of triggers. The first two categories rely on auditory stimulation. While the others rely on visual stimulation, the person making the video (called an "ASMRtist") will often whisper and add other sounds related to the simulation.

The personal attention videos place the viewer as the focal point of the video. The ASMRtist is usually very close to and facing the camera. This creates the illusion that you are in the room with them. They proceed to perform an activity on you, like brushing your hair or stroking your face while they whisper affirming statements.

Some people find this kind of stimulation unsettling. One study found that mouth sounds were polarizing; the participants found them to either be pleasing or irritating. Not all triggers are created equal, and it will take some trial and error to find sounds or experiences that work to make you feel relaxed. (This is true even if you don't experience ASMR.)

There is a caution to consider with ASMR triggers. Although you may find some sounds unpleasant, a small percentage of people react to certain sounds with intense anxiety or anger. This reaction may be due to a neurologic condition called *misophonia*. Some researchers believe ASMR may be on the opposite end of the spectrum from misophonia.

With misophonia, people react negatively to common sounds like breathing and eating. If you have this condition, you can become unglued, intensely angry, and even self-harming when hearing these sounds that other people hardly notice. This condition usually appears around age 12 and is sometimes related to OCD. A person with OCD can hear a sound and then need to perform rituals to manage the anxiety created by the sound. If you have this problem, you would probably already know to stay away from trying the ASMR triggers.

Even if you find the ASMR triggers neutral or positive, you still may not experience the tingling or euphoric feelings that some people can achieve. One thing that may improve your chances of having the physiologic response is getting into a flow state. A flow state is when you are intensely focused on something to the extent that you block out other things in your environment and even lose track of time. It's what some refer to as "being in the zone." You can think of flow as a form of intense mindfulness. Try bringing all your attention to the sounds or visuals to get more out of the experience. So for example, if someone is crinkling paper, focus on the paper and how it sounds. If your mind drifts to the color of the person's nail polish, and you wonder if they had a manicure for the video, you're losing your focus. Simply bring your awareness back to the active focus of the video.

The research on ASMR is still new, so there are a lot of unanswered questions about it. Even if you never achieve ASMR, you may still find it calming to immerse yourself in the visual activity or soak in the sounds. At its most basic level, it's a way to engage your senses in a mindful experience.

Coloring

When I was young and no longer had the company of Melanie the Mop, I had to find another activity to keep me busy during consecutive hours of watching my grandmother's "stories." Art and drawing became my escape. After drawing scores of family portraits and picture books, my parents bought me a Spirograph. Spirograph is an art kit with colored pens, paper, and several plastic circles of varying sizes. The circles have jagged edges and fit together like gears.

This kit definitely took my drawing to the next level. To create a design, I would pick a circle that I used as a frame and then used a second circle with a hole in it to fit my pen. I would hold down the outer circle while using my pen to draw with the inner circle. The result was a unique spiral design. I could create endless designs by varying the size of the circles and my pen placement.

What I didn't know then was that I was creating mandala designs. Mandalas are complex, symmetrical designs that typically include radial lines and colorful shapes or patterns. They can vary widely in color and shape, but the consistent theme is their symmetry and circular layouts. Coloring mandalas has been a part of art therapy and spiritual practices for many years.

The theory behind how coloring works to relieve stress is similar to how music works. As I stated earlier, the rhythmic pattern of music is like a lattice framework upon which new mental processes can attach. Similarly, if we think of anxiety as mental turmoil, the complex designs used for mindful coloring provide the structure against which your mind can untangle itself.

As you color the complex designs, you are drawn into a meditative state that is relaxing and calming. To get the full benefit of the activity, turn your attention fully to the activity of coloring. Notice the feel of the pens, the texture of the paper, and the sound of the strokes as you color.

One study that analyzed different types of coloring showed that freestyle coloring, where you draw and color whatever you want, did not keep people's attention as well as coloring mandalas or something with similar complexity. Because coloring has become a popular activity in recent years, many options are available to purchase mandala coloring books and pens. If you don't think coloring is your style but are intrigued by the designs, there are ASMR videos online where you can watch people draw and color mandalas.

Laughter

This is not a joke. Laughter therapy is a real thing. You may think, "When I feel anxious, the last thing I think about is laughing." You may feel so stiff and uncomfortable that you don't feel you have the capacity to find anything funny. Let me tell you what the science says about laughter and how you can (and should) integrate it into your lifestyle.

Researchers distinguish between spontaneous laughter (also called *humorous laughter*) and forced laughter (also called *simulated laughter*) that is nonhumorous. Spontaneous laughter is more associated with positive moods, but the brain and body don't distinguish between the two types of laughter. You can get the same benefits from laughter that comes naturally as you can from forced laughter.

Studies have shown that laughter has several therapeutic effects. It reduces the stress hormones cortisol and epinephrine, which lowers your blood pressure. Laughter also reduces pain perception through endorphin release. Endorphins are your body's "feel-good" chemicals, and they bind to opioid (pain) receptors. Laughter also boosts immunity by triggering the release of immune cells that help you fight infection.

If you want to laugh spontaneously, you could schedule a time to watch a comedy show. An advantage to this approach is that some studies found that even anticipating laughter reduces stress. So even if you don't roar with laughter from the show, waiting and expecting to laugh can be beneficial.

What makes you laugh depends on your personality and experience. There are a few theories about why we laugh.

According to the release theory, we laugh at things that represent repressed desires and motivations. An example of this would be laughing at a scene where an employee passes gas in an office meeting. Passing gas is socially inappropriate, but you may wish you had the freedom to let loose in front of an uptight crowd.

Then there is the superiority theory, which proposes that we laugh at things that boost our self-esteem at the expense of someone else's. You see this with some stand-up routines that rely heavily on ethnic or gender-based jokes. Some people are only amused by statements that insult others, and they justify the humor by saying that "it's only a joke."

The last humor theory is the incongruity theory, which posits that we laugh when we realize the absurdity of a situation. An example of this would be laughing at the sight of a circus elephant wearing a ballerina tutu. An animal rights activist may not find this sight funny. This example illustrates how personal values factor into what you find funny.

Forced Laughter

You don't have to wait until you're in a good mood to laugh; you can use laughter as a tool to improve your mood or reduce your stress at any time. Laughter yoga has become a popular way to engage in simulated laughter as a therapeutic exercise.

Laughter yoga is not the same as laughing during a yoga session. It combines laughing exercises with yogic breathing. Practitioners actively move during the laughter exercises, but they do not perform yoga poses. Laughter yoga strengthens your ability to laugh on command without the need for humor.

Here are the basics of how it works. You can attend a laughing club for guided exercises in a group setting, or you can practice it on your own. In the group setting, you have the advantage of playing off the energy of others in the room. Forcing yourself to laugh in front of other people may initially feel uncomfortable, but you will often loosen up quickly once the laughing starts.

Online videos can guide you through laughter yoga exercises that you perform either alone or with others. If you choose to do it yourself, there are four general steps to laughter yoga:

1. **Clapping and chanting**

   This is a warmup activity where you clap so that your whole palm and all fingers touch each other. The open palm helps you take advantage of acupressure points in the hand. Your clapping and chanting follow the rhythm of 1-2, pause, 1-2-3. Then you repeat: 1-2, pause, 1-2-3. While you clap, you say "ho-ho" (pause) "ha-ha-ha."

   You perform this clapping chant in sets of twos for three sets (clapping six times altogether).

2. **Yoga breathing**

   At the second step, you breathe deeply from your abdomen. The first two breathing cycles can include normal breaths, in and out.

Then, change to a laugh when you exhale. People typically vocalize their laugh with "ha ha," "ho ho," or "hee hee." Do the laughing exhale for two breathing cycles.

An alternative style of exhaling is to use the yoga lion's breath. With this breath, you inhale and on the exhale, you open your mouth wide, stick out your tongue, and laugh ("ha ha ha") as you expel your breath.

3. Childlike play

Clap your hands together twice, and with each clap, say, "very good, very good." Then, bring your arms above your head with your palms facing outward and say, "Yay." Repeat this twice.

4. Laughter yoga exercises

Open your mouth wide and say "ho ho, ha ha" while pushing your hands in front of your chest, as if you were pushing someone away from you. Turn to each side and repeat. Do this a second time a little faster, then a third time even faster, as if you are almost panting. Then bring your arms above your head again and force yourself to laugh the words "ha, ha, ha, ha, ha …."

If you have a partner, you can do the laughter greeting exercise. Look the person in the eye, and instead of saying hello, laugh while you shake their hand or pretend to shake their hand. In a group setting, you move from person to person, exchanging laughing greetings. This laughter becomes contagious and eventually spontaneous.

Here are a few other laughing exercises:

- **Driving laughter:** Laugh as you walk around with your hands on a pretend steering wheel. Turn the wheel as you laugh.
- **Cell phone laughter:** pretend to hold a cell phone to your ear or in your hand (if you talk with the speakerphone) and laugh instead of talking. Change the tone of your laugh or your laughing words (ha ha vs. ho ho vs. hee hee) to reflect different aspects of the conversation.

- **Hula-Hoop laughter:** Move your hips in circular gyration (as if you were moving a Hula-Hoop around your waist) while simultaneously saying "ooh, aah," and then laugh. There is no pelvic thrusting with this activity, just gentle circular movements.

It's hard to laugh when you feel irked. But forcing the laugh diffuses tension and loosens you up. The childlike activities also strip away your defenses and allow you to feel more open. The emotional openness lowers the bar for what you find funny. Although these exercises don't require humor for you to laugh, I think the induced laughter generates spontaneous laughter. The spontaneous laughter creates a positive mood and leaves you feeling like the process was enjoyable.

Exposure Exercises

The last behavioral tool we will discuss is exposure exercises. Behavior therapy is part of the cognitive and behavior therapy (CBT) approach. Anxiety disorders, such as specific phobias, social phobia, and obsessive-compulsive disorder, respond well to exposure therapy. For these disorders, exposure therapy works best administered by a therapist who can customize the exercises to fit your needs.

But for mild to moderate situational anxiety, you can apply behavioral techniques to help overcome some fear-based anxiety situations. Although there are many behavioral techniques, this discussion will be limited to graded exposure and interoceptive exposure.

Graded Exposure

This involves ranking fear triggers from easy to difficult and gradually exposing yourself to progressively more difficult triggers.

I mentioned earlier that it's common for people with anxiety to avoid situations that make them anxious. Unfortunately, avoidance behaviors strengthen the fear and allow it to grow. Gradually exposing yourself to the object or situation in stages desensitizes you to its adverse effects.

Part of the strategy of exposure is to recognize and extinguish safety behaviors: the things you do to prevent anxiety. Safety behaviors can do more harm than good. When you engage in them, you believe your actions prevented you from experiencing the negative outcome you fear. You never learn that these behaviors are unnecessary to manage your anxiety. You also prevent yourself from learning that anxiety, though unpleasant, can coexist with your daily activities.

How do you identify safety behaviors? Some examples are staying away from situations or places that stir up your anxiety, using companions, checking, seeking reassurance from people, or using alcohol or drugs to dampen the effect. If you have trouble deciding if something is a safety behavior, think about some of the things you do and ask yourself, "Does this make me feel more comfortable about the situation? How anxious would I get if I didn't do this?" If removing the activity would make you more anxious, it's probably a safety behavior.

Let's look at a typical example of social anxiety. You become extremely uncomfortable in groups where people talk and share details about themselves. Your primary fear is being criticized or humiliated when interacting with others.

Here are some strategies you might use to avoid experiencing the negative outcome you expect:

- Talking fast or nonstop to prevent uncomfortable silences.
- Looking down at your phone to keep people from asking you questions.
- Talking very softly so that people ignore you.
- Avoiding sharing personal information by giving superficial answers, then changing the subject.
- Holding your arms or hands stiffly by your sides to hide your trembling hands.

Before proceeding with the exposure exercise, you want to identify and eliminate your safety behaviors. They will only hold back your progress and make the exercises less effective. Don't worry if you can't eliminate them all at once. You may have to do it in a phase-out approach.

The next step is to create your hierarchy of fears that you assign to a fear ladder. The bottom rung of the ladder will be a situation that provokes a little fear, while the top rung holds the greatest threat.

Here's an example. Let's say you fear going to small social gatherings where there will be a lot of small talk. You can't refuse to go, because networking is part of your job. To determine how to break the situation into steps, set a reasonable endpoint goal you want to reach at the top of the ladder. In your case, you want to attend a networking function and have conversations with at least three people.

Here's how your ladder might look:

1. Look at pictures of people chatting at a party.
2. Ask a stranger at the store for the time.
3. Compliment a stranger while looking them in the eye.
4. Ask a cashier something about themselves.
5. Ask a coworker or classmate about their weekend.
6. Attend a social event and make eye contact with each person while they are talking.
7. Join a conversation of people talking and have something to say.
8. Invite people to your home for an intimate get-together, or invite a small group out to a restaurant.

Notice how the steps advance from least to most threatening. Step 1 involves no direct contact with people, but it's an image of your ultimate goal: comfortably socializing in a group. With step 2, you speak to a stranger, but you're asking a generic, nonintrusive question. With steps 3 and 4, you are engaging in limited small talk with strangers. Although it's presumed that the cashier may be familiar to you if you frequent the same store. This familiarity is why the cashier gets a personal question. This step is also riskier because you will probably see the cashier again, which raises the stakes for negative consequences if the interaction doesn't go as planned.

Step 5 raises the stakes even higher as you ask personal questions of someone you will definitely see again. Step 6 gets you closer to your goal, but all you have to do is make eye contact. The greatest challenge for this step and step 7 is doing them without your safety behaviors. With step 7, you only need to have one thing to say spontaneously, although someone may pull you into a more extensive conversation. With step 8, you reach your eventual goal of networking master by hosting the gathering. As a host, you'll be front and center and unable to hide behind safety behaviors.

It's alright to linger on each wrung until you feel comfortable with the activity. Expect to feel anxious when you start the step, but know that eventually, the anxiety will level off. As you move up the ladder, each step will generate more anxiety. However, the anxiety should not be overwhelming, because it represents an incremental change from the previous step that you've already mastered. If you have trouble moving to the next step because the anxiety feels much worse, you may need to create an intermediate step that is not as threatening as the one that gives you difficulty.

In the above example, let's say you complete step 4, where you talk to the cashier, but you choke when you try to get personal with your coworker. Here, you can add a step of complimenting your coworker. You can even break that step into two by complimenting them with and without eye contact. Paying someone a compliment is different from asking them a question. You make a closed-end statement with a compliment that doesn't necessarily invite conversation.

Suppose you say, "That color looks great on you," and the person responds, "Thanks, I got this shirt on sale." If you were ready for conversation, you could inquire where they purchased the shirt and how much money they saved. Then you could follow up with how you love a good sale and how you don't have a lot of time for shopping. Alternatively, you could shut things down quickly by saying, "That was a good buy," and walk away or continue working. Paying compliments is an easy way to speak to someone without the conversation becoming too personal. Compliments also make people feel good and more receptive to future conversations.

You'll probably need to practice the steps until they feel natural. A typical recommendation is to practice one exposure exercise a day.

Interoceptive Exposure

This is another type of exposure exercise that focuses on the anxiety-driven body sensations that can cause you a lot of distress. Interoception is a term that means "awareness of your internal body state." When you have physical symptoms with your anxiety, you can become hyperaware of every body sensation you associate with feeling anxious. This association is called *conditioning*. The physical sensations become conditioned stimuli that trigger more anxiety. When you experience these sensations, you become conditioned to associate them with a fearful state, and your anxiety can spiral.

For example, if you have panic attacks, you can become conditioned to expect certain physical sensations that come along with a panic attack, like feeling lightheaded. Then anytime you have the slightest odd feeling in your head, your anxiety escalates into a panic attack. It's as though you become anxious about the possibility of becoming anxious. You can even fall into the practice of being on alert as you scan your body for abnormal sensations. Eventually, any physical arousal triggers panic.

For some people, body sensations get misinterpreted as precursors to something more ominous, and this fear leads to a panic attack. You may see a palpitation as an impending heart attack, and any sensation in your chest makes you panic about having a heart attack.

Interoceptive exposure is a type of exposure exercise where you intentionally provoke a physical sensation and tolerate the distress the sensation causes. You disprove your false beliefs about the catastrophic consequences you expected by tolerating the distress. You also desensitize yourself to the extreme reactions to the body sensations. Dizziness is still a bothersome experience, but desensitization allows you to experience it mainly as bothersome and not assume it's a precursor to something more dangerous.

To practice interoceptive exposure, you identify the body sensations you find most problematic. Here are some questions to help you identify the sensations.

- What physical sensations make you believe you have a severe condition?
- What physical sensations signal that you're getting ready to have an attack of panic?
- What sensations are you afraid to experience because you fear they will lead to a more considerable negative consequence?

Once you have your list of sensations, group them by body system or types of sensations. Here are the categories you can use:

Head	Dizziness, lightheadedness, head rush
Heart	Palpitations, chest tightness
Stomach	Nausea
Lungs	Shortness of breath, choking, throat closing
Nerves	Tingling in upper or lower limbs
Body	Sweating
Mind	Feeling unreal, environment is unreal

Next, choose an activity that triggers the sensation you fear. It's important to note that these activities are not dangerous for people who do not have serious medical conditions. If you have a health condition that you feel may be aggravated by these exercises, check with your doctor about your ability to engage in them.

Symptom to provoke	Activity and duration
Dizziness, lightheadedness	Spin in a swivel chair for 1 minute.
	Shake your head from side to side for thirty seconds.
	Spin around while standing for 30 seconds.
Palpitations, chest pain, sweating	Jog in place for 1 minute.
Choking	Breathe through a straw while holding your nose for 1 minute.
	Pinch your nose closed and hold your breath for as long as you can. If it is less than 1 minute, take a quick breath and hold again.
Shortness of breath	Breathe through a straw while holding your nose for 1 minute.
	Pinch your nose closed and hold your breath for as long as you can. If it is less than 1 minute, take a quick breath and hold again.
	Jog in place for 1 minute.

Head rush	Sit with your head between your legs for 30 seconds, then stand quickly.
	Lie flat for one minute, then stand up quickly.
Throat closing	Swallow quickly 10 times in a row (without drinking anything).
	Breathe through a straw while holding your nose for 1 minute.
Nausea	Spin in a swivel chair for 1 minute.
	Spin around while standing for 30 seconds.
Tingling in limbs	Breathe in and out fast and deeply for 1 minute.
Unreality	Breathe in and out fast and deeply for 1 minute.
	Stare into a mirror without blinking for 2 minutes (try not to blink for as long as you can).
	Stare at a spot on a wall for 1 minute.

After you perform the activity, notice how you feel. Write down what you noticed in your body and write what thoughts went through your mind during the activity. Then, rate the intensity of your anxiety using the Subjective Measure of Distress Scale (SUDS). Joseph Wolpe developed this scale in his 1969 book, *The Practice of Behavior Therapy*. A rating of 0 means you have no anxiety, and a rating of 10 means you're experiencing unbearable anxiety. Some references to this scale use the number system as 0 to 100. Whichever number system you use, you don't have to worry about being exact.

The writing part of the exercise helps you notice your thoughts and feelings during the experience and measures the intensity of your anxiety. As you continue to practice the exercises, you'll notice the intensity waning. As discussed in Chapter 8, assigning an emotional label to your feelings helps extinguish the anxiety reaction.

Interoceptive exposure works best for people with anxiety triggered by body sensations. This includes panic disorder, health anxiety, and generalized anxiety. General exposure therapy, of which we discussed the graded type, works well for anxiety driven by a fear of uncertainty. Fear of unknown consequences can feel crippling to people with anxiety and is the basis of avoidance behaviors. The exposure exercises acquaint you with the feared symptoms and prove that your worst fears won't come to pass.

This chapter discussed how to use music, ASMR triggers, coloring, laughter, and exposure to address your anxiety. Although these are behavioral tools, you can turn them into journaling tools by rating your SUDS before and after each activity. You can also document your safety behaviors and mark them as "archived" when you no longer rely on them. Journaling these activities can help you keep an account of how you are using your tools and allow you to see what works, what doesn't, and what progress you've made.

It's been a fun process guiding you through the maze of anxiety and helping you understand what you experience and how to put what you feel into words. I've included some quick references and worksheets in the appendices to help you organize your tools. I hope you find this information a helpful companion for your life journey.

It's goodbye for now, but you can always visit me on my YouTube channel, DrTraceyMarks. Drop in and say hello. I wish you all the best for your future. Stay well.

How to Recognize
Target Symptoms

Prompts to Ask Yourself

What Do You Feel Physically That's Not Normal for You?

These symptoms may be helped by the body tools:

- Palpitations (feeling your heartbeat or a thump in your chest)
- Sweating at rest
- Nausea
- Dizziness (feeling unsteady)
- Feeling faint (like the lights are getting dim)
- Dry mouth
- Hot or cold flashes
- Tightness in your chest
- Shortness of breath (you can't breathe deeply enough)
- Sensation that your throat is closing
- Weak legs
- Trembling
- Blurred or double vision
- Gurgling stomach
- Loose stools
- Numbness or tingling in your face or fingers
- Feeling as though you're floating
- Tightness across your forehead
- Feeling unreal
- Feeling tense all over or unable to unwind
- Mind racing

What Thoughts Cause You Distress?

These symptoms may be helped by the mind tools:

- Fear of a future negative event
- Fear of having contact with something dangerous or disgusting
- Beliefs that other people may think are unreasonable or unrealistic
- Ideas or images that you can't get out of your head
- Beliefs about yourself that undermine your motivation

What Are You Doing That Is Not Normal for You or Is Causing Problems?

These actions may be helped by the behavior and body tools:

- Pacing
- Not eating or overeating (especially junk food)
- Not finishing tasks or falling behind on responsibilities
- Self-harm behaviors, like cutting or picking your skin
- Overindulging in substances like alcohol to drown out negative thoughts or feelings
- Starting arguments with people
- Aggravating or alarming people around you with your worries
- Engaging in compulsive behaviors (checking, counting, cleaning, etc.) to the degree that it interferes with your usual activities
- Avoiding people, places, or situations that make you feel anxious, even if avoiding has negative consequences
- Jumping to conclusions that lead to bad decisions

What Things Are You Unable to Do or Are Not Doing Well?

These symptoms may be helped by the behavior and body tools:

- Poor concentration and focus
- Can't sleep
- No sex drive
- Poor social relationships
- Can't follow through with performance-related obligations, like presenting to a group
- Limited ability to drive
- Social isolation

Worksheet

Make a list of your symptoms. The items on this list are the things you want to improve. Then take a look at the *What Tool Helps What* chart to see what tools you should use to address each of these symptoms. If a symptom has more than one possible tool, try one or two to see what works best. If a tool works for more than one of your symptoms, you may want to use that tool preferentially.

Target symptoms	Tool to use	Helpfulness (1-amazing, 3-partially helpful, 5-no help at all)

APPENDIX B

Which Tools Help What

Below are symptoms or situations that cause anxiety and the tools that work best in these instances. These tools do not include medication, therapy, supplements, or complementary and alternative treatments, aside from aromatherapy.

Problem/Situation	Tool(s)
Decreasing the effects of stress and reducing your stress response	Diet, probiotics, intermittent fasting, exercise, mindfulness, meditation, deep breathing, yoga, relaxation exercises, coloring, laughter
Turning down the dial when feeling uptight and tense	Mindfulness, meditation, deep breathing, yoga, relaxation exercises, music, ASMR, coloring, laughter, aromatherapy, weighted blanket
Health anxiety (worry about your health and physical problems)	Applied relaxation, interoceptive exposure, deep breathing, mindfulness, affirmation journaling, worry journal, reframing automatic negative thoughts
Reducing acute, intense anxiety like a panic attack (with or without physical symptoms), intense situational nervousness	Vagal maneuvers, applied relaxation (for prevention), grounding, deep breathing, relaxing essential oil inhaler
Taking the edge off a bad day	Mindfulness, deep breathing, yoga, coloring, laughter, weighted blanket, aromatherapy, music
Helping you relax for sleep	Aromatherapy (e.g., Peaceful Sleep Oil), weighted blanket, meditation, yoga, relaxation exercises, music, ASMR
Deepening your sleep	Aromatherapy, exercise, weighted blanket, probiotics, yoga
Social or performance anxiety with avoidance	Graded exposure, affective labeling, affirmation journaling, worry journal, reframing automatic negative thoughts
Anxious ruminations (worries and fears)	Gratitude journaling, affective labeling, affirmation journaling, worry journal, reframing automatic negative thoughts, mindfulness, meditation, grounding
Compulsions	Graded exposure,* reframing automatic negative thoughts, affective labeling

Problem/Situation	Tool(s)
Mind racing	Mindfulness, meditation, gratitude journaling, affirmation journaling, worry journal, aromatherapy, music, ASMR, coloring, yoga
Slowing the effects of stress-related aging	Diet, probiotics, intermittent fasting, exercise, mindfulness, meditation, yoga
Poor focus and concentration	Intermittent fasting, stimulating essential oil inhaler (e.g., sweet orange and peppermint), meditation
Feeling unreal or detached from your environment	Grounding, mindfulness, meditation, yoga, essential oil inhaler (as part of grounding)

* Exposure for compulsions works best in combination with response prevention. Build your fear ladder using triggers that make you feel anxious and want to perform your compulsion. Then expose yourself to the trigger without engaging in the compulsion. If you cannot entirely refrain from performing the compulsion, start by waiting for a specified amount of time and then reduce the number of times you perform the compulsion. Keep exposing yourself to the trigger until you can eliminate the compulsion.

Aromatherapy Recipes and Tips

Single Oils:

- For an inhaler, apply 10 to 15 drops to a cotton wick.
- Add 1–2 drops to a diffuser, the shower wall, or your sheets.
- You can purchase plastic, single-use inhalers, or reusable metal containers. An inhaler can remain effective for 6 months.
- Oils to use in the inhaler: lavender, sandalwood, neroli, vetiver, Roman chamomile, spikenard, patchouli, ylang-ylang, bergamot.

Oil Blends:

(Use these on your skin to inhale or for soothing massages.)

- Measurement conversions: 1 ounce = 2 tablespoons = 30 milliliters.
- When applying the essential oil to your skin, use a carrier oil to stabilize the essential oil. Wherever possible, use organic cold-pressed and unfiltered oils from vegetables, seeds, or nuts.
- Good carrier oils include apricot, coconut, grapeseed, safflower, sesame seed, shea butter, sweet almond, and sunflower. (Coconut and shea butter are solids at room temperature and will need to be melted before you add the essential oil.)
- You can apply the oil to your skin using a roll-on applicator or spray bottle. Use a 2% dilution, which is 1-ounce carrier oil plus 12 drops of essential oil.

Calming Oil Blend Combinations

One way to combine oils with optimal synergy is to consider their evaporation rates. Top notes evaporate quickly, middle notes at a moderate rate, and base notes linger the longest and evaporate slowly. Top notes tend to have a light aroma that you smell immediately before it fades. You notice the middle note scent after the top note evaporates, and they add body to the oil. The base notes tend to be heavier scents and are the foundation of the blend. When choosing oils to blend, add them in a ratio of 5:4:3. Therefore, for a 2% dilution, you use 1 ounce of carrier oil with five drops of a top note, four drops of a middle note, and three drops of a base note.

Here are calming oils grouped by their evaporation rates. You can use this chart to experiment with your own blends.

Top notes (5 drops)	Middle notes (4 drops)	Base notes (3 drops)
Bergamot*	Roman or German chamomile	Cedar
Cardamom	Cypress	Frankincense
Clary sage	Fir	Ginger
Grapefruit	Ginger	Neroli
Mandarin	Lavender	Patchouli
Myrtle*	Marjoram	Sandalwood
Palmarosa	Melissa*	Valerian
Petitgrain		Vetiver
Sweet orange		Ylang-ylang*
Tea tree		
Thyme		

Be cautious when using these oils in the bath, as they may cause skin irritation.

Peaceful Sleep Oil

I use this every night by putting some on my finger and dabbing it on the front of my neck and chest. On a few occasions, I have fallen asleep shortly after applying it (while watching television), so you may want to wait until you are ready for bed.

This blend is a 4% dilution, which is stronger than the recommended 2% dilution for long-term general use. Even if you use this oil long term, 4% is not too strong, because you're only using it on a small area of your skin. If you were using it for a daily, full-body massage (lucky you!), you should consider a 1% to 2% dilution.

Sunflower oil	1 ounce
Clary sage	8 drops
Spikenard	4 drops
Green mandarin	6 drops
Ylang-ylang	6 drops

Mix all oils together in a glass jar with a spray top, dropper, or open top. If it has a narrow open top, you can cover the opening with your finger and turn it upside down to get some on your finger. Then use your finger to rub the oil on your neck or palms.

Caution: Ylang-ylang is one of the oils that can cause skin irritation. If you have sensitive skin, you can substitute the ylang-ylang for another middle or base note, like ginger.

Relaxing Bath Salt

The template is one-half cup of salt + 12 drops of essential oil + 2 tablespoons of carrier oil.

Salt options include Epsom salt, Dead Sea salt, and Himalayan salt.

Epsom salt is magnesium sulfate. (Remember the relaxing effects of magnesium?). Dead Sea salt comes from the Dead Sea in the Middle East, which is a unique body of water in that it has a lower sodium concentration than oceanic water. It also has a high magnesium concentration, and contains other minerals. Himalayan salt is mined from a small Himalayan mountain chain in the Punjab province of Pakistan. Himalayan salt is used as table salt and has a lower sodium concentration than table salt. It also contains several trace elements, including magnesium, that give it a pink color.

You can add a single oil or an oil blend to the carrier oil. Mix the oils, then add to the salt, and stir well. If the salt crystals are fine, you can use them as a scrub. If they are large and coarse, you can drop the salt in your bath.

Bath Oil

Since water and oil don't mix, you will need to add your essential oil to a water-soluble fixative like vegetable glycerin or aloe vera. Prepare the mixture the same way you'd prepare an oil blend for your skin. Once the oil is mixed with the glycerin, you can add this mixture to your bathwater. You should use a 1% dilution for the bath oil. Add six drops of essential oil(s) to 1 ounce of vegetable glycerin or aloe vera with this dilution.

Room Spray

Add your oil to the vegetable glycerin fixative in a spray bottle and
mix. Fill the bottle with water and shake well. (The room spray will be
a 3% dilution.)

APPENDIX D

Emotions Chart

If you have trouble recognizing your emotions, these charts can help you identify what you feel. For each primary emotion, like happy or fearful, the related emotions are categorized as mild, moderate, or intense versions of the primary emotion.

Happy		
Mild	**Moderate**	**Intense**
Content	Blissful	Excited
Peaceful	Cheerful	Thrilled
Satisfied	Delighted	Ecstatic
Glad	Elated	Stoked
Pleased	Gratified	Euphoric
Joyful	Optimistic	Radiant

Fearful		
Mild	**Moderate**	**Intense**
Shy	Afraid	Terrified
Nervous	Scared	Intimidated
Anxious	Threatened	Horrified
Self-conscious	Mistrustful	Panicked
Worried	Defensive	Dread
Edgy	Alarmed	Unglued

Hurt		
Mild	**Moderate**	**Intense**
Neglected	Belittled	Destroyed
Minimized	Criticized	Degraded
Unappreciated	Disparaged	Wounded
Slighted	Ridiculed	Humiliated
Disrespected	Exploited	Forsaken
Insulted	Aggrieved	Rejected

Sad		
Mild	**Moderate**	**Intense**
Unhappy	Upset	Hopeless
Disappointed	Miserable	Depressed
Low	Pessimistic	Empty
Downcast	Blue	Miserable
Somber	Gloomy	Broken
Lonely	Crestfallen	Dejected

Inadequate		
Mild	**Moderate**	**Intense**
Unsure	Defeated	Worthless
Ineffective	Incapable	Powerless
Weak	Deficient	Helpless
Nonconfident incompetent	Shamed	Useless
Embarrassed	Humiliated	Inferior
	Lame	Mortified

Angry		
Mild	**Moderate**	**Intense**
Uptight	Resentful	Furious
Offended	Irritable	Enraged
Irked	Annoyed	Irate
Chagrined	Miffed	Bitter
Flustered	Indignant	Livid
Perturbed	Disgusted	Incensed

APPENDIX E

Grounding Exercises

Grounding exercises are helpful when you feel afraid, have a dissociative experience, or feel panicked. Find a few exercises that you find calming and keep them ready to use when you need them.

Orientation Exercises

Recite identifying information about yourself:

> I am [full name]. I am [x] years old. I live in [city, state].
> Today is [day, date]. I am currently in/at [location].
> I am safe.

5-4-3-2-1 Environment Awareness

This technique uses your five senses to help you notice your environment.

- Name five things you can see.
- Name four things you can feel.
- Name three things you can hear.
- Name two things you can smell.
- Name one thing you can taste or name one good quality about yourself.

Body Awareness

- Clench your fists tightly and then release them. Do this five times.
- Wiggle your toes.
- Rub your palms together and notice the sound and the warmth this action creates.
- Open your mouth wide and stretch your jaw are far as is comfortable for you; then release and close. Notice the release of tension in your lower face.

Breath Awareness

Take notice of your breathing pattern without trying to change it:

- Are you breathing slowly, quickly?
- Are you breathing out of your nose or mouth?
- Can you see your body move with your breaths?

Color Awareness

Pick a color and name all the objects around you that have that color.

Smell Awareness

Carry a strong but pleasant smell. This smell can be in an aromatherapy inhaler with a scent of your choice or it can be something else with a fragrance, like a hand lotion.

Deep Breaths

Breathe in slowly and deeply while counting to five on your inhale and five on your exhale. When you exhale, imagine your breath is releasing all tension from your body.

Bare Earth Sensation

Stand on the ground (or in the grass) with your bare feet. Close your eyes and notice the texture of the ground and how it feels against your feet.

Mental Exercises

- Name as many states as you can.
- Say the months of the year backward.
- Recite multiplication tables.
- Recite the lyrics to a song you like.
- Count down from 100.

Alphabet Geography

Name a country, state, or city for each letter of the alphabet. For example, "A is for Afghanistan, B is for Belgium, C is for Columbia, D is for Denmark …" Feel free to mix countries, states, and cities. Try starting with countries as the top-level answer, but if you can't think of a country to match the letter, move to a state or province, then a city as a last resort answer. Another variation of this exercise is limiting your answers to states/provinces within a country or cities within a single state/province.

Sensory Objects

Carry an object or have easy access to an object with an interesting texture like a smooth stone or squishy stress ball. When you feel anxious, manipulate the object in your hand and remind yourself that you are safe at the moment. Think about how the object is with you in the present; whereas your anxiety or agitation is about the past or future.

Meaningful Object

Carry an object with sentimental meaning that gives you a warm and pleasant feeling when you look at it. This object could be a picture of someone you love or a memento from an activity you enjoyed.

Elastic Band

Wear an elastic band around your wrist and snap it (gently) against your wrist.

Body Movements

Stretch your arms up toward the ceiling and then bend at the waist and touch the floor.

Cooling Sensations

Run cool water over your hands or splash cool water on your face. You can also place a cool cloth on your neck. Another option is to sip a cool drink and notice the cooling sensation in your mouth, throat, and chest.

Grounding Safety Statements

Remind yourself that you are safe. Remind yourself that your anxiety will pass as it always does. Remind yourself that your anxiety is your mind playing tricks on you, and it doesn't mean something is physically wrong with you.

Repeat Coping Statements

Say affirming statements like "This will pass," or "This is a part of life that I can handle," or "I've got this," etc.

Glitter Jar

Shake your glitter jar and feel your thoughts settle as the glitter settles. You can also use the glitter as a timer while focusing on your breaths.

Interoceptive Exposure Worksheet

Use this worksheet to practice your interoceptive exposure exercises. For each symptom, you can do more than one activity. Continue to practice until your SUDS (Subjective Measure of Distress Scale) score is two or less.

Symptom	Activity	Related emotion (see Emotion Chart)	SUDS (1-10)
Dizziness	Spin in a swivel chair for 1 minute	Alarmed	5

Symptoms by Body System

Head	Dizziness, lightheadedness, head rush
Heart	Palpitations, chest tightness
Stomach	Nausea
Lungs	Short of breath, choking, throat closing
Nerves	Tingling in upper or lower limbs
Body	Sweating
Mind	Feeling unreal, or that the environment is unreal

Interoceptive Exercises

Symptom to provoke	Activity and duration
Dizziness, lightheadedness	Spin in a swivel chair for 1 minute.
	Shake your head from side to side for 30 seconds.
	Spin around while standing for 30 seconds.
Palpitations, chest pain, sweating	Jog in place for 1 minute.
Choking	Breathe through a straw while holding your nose for 1 minute.
	Pinch your nose closed and hold your breath for as long as you can. If it is less than 1 minute, take a quick breath and hold again.
Shortness of breath	Breathe through a straw while holding your nose for 1 minute.
	Pinch your nose closed and hold your breath for as long as you can. If it is less than 1 minute, take a quick breath and hold again.
	Jog in place for 1 minute.
Head rush	Sit with your head between your legs for 30 seconds, then stand quickly.
	Lie flat for 1 minute, then stand up quickly.
Throat closing	Swallow quickly 10 times in a row without drinking anything.
	Breathe through a straw while holding your nose for 1 minute.
Nausea	Spin in a swivel chair for 1 minute.
	Spin around while standing for 30 seconds.
Tingling in limbs	Breathe in and out fast and deeply for 1 minute.
Unreality	Breathe in and out fast and deeply for 1 minute.
	Stare into a mirror without blinking for 2 minutes (try not to blink for as long as you can).
	Stare at a spot on a wall for 1 minute.

Subjective Measure of Distress Scale (SUDS)

Example rating	
0	No anxiety; life is a beach.
1	On guard, but not distressed.
2	Feeling a little tense with some vague uneasiness.
3	Mild anxiety, with some mental or physical symptoms, but I'm still performing my usual duties.
4	Mild-moderate anxiety; this is becoming a problem and distracting me.
5	Moderate anxiety; I'm very uncomfortable, but I can still perform.
6	My performance is affected; I'm falling behind or not able to do things.
7	Very anxious and having trouble staying focused; I feel close to the edge.
8	Extremely anxious and feeling discombobulated.
9	Overwhelmed with anxiety and on the verge of a complete meltdown.
10	Anxiety is so bad; disaster is staring me in the face. I may need to go to the hospital.

APPENDIX G

References

Chapter 1

Aktar, E., and Bögels, S. M. (2017). Exposure to Parents' Negative Emotions as a Developmental Pathway to the Family Aggregation of Depression and Anxiety in the First Year of Life. *Clinical Child and Family Psychology Review*, 20(4), 369–390. https://doi.org/10.1007/s10567-017-0240-7.

Al-Ezzi, A., Kamel, N., Faye, I., and Gunaseli, E. (2021). Analysis of Default Mode Network in Social Anxiety Disorder: EEG Resting-State Effective Connectivity Study. *Sensors* (Basel, Switzerland), 21(12), 4098. https://doi.org/10.3390/s21124098.

Banerjee, A., Sarkhel, S., Sarkar, R., and Dhali, G. K. (2017). Anxiety and Depression in Irritable Bowel Syndrome. *Indian Journal of Psychological Medicine*, 39(6), 741–745. https://doi.org/10.4103/IJPSYM.IJPSYM_46_17.

Bansal, T., and Hooda, S. (2016). Hyperventilation syndrome after general anesthesia: Our experience. *Journal of Anaesthesiology, Clinical Pharmacology*, 32(4), 536–537. https://doi.org/10.4103/0970-9185.168192.

Bansal, T., and Hooda, S. (2013). Teena Bansal, Sarla Hooda, Hyperventilation causing symptomatic hypocalcaemia during labour in a parturient: *Egyptian Journal of Anaesthesia*, 29,(4), 333-335.

Constantino, J. N., Cloninger, C. R., Clarke, A. R., Hashemi, B., and Przybeck, T. (2002). Application of the seven-factor model of personality to early childhood. *Psychiatry Research*, 109(3), 229–243. https://doi.org/10.1016/s0165-1781(02)00008-2.

Crosby Budinger, M., Drazdowski, T. K., and Ginsburg, G. S. (2013). Anxiety-promoting parenting behaviors: a comparison of anxious parents with and without social anxiety disorder. *Child Psychiatry and Human Development*, 44(3), 412–418. https://doi.org/10.1007/s10578-012-0335-9.

Etkin, A., and Wager, T.D.: Functional neuroimaging of anxiety: a meta-analysis of emotional processing in PTSD, social anxiety disorder, and specific phobia. *American Journal of Psychiatry* 2007; 164:1476–1488.

Fountoulakis, K. N., and Gonda, X. (2019). Modeling human temperament and character on the basis of combined theoretical approaches. *Annals of General Psychiatry*, 18(1). https://doi.org/10.1186/s12991-019-0247-1.

Fox, A. S., Harris, R. A., Rosso, L. D., Raveendran, M., Kamboj, S., Kinnally, E. L., Capitanio, J. P., and Rogers, J. (2021). Infant inhibited temperament in primates predicts adult behavior, is heritable, and is associated with anxiety-relevant genetic variation. *Molecular Psychiatry*, 26(11), 6609–6618. https://doi.org/10.1038/s41380-021-01156-4.

Garcia, K. M., Carlton, C. N., and Richey, J. A. (2021). Parenting Characteristics among Adults With Social Anxiety and their Influence on Social Anxiety Development in Children: A Brief Integrative Review. *Frontiers in Psychiatry*, 12, 614318. https://doi.org/10.3389/fpsyt.2021.614318.

Grillon, C., Robinson, O. J., Cornwell, B., and Ernst, M. (2019). Modeling anxiety in healthy humans: a key intermediate bridge between basic and clinical sciences. *Neuropsychopharmacology: official publication of the American College of Neuropsychopharmacology*, 44(12), 1999–2010. https://doi.org/10.1038/s41386-019-0445-1.

Gusnard, D.A., Akbudak, E., Shulman, G.L., and Raichle, M.E. Medial prefrontal cortex and self-referential mental activity: relation to a default mode of brain function. *Proceedings of the National Academy of Sciences* March 2001, 98 (7) 4259-4264; DOI: 10.1073/pnas.071043098.

Hermann, R., Lay, D., Wahl, P., Roth, W. T., and Petrowski, K. (2019). Effects of psychosocial and physical stress on lactate and anxiety levels. *Stress* (Amsterdam, Netherlands), 22(6), 664–669. https://doi.org/10.1080/10253890.2019.1610743.

Hettema, J. M., Neale, M. C., and Kendler, K. S. (2001). A review and meta-analysis of the genetic epidemiology of anxiety disorders. *American Journal of Psychiatry*, 158(10), 1568–1578. https://doi.org/10.1176/appi.ajp.158.10.1568.

Holzschneider, K., and Mulert, C. (2011). Neuroimaging in anxiety disorders. *Dialogues in Clinical Neuroscience*, 13(4), 453–461. https://doi.org/10.31887/DCNS.2011.13.4/kholzschneider.

Hyland, P., Shevlin, M., Elklit, A., Christoffersen, M., and Murphy, J. (2016). Social, familial and psychological risk factors for mood and anxiety disorders in childhood and early adulthood: a birth cohort study using the Danish Registry System. *Social Psychiatry and Psychiatric Epidemiology*, 51(3), 331–338. https://doi.org/10.1007/s00127-016-1171-1.

Jokela, M., Keltikangas-Järvinen, L., Kivimäki, M., Puttonen, S., Elovainio, M., Rontu, R., and Lehtimäki, T. (2007). Serotonin receptor 2A gene and the influence of childhood maternal nurturance on adulthood depressive symptoms. *Archives of General Psychiatry*, 64(3), 356–360. https://doi.org/10.1001/archpsyc.64.3.356.

Kagan J. (2002). Childhood predictors of states of anxiety. Dialogues in clinical neuroscience, 4(3), 287–293. https://doi.org/10.31887/DCNS.2002.4.3/jkagan.

Lamm, C., Walker, O. L., Degnan, K. A., Henderson, H. A., Pine, D. S., McDermott, J. M., and Fox, N. A. (2014). Cognitive control moderates early childhood temperament in predicting social behavior in 7-year-old children: an ERP study. *Developmental Science*, 17(5), 667–681. https://doi.org/10.1111/desc.12158.

Lebowitz, E. R., Leckman, J. F., Silverman, W. K., and Feldman, R. (2016). Cross-generational influences on childhood anxiety disorders: pathways and mechanisms. *Journal of Neural Transmission* (Vienna, Austria: 1996), 123(9), 1053–1067. https://doi.org/10.1007/s00702-016-1565-y.

LeDoux, Joseph E. and Daniel S. Pine. Using Neuroscience to Help Understand Fear and Anxiety: A Two-System Framework. *American Journal of Psychiatry* 2016. 173:11, 1083-1093 doi: 10.1176/appi.ajp.2016.16030353.

Li, X., Sundquist, J., and Sundquist, K. (2008). Age-specific familial risks of anxiety. A nationwide epidemiological study from Sweden. *European Archives of Psychiatry and Clinical Neuroscience*, 258(7), 441–445. https://doi.org/10.1007/s00406-008-0817-8.

Lieb, R., Wittchen, H. U., Höfler, M., Fuetsch, M., Stein, M. B., and Merikangas, K. R. (2000). Parental psychopathology, parenting styles, and the risk of social phobia in offspring: a prospective-longitudinal community study. *Archives of General Psychiatry*, 57(9), 859–866. https://doi.org/10.1001/archpsyc.57.9.859.

Parasa, M., Saheb, S. M., and Vemuri, N. N. (2014). Cramps and tingling: A diagnostic conundrum. *Anesthesia, Essays and Researches*, 8(2), 247–249. https://doi.org/10.4103/0259-1162.134524.

van Laere, K., Goffin, K., Bormans, G., Casteels, C., Mortelmans, L., de Hoon, J., Grachev, I., Vandenbulcke, M., and Pieters, G. (2009). Relationship of type 1 cannabinoid receptor availability in the human brain to novelty-seeking temperament. *Archives of General Psychiatry*, 66(2), 196–204. https://doi.org/10.1001/archgenpsychiatry.2008.530.

van Tilburg, M. A., Palsson, O. S., and Whitehead, W. E. (2013). Which psychological factors exacerbate irritable bowel syndrome? Development of a comprehensive model. *Journal of Psychosomatic Research*, 74(6), 486–492. https://doi.org/10.1016/j.jpsychores.2013.03.004.

Weissman, M. M., Leckman, J. F., Merikangas, K. R., Gammon, G. D., and Prusoff, B. A. (1984). Depression and anxiety disorders in parents and children. Results from the Yale family study. *Archives of General Psychiatry*, 41(9), 845–852. https://doi.org/10.1001/archpsyc.1984.01790200027004.

Chapter 2

Aktar, E., and Bögels, S. M. (2017). Exposure to Parents' Negative Emotions as a Developmental Pathway to the Family Aggregation of Depression and Anxiety in the First Year of Life. *Clinical Child and Family Psychology Review*, 20(4), 369–390. https://doi.org/10.1007/s10567-017-0240-7.

Balaram, K., Marwaha, R., *Agoraphobia*. Treasure Island, Florida: StatPearls Publishing; 2021. https://www.ncbi.nlm.nih.gov/books/NBK554387/.

Blair, K., Geraci, M., Devido, J., McCaffrey, D., Chen, G., Vythilingam, M., Ng, P., Hollon, N., Jones, M., Blair, R. J. R., and Pine, D. S. (2008). Neural Response to Self- and Other Referential Praise and Criticism in Generalized Social Phobia. *Archives of General Psychiatry*, 65(10), 1176. https://doi.org/10.1001/archpsyc.65.10.1176.

De Cort, K., Griez, E., Büchler, M., and Schruers, K. (2012). The role of "interoceptive" fear conditioning in the development of panic disorder. *Behavior Therapy*, 43(1), 203–215. https://doi.org/10.1016/j.beth.2011.06.005.

Eaton, W. W., Bienvenu, O. J., and Miloyan, B. (2018). Specific phobias. *The Lancet, Psychiatry*, 5(8), 678–686. https://doi.org/10.1016/S2215-0366(18)30169-X.

Handley, A. K., Egan, S. J., Kane, R. T., and Rees, C. S. (2014). The relationships between perfectionism, pathological worry and generalised anxiety disorder. *BMC Psychiatry*, 14, 98. https://doi.org/10.1186/1471-244X-14-98.

Hanisch, L. J., Hantsoo, L., Freeman, E. W., Sullivan, G. M., and Coyne, J. C. (2008). Hot flashes and panic attacks: a comparison of symptomatology, neurobiology, treatment, and a role for cognition. *Psychological Bulletin*, 134(2), 247–269. https://doi.org/10.1037/0033-2909.134.2.247.

Hirsch, C. R., and Mathews, A. (2012). A cognitive model of pathological worry. *Behaviour Research and Therapy*, 50(10), 636–646. https://doi.org/10.1016/j.brat.2012.06.007.

Hoffman, Y., Pitcho-Prelorentzos, S., Ring, L., and Ben-Ezra, M. (2019). "Spidey Can": Preliminary Evidence Showing Arachnophobia Symptom Reduction Due to Superhero Movie Exposure. *Frontiers in Psychiatry*, 10, 354. https://doi.org/10.3389/fpsyt.2019.00354.

Jarcho, J. M., Romer, A. L., Shechner, T., Galvan, A., Guyer, A. E., Leibenluft, E., Pine, D. S., and Nelson, E. E. (2015). Forgetting the best when predicting the worst: Preliminary observations on neural circuit function in adolescent social anxiety. *Developmental Cognitive Neuroscience*, 13, 21–31. https://doi.org/10.1016/j.dcn.2015.03.002.

Kessler, R. C., Chiu, W. T., Jin, R., Ruscio, A. M., Shear, K., and Walters, E. E. (2006). The epidemiology of panic attacks, panic disorder, and agoraphobia in the National Comorbidity Survey Replication. *Archives of General Psychiatry*, 63(4), 415–424. https://doi.org/10.1001/archpsyc.63.4.415.

Kessler, R. C., Petukhova, M., Sampson, N. A., Zaslavsky, A. M., and Wittchen, H. (2012). Twelve-month and lifetime prevalence and lifetime morbid risk of anxiety and mood disorders in the United States. *International Journal of Methods in Psychiatric Research*, 21(3), 169–184. https://doi.org/10.1002/mpr.1359.

Kessler, R. C., Stein, M. B., and Berglund, P. (1998). Social phobia subtypes in the National Comorbidity Survey. *American Journal of Psychiatry*, 155(5), 613–619. https://doi.org/10.1176/ajp.155.5.613.

Lieb, R., Wittchen, H. U., Höfler, M., Fuetsch, M., Stein, M. B., and Merikangas, K. R. (2000). Parental psychopathology, parenting styles, and the risk of social phobia in offspring: a prospective-longitudinal community study. *Archives of General Psychiatry*, 57(9), 859–866. https://doi.org/10.1001/archpsyc.57.9.859.

Manicavasagar, V., Silove, D., Wagner, R., and Hadzi-Pavlovic, D. (1999). Parental representations associated with adult separation anxiety and panic disorder-agoraphobia. *The Australian and New Zealand Journal of Psychiatry*, 33(3), 422–428. https://doi.org/10.1046/j.1440-1614.1999.00566.x.

Milrod, B., Markowitz, J. C., Gerber, A. J., Cyranowski, J., Altemus, M., Shapiro, T., Hofer, M., and Glatt, C. (2014). Childhood separation anxiety and the pathogenesis and treatment of adult anxiety. *American Journal of Psychiatry*, 171(1), 34–43. https://doi.org/10.1176/appi.ajp.2013.13060781.

Mitchell, J. P., Banaji, M. R., and Macrae, C. N. (2005). The link between social cognition and self-referential thought in the medial prefrontal cortex. *Journal of Cognitive Neuroscience*, 17(8), 1306–1315. https://doi.org/10.1162/0898929055002418.

Nakamura, M., Sugiura, T., Nishida, S., Komada, Y., and Inoue, Y. (2013). Is nocturnal panic a distinct disease category? Comparison of clinical characteristics among patients with primary nocturnal panic, daytime panic, and coexistence of nocturnal and daytime panic. *Journal of clinical sleep medicine: JCSM: Official Publication of the American Academy of Sleep Medicine*, 9(5), 461–467. https://doi.org/10.5664/jcsm.2666.

Olatunji, B. O., and Sawchuk, C. N. (2005). Disgust: Characteristic features, social manifestations, and clinical implications. *Journal of Social and Clinical Psychology*, 24(7), 932–962. https://doi.org/10.1521/jscp.2005.24.7.932.

Pickering, L., Hadwin, J. A. and Kovshoff, H. The Role of Peers in the Development of Social Anxiety in Adolescent Girls: A Systematic Review. *Adolescent Res Rev* 5, 341–362 (2020). https://doi.org/10.1007/s40894-019-00117-x.

Pini, S., Abelli, M., Troisi, A., Siracusano, A., Cassano, G. B., Shear, K. M., and Baldwin, D. (2014). The relationships among separation anxiety disorder, adult attachment style and agoraphobia in patients with panic disorder. *Journal of Anxiety Disorders*, 28(8), 741–746. https://doi.org/10.1016/j.janxdis.2014.06.010.

Polák, J., Sedláčková, K., Landová, E., and Frynta, D. (2020). Faster detection of snake and spider phobia: revisited. *Heliyon*, 6(5), e03968. https://doi.org/10.1016/j.heliyon.2020.e03968.

Ruscio, A. M., Brown, T. A., Chiu, W. T., Sareen, J., Stein, M. B., and Kessler, R. C. (2008). Social fears and social phobia in the USA: results from the National Comorbidity Survey Replication. *Psychological medicine*, *38*(1), 15–28. https://doi.org/10.1017/S0033291707001699.

Silove, D., Alonso, J., Bromet, E., Gruber, M., Sampson, N., Scott, K., Andrade, L., Benjet, C., Caldas de Almeida, J. M., De Girolamo, G., de Jonge, P., Demyttenaere, K., Fiestas, F., Florescu, S., Gureje, O., He, Y., Karam, E., Lepine, J. P., Murphy, S., Villa-Posada, J., and Kessler, R. C. (2015). Pediatric-Onset and Adult-Onset Separation Anxiety Disorder Across Countries in the World Mental Health Survey. *American Journal of Psychiatry*, 172(7), 647–656. https://doi.org/10.1176/appi.ajp.2015.14091185.

Simons, M., and Vloet, T. D. (2018). Emetophobia - A Metacognitive Therapeutic Approach for an Overlooked Disorder. *Zeitschrift fur Kinder- und Jugendpsychiatrie und Psychotherapie*, 46(1), 57–66. https://doi.org/10.1024/1422-4917/a000464.

Stöber, J., Joormann, J. Worry, Procrastination, and Perfectionism: Differentiating Amount of Worry, Pathological Worry, Anxiety, and Depression. *Cognitive Therapy and Research* 25, 49–60 (2001). https://doi.org/10.1023/A:1026474715384.

Tybur, J. M., Çınar, Ç., Karinen, A. K., and Perone, P. (2018). Why do people vary in disgust?. *Philosophical transactions of the Royal Society of London. Series B, Biological Sciences*, 373(1751), 20170204. https://doi.org/10.1098/rstb.2017.0204.

Ziemann, A. E., Allen, J. E., Dahdaleh, N. S., Drebot, I. I., Coryell, M. W., Wunsch, A. M., Lynch, C. M., Faraci, F. M., Howard, M. A., Welsh, M. J., and Wemmie, J. A. (2009). The amygdala is a chemosensor that detects carbon dioxide and acidosis to elicit fear behavior. *Cell*, 139(5), 1012–1021. https://doi.org/10.1016/j.cell.2009.10.029.

Chapter 3

Agarwal, S., Guntuku, S. C., Robinson, O. C., Dunn, A., and Ungar, L. H. (2020). Examining the Phenomenon of Quarter-Life Crisis Through Artificial Intelligence and the Language of Twitter. *Frontiers in Psychology*, 11, 341. https://doi.org/10.3389/fpsyg.2020.00341.

Clarke C. Can Occupational Therapy Address the Occupational Implications of Hoarding?. *Occupational Therapy International*, 2019; 2019:5347403. Published 2019, March 4. doi:10.1155/2019/5347403.

Davidson, E. J., Dozier, M. E., Pittman, J., Mayes, T. L., Blanco, B. H., Gault, J. D., Schwarz, L. J., and Ayers, C. R. (2019). Recent Advances in Research on Hoarding. *Current Psychiatry Reports*, 21(9), 91. https://doi.org/10.1007/s11920-019-1078-0.

Davidson, E. J., Dozier, M. E., Pittman, J. O. E., Mayes, T. L., Blanco, B. H., Gault, J. D., Schwarz, L. J., and Ayers, C. R. (2019). Recent Advances in Research on Hoarding. *Current Psychiatry Reports*, 21(9). https://doi.org/10.1007/s11920-019-1078-0.

Foa, E. B., Kozak, M. J., Goodman, W. K., Hollander, E., Jenike, M. A., and Rasmussen, S. A. (1995). DSM-IV field trial: obsessive-compulsive disorder. *American Journal of Psychiatry*, 152(1), 90–96. https://doi.org/10.1176/ajp.152.1.90.

Frost, R. O., Patronek, G., and Rosenfield, E. (2011). Comparison of object and animal hoarding. *Depression and Anxiety*, 28(10), 885–891. https://doi.org/10.1002/da.20826.

Grant, J. E., Odlaug, B. L., Chamberlain, S. R., Keuthen, N. J., Lochner, C., and Stein, D. J. (2012). Skin picking disorder. *American Journal of Psychiatry*, 169(11), 1143–1149. https://doi.org/10.1176/appi.ajp.2012 12040508.

Grisham, J.R., Baldwin, P.A. Neuropsychological and neurophysiological insights into hoarding disorder. *Neuropsychiatric Disease and Treatment*, 2015;11:951-962. Published 2015 Apr 2. doi:10.2147/NDT.S62084.

Gu, Y., Gu, S., Lei, Y., and Li, H. (2020). From Uncertainty to Anxiety: How Uncertainty Fuels Anxiety in a Process Mediated by Intolerance of Uncertainty. *Neural Plasticity*, 2020, 8866386. https://doi.org/10.1155/2020/8866386.

Jenike, M. A. (2004). Clinical practice. Obsessive-compulsive disorder. *The New England Journal of Medicine*, 350(3), 259–265. https://doi.org/10.1056/NEJMcp031002.

Keefer, L. A., Landau, M. J., Rothschild, Z. K., and Sullivan, D. (2012). Attachment to objects as compensation for close others' perceived unreliability. *Journal of Experimental Social Psychology*, 48(4), 912-917. https://doi.org/10.1016/j.jesp.2012.02.007.

Keshen A. (2006). A new look at existential psychotherapy. *American Journal of Psychotherapy*, 60(3), 285–298. https://doi.org/10.1176/appi.psychotherapy.2006.60.3.285.

Koch, K., Reeß, T. J., Rus, O. G., Gürsel, D. A., Wagner, G., Berberich, G., and Zimmer, C. (2018). Increased Default Mode Network Connectivity in Obsessive-Compulsive Disorder During Reward Processing. *Frontiers in Psychiatry*, 9, 254. https://doi.org/10.3389/fpsyt.2018.00254.

Mackin, R. S., Vigil, O., Insel, P., Kivowitz, A., Kupferman, E., Hough, C. M., Fekri, S., Crothers, R., Bickford, D., Delucchi, K. L., and Mathews, C. A. (2016). Patterns of Clinically Significant Cognitive Impairment in Hoarding Disorder. *Depression and Anxiety*, 33(3), 211–218. https://doi.org/10.1002/da.22439.

Maheu, C., Singh, M., Tock, W. L., Eyrenci, A., Galica, J., Hébert, M., Frati, F., and Estapé, T. (2021). Fear of Cancer Recurrence, Health Anxiety, Worry, and Uncertainty: A Scoping Review About Their Conceptualization and Measurement Within Breast Cancer Survivorship Research. *Frontiers in Psychology*, 12, 644932. https://doi.org/10.3389/fpsyg.2021.644932.

Moritz, S., Rufer, M. Movement decoupling: A self-help intervention for the treatment of trichotillomania. *Journal of Behavior Therapy and Experimental Psychiatry*. 2011 March; 42(1): 74-80. doi: 10.1016/j.jbtep.2010.07.001. Epub 2010 Jul 14. PMID: 20674888.

Robinson, O. C., Wright, G. R. T. (2013). The prevalence, types and perceived outcomes of crisis episodes in early adulthood and midlife: a structured retrospective-autobiographical study. *International Journal of Behavioral Development*, 37 407–416. 10.1177/0165025413492464.

Spitzenstätter, D., and Schnell, T. (2020). The existential dimension of the pandemic: Death attitudes, personal worldview, and coronavirus anxiety. *Death Studies*, 1–11. Advance online publication. https://doi.org/10.1080/07481187.2020.1848944.

Stein, D. J., Costa, D., Lochner, C., Miguel, E. C., Reddy, Y., Shavitt, R. G., van den Heuvel, O. A., and Simpson, H. B. (2019). Obsessive-compulsive disorder. *Nature Reviews. Disease Primers*, 5(1), 52. https://doi.org/10.1038/s41572-019-0102-3.

Stonnington, C. M., Barry, J. J., and Fisher, R. S. (2006). Conversion Disorder. *American Journal of Psychiatry*, 163(9), 1510–1517. https://doi.org/10.1176/ajp.2006.163.9.1510.

Torales, J., Barrios, I., Villalba, J. Alternative Therapies for Excoriation (Skin Picking) Disorder: A Brief Update. *Advances in Mind-Body Medicine*, 2017 Winter;31(1):10-13. PMID: 28183072.

Thorpe, S., Bolster, A., Neave N. Exploring aspects of the cognitive behavioural model of physical hoarding in relation to digital hoarding behaviours. *Digit Health*. 2019;5:2055207619882172. Published 2019 Oct 9. doi:10.1177/2055207619882172.

Tomaszek, K., and Muchacka-Cymerman, A. (2020). Thinking about My Existence during COVID-19, I Feel Anxiety and Awe-The Mediating Role of Existential Anxiety and Life Satisfaction on the Relationship between PTSD Symptoms and Post-Traumatic Growth. *International Journal of Environmental Research and Public Health*, 17(19), 7062. https://doi.org/10.3390/ijerph17197062.

Wong P. (2020). Existential positive psychology and integrative meaning therapy. *International Review of Psychiatry* (Abingdon, England), 32(7-8), 565–578. https://doi.org/10.1080/09540261.2020.1814703.

Yalom, I. D. (1980). *Existential Psychotherapy*. Basic Books, New York, N.Y.

Zafirides, P., Markman, K.D., Proulx, T., Lindberg, M.J. *American Psychological Association;* 2013. Psychotherapy and the restoration of meaning: Existential philosophy in clinical practice.

Chapter 4

American Psychiatric Association. (2013). *Diagnostic and Statistical Manual of Mental Disorders, fifth ed.* https://doi.org/10.1176/appi.books.9780890425596.

Auchincloss, E. L. (2015). *The Psychoanalytic Model of the Mind* (1st ed.). American Psychiatric Association Publishing, Washington, D.C.

Donne, John. *The Works of John Donne. vol III.* Henry Alford, ed. London: John W. Parker, 1839. 574-5. http://www.luminarium.org/sevenlit/donne/meditation17.php.

Eikenaes, I., Egeland, J., Hummelen, B., and Wilberg, T. (2015). Avoidant personality disorder versus social phobia: the significance of childhood neglect. *PloS one*, 10(3), e0122846. https://doi.org/10.1371/journal.pone.0122846.

Eisen, J. L., Coles, M. E., Shea, M. T., Pagano, M. E., Stout, R. L., Yen, S., Grilo, C. M., and Rasmussen, S. A. (2006). Clarifying the convergence between obsessive-compulsive personality disorder criteria and obsessive-compulsive disorder. *Journal of Personality Disorders*, 20(3), 294–305. https://doi.org/10.1521/pedi.2006.20.3.294.

Gecaite-Stonciene, J., Lochner, C., Marincowitz, C., Fineberg, N. A., and Stein, D. J. (2021). Obsessive-Compulsive (Anankastic) Personality Disorder in the ICD-11: A Scoping Review. *Frontiers in Psychiatry*, 12, 646030. https://doi.org/10.3389/fpsyt.2021.646030.

Granieri, A., La Marca, L., Mannino, G., Giunta, S., Guglielmucci, F., and Schimmenti, A. (2017). The Relationship between Defense Patterns and DSM-5 Maladaptive Personality Domains. *Frontiers in Psychology*, 8, 1926. https://doi.org/10.3389/fpsyg.2017.01926.

Hemmati, A., Mirghaed, S. R., Rahmani, F., and Komasi, S. (2019). The Differential Profile of Social Anxiety Disorder (SAD) and Avoidant Personality Disorder (APD) on the Basis of Criterion B of the DSM-5-AMPD in a College Sample. *The Malaysian Journal of Medical Sciences*, 26(5), 74–87. https://doi.org/10.21315/mjms2019.26.5.7.

Loas, G., Cormier, J., and Perez-Diaz, F. (2011). Dependent personality disorder and physical abuse. *Psychiatry Research*, 185(1-2), 167–170. https://doi.org/10.1016/j.psychres.2009.06.011.

Ni, C., Ma, L., Wang, B., Yan, Y., Huang, Y., Wallen, G. R., Li, L., Lang, H., and Hua, Q. (2014). Neurotic Disorders of General Medical Outpatients in Xi'an, China: Knowledge, Attitudes, and Help-Seeking Preferences. *Psychiatric Services*, 65(8), 1047–1053. https://doi.org/10.1176/appi.ps.201300071.

Pinkofsky H. B. (1997). Mnemonics for DSM-IV personality disorders. *Psychiatric Services (Washington, D.C.)*, 48(9), 1197–1198. https://doi.org/10.1176/ps.48.9.1197.

Poropat, A. E. (2009). A meta-analysis of the five-factor model of personality and academic performance. *Psychological Bulletin*, 135(2), 322–338. https://doi.org/10.1037/a0014996.

Reich, J., Noyes, R., Jr, and Troughton, E. (1987). Dependent personality disorder associated with phobic avoidance in patients with panic disorder. *American Journal of Psychiatry*, 144(3), 323–326. https://doi.org/10.1176/ajp.144.3.323.

Reichborn-Kjennerud, T., Czajkowski, N., Torgersen, S., Neale, M. C., Ørstavik, R. E., Tambs, K., and Kendler, K. S. (2007). The relationship between avoidant personality disorder and social phobia: a population-based twin study. *American Journal of Psychiatry*, 164(11), 1722–1728. https://doi.org/10.1176/appi.ajp.2007.06101764.

Sansone, R. A., and Sansone, L. A. (2011). Personality disorders: a nation-based perspective on prevalence. *Innovations in Clinical Neuroscience*, 8(4), 13–18.

Swaminath G. (2006). "Joke's A Part": In defence of humour. *Indian Journal of Psychiatry*, 48(3), 177–180. https://doi.org/10.4103/0019-5545.31581.

Chapter 5

Chakraborty, A. (2019). Role of Cyproheptadine in Various Psychiatric Conditions. *Indian Journal of Private Psychiatry*, 13(2), 58–61. https://doi.org/10.5005/jp-journals-10067-0034.

Dabaghzadeh, F., Ghaeli, P., Khalili, H., Alimadadi, A., Jafari, S., Akhondzadeh, S., and Khazaeipour, Z. (2013). Cyproheptadine for prevention of neuropsychiatric adverse effects of efavirenz: a randomized clinical trial. *AIDS Patient Care and STDs*, 27(3), 146–154. https://doi.org/10.1089/apc.2012.0410.

Deshmukh, R., and Franco, K. (2003). Managing weight gain as a side effect of antidepressant therapy. *Cleveland Clinic Journal of Medicine*, 70(7). https://doi.org/10.3949/ccjm.70.7.614.

Garakani, A., Murrough, J. W., Freire, R. C., Thom, R. P., Larkin, K., Buono, F. D., and Iosifescu, D. V. (2020). Pharmacotherapy of Anxiety Disorders: Current and Emerging Treatment Options. *Frontiers in Psychiatry*, 11, 595584. https://doi.org/10.3389/fpsyt.2020.595584.

Li, Z., Pfeiffer, P. N., Hoggatt, K. J., Zivin, K., Downing, K., Ganoczy, D., and Valenstein, M. (2011). Emergent Anxiety after Antidepressant Initiation: A Retrospective Cohort Study of Veterans Affairs Health System Patients With Depression. *Clinical Therapeutics*, 33(12), 1985–1992.e1. https://doi.org/10.1016/j.clinthera.2011.11.010.

Marcinkiewcz, C. A., Mazzone, C. M., D'Agostino, G., Halladay, L. R., Hardaway, J. A., DiBerto, J. F., Navarro, M., Burnham, N., Cristiano, C., Dorrier, C. E., Tipton, G. J., Ramakrishnan, C., Kozicz, T., Deisseroth, K., Thiele, T. E., McElligott, Z. A., Holmes, A., Heisler, L. K., and Kash, T. L. (2016). Serotonin engages an anxiety and fear-promoting circuit in the extended amygdala. *Nature*, 537(7618), 97–101. https://doi.org/10.1038/nature19318.

Slee, A., Nazareth, I., Bondaronek, P., Liu, Y., Cheng, Z., and Freemantle, N. (2019). Pharmacological treatments for generalised anxiety disorder: a systematic review and network meta-analysis. *Lancet* (London, England), 393(10173), 768–777. https://doi.org/10.1016/S0140-6736(18)31793-8.

Chapter 6

Akhondzadeh, S., Naghavi, H. R., Vazirian, M., Shayeganpour, A., Rashidi, H., and Khani, M. (2001). Passionflower in the treatment of generalized anxiety: a pilot double-blind randomized controlled trial with oxazepam. *Journal of Clinical Pharmacy and Therapeutics*, 26(5), 363–367. https://doi.org/10.1046/j.1365-2710.2001.00367.x.

Amico-Ruvio, S. A., Murthy, S. E., Smith, T. P., and Popescu, G. K. (2011). Zinc effects on NMDA receptor gating kinetics. *Biophysical Journal*, 100(8), 1910–1918. https://doi.org/10.1016/j.bpj.2011.02.042.

Amsterdam, J. D., Li, Y., Soeller, I., Rockwell, K., Mao, J. J., and Shults, J. (2009). A randomized, double-blind, placebo-controlled trial of oral Matricaria recutita (chamomile) extract therapy for generalized anxiety disorder. *Journal of Clinical Psychopharmacology*, 29(4), 378–382. https://doi.org/10.1097/JCP.0b013e3181ac935c.

Anjom-Shoae, J., Sadeghi, O., Hassanzadeh Keshteli, A., Afshar, H., Esmaillzadeh, A., and Adibi, P. (2018). The association between dietary intake of magnesium and psychiatric disorders among Iranian adults: a cross-sectional study. *The British Journal of Nutrition*, 120(6), 693–702. https://doi.org/10.1017/S0007114518001782.

Benjamin, J., Levine, J., Fux, M., Aviv, A., Levy, D., and Belmaker, R. H. (1995). Double-blind, placebo-controlled, crossover trial of inositol treatment for panic disorder. *American Journal of Psychiatry*, 152(7), 1084–1086. https://doi.org/10.1176/ajp.152.7.1084.

Black, N., Stockings, E., Campbell, G., Tran, L. T., Zagic, D., Hall, W. D., Farrell, M., and Degenhardt, L. (2019). Cannabinoids for the treatment of mental disorders and symptoms of mental disorders: a systematic review and meta-analysis. *The Lancet. Psychiatry*, 6(12), 995–1010. https://doi.org/10.1016/S2215-0366(19)30401-8.

Cândido Dos Reis, A., Theodoro de Oliveira, T., Vidal, C. L., Borsatto, M. C., and Lima da Costa Valente, M. (2021). Effect of Auricular Acupuncture on the Reduction of Symptoms Related to Sleep Disorders, Anxiety and Temporomandibular Disorder (TMD). *Alternative Therapies in Health and Medicine*, 27(2), 22–26.

Carey, P. D., Warwick, J., Harvey, B. H., Stein, D. J., and Seedat, S. (2004). Single photon emission computed tomography (SPECT) in obsessive-compulsive disorder before and after treatment with inositol. *Metabolic Brain Disease*, 19(1-2), 125–134. https://doi.org/10.1023/b:mebr. 0000027423.34733.12.

Chandrasekhar, K., Kapoor, J., and Anishetty, S. (2012). A prospective, randomized double-blind, placebo-controlled study of safety and efficacy of a high-concentration full-spectrum extract of ashwagandha root in reducing stress and anxiety in adults. *Indian Journal of Psychological Medicine*, 34(3), 255–262. https://doi.org/10.4103/0253-7176.106022.

Cheong, M. J., Kim, S., Kim, J. S., Lee, H., Lyu, Y. S., Lee, Y. R., Jeon, B., and Kang, H. W. (2021). A systematic literature review and meta-analysis of the clinical effects of aroma inhalation therapy on sleep problems. *Medicine*, 100(9), e24652. https://doi.org/10.1097/MD.0000000000024652.

Cooley, K., Szczurko, O., Perri, D., Mills, E. J., Bernhardt, B., Zhou, Q., and Seely, D. (2009). Naturopathic Care for Anxiety: A Randomized Controlled Trial ISRCTN78958974. *PLoS ONE*, 4(8), e6628. https://doi.org/10.1371/journal.pone.0006628.

Dietzel, J., Cummings, M., Hua, K., Hahnenkamp, K., Brinkhaus, B., and Usichenko, T. I. (2020). Auricular Acupuncture for Preoperative Anxiety-Protocol of Systematic Review and Meta-Analysis of Randomized Controlled Trials. *Medicines* (Basel, Switzerland), 7(12), 73. https://doi.org/10.3390/medicines7120073.

ElSohly, M. A., Mehmedic, Z., Foster, S., Gon, C., Chandra, S., and Church, J. C. (2016). Changes in Cannabis Potency Over the Last 2 Decades (1995-2014): Analysis of Current Data in the United States. *Biological Psychiatry*, 79(7), 613–619. https://doi.org/10.1016/j.biopsych.2016.01.004.

Ernst E. (2008). How the public is being misled about complementary/alternative medicine. *Journal of the Royal Society of Medicine*, 101(11), 528–530. https://doi.org/10.1258/jrsm.2008.080233.

Ernst E. (2000). The role of complementary and alternative medicine. *BMJ* (Clinical research ed.), 321(7269), 1133–1135. https://doi.org/10.1136/bmj.321.7269.1133.

Errington-Evans, N. (2015). Randomised Controlled Trial on the Use of Acupuncture in Adults with Chronic, Non-Responding Anxiety Symptoms. *Acupuncture in Medicine*, 33(2), 98–102. https://doi.org/10.1136/acupmed-2014-010524.

Farrar, A. J., and Farrar, F. C. (2020). Clinical Aromatherapy. *The Nursing Clinics of North America*, 55(4), 489–504. https://doi.org/10.1016/j.cnur.2020.06.015.

Fux, M., Levine, J., Aviv, A., and Belmaker, R. H. (1996). Inositol treatment of obsessive-compulsive disorder. *American Journal of Psychiatry*, 153(9), 1219–1221. https://doi.org/10.1176/ajp.153.9.1219.

Gendle, M. H., and O'Hara, K. P. (2015). Oral magnesium supplementation and test anxiety in University undergraduates. *Journal of Articles in Support of the Null Hypothesis*, 11(2), 21+.

Han, X., Beaumont, C., and Stevens, N. (2017). Chemical composition analysis and in vitro biological activities of ten essential oils in human skin cells. *Biochimie Open*, 5, 1–7. https://doi.org/10.1016/j.biopen.2017.04.001.

Janda, K., Wojtkowska, K., Jakubczyk, K., Antoniewicz, J., and Skonieczna-Zydecka, K. (2020). Passiflora incarnata in Neuropsychiatric Disorders-A Systematic Review. *Nutrients*, 12(12), 3894. https://doi.org/10.3390/nu12123894.

Jensen, M. P., Adachi, T., Tomé-Pires, C., Lee, J., Osman, Z. J., and Miró, J. (2015). Mechanisms of hypnosis: toward the development of a biopsychosocial model. *The International Journal of Clinical and Experimental Hypnosis*, 63(1), 34–75. https://doi.org/10.1080/00207144.2014.961875.

Kasper, S., Gastpar, M., Müller, W. E., Volz, H. P., Möller, H. J., Schläfke, S., and Dienel, A. (2014). Lavender oil preparation Silexan is effective in generalized anxiety disorder--a randomized, double-blind comparison to placebo and paroxetine. *The International Journal of Neuropsychopharmacology*, 17(6), 859–869. https://doi.org/10.1017/S1461145714000017.

Kasper, S., Müller, W. E., Volz, H. P., Möller, H. J., Koch, E., and Dienel, A. (2018). Silexan in anxiety disorders: Clinical data and pharmacological background. *The World Journal of Biological Psychiatry: World Federation of Societies of Biological Psychiatry*, 19(6), 412–420. https://doi.org/10.1080/15622975.2017.1331046.

Kuriyama, K., and Sze, P. Y. (1971). Blood-brain barrier to H3-gamma-aminobutyric acid in normal and amino oxyacetic acid-treated animals. *Neuropharmacology*, 10(1), 103–108. https://doi.org/10.1016/ 0028-3908(71)90013-x.

Lafaye, G., Karila, L., Blecha, L., and Benyamina, A. (2017). Cannabis, cannabinoids, and health. *Dialogues in Clinical Neuroscience*, 19(3), 309–316. https://doi.org/10.31887/DCNS.2017.19.3/glafaye.

Lakhan, S. E., and Vieira, K. F. (2010). Nutritional and herbal supplements for anxiety and anxiety-related disorders: systematic review. *Nutrition Journal*, 9, 42. https://doi.org/10.1186/1475-2891-9-42.

Lee, Y.-L., Wu, Y., Tsang, H. W. H., Leung, A. Y., and Cheung, W. M. (2011). A systematic review on the anxiolytic effects of aromatherapy in people with anxiety symptoms. *The Journal of Alternative and Complementary Medicine*, 17(2), 101–108. https://doi.org/10.1089/acm.2009.0277.

Longhurst J. C. (2010). Defining meridians: a modern basis of understanding. *Journal of Acupuncture and Meridian Studies*, 3(2), 67–74. https://doi.org/10.1016/S2005-2901(10)60014-3.

Malsch, U., and Kieser, M. (2001). Efficacy of kava-kava in the treatment of non-psychotic anxiety, following pretreatment with benzodiazepines. *Psychopharmacology*, 157(3), 277–283. https://doi.org/10.1007/ s002130100792.

Mao, J. J., Xie, S. X., Keefe, J. R., Soeller, I., Li, Q. S., and Amsterdam, J. D. (2016). Long-term chamomile (*Matricaria chamomilla* L.) treatment for generalized anxiety disorder: A randomized clinical trial. *Phytomedicine: International Journal of Phytotherapy and Phytopharmacology*, 23(14), 1735–1742. https://doi. org/10.1016/j.phymed.2016.10.012.

Melvin A. Gravitz Ph.D. (1994) The First Use of Self-Hypnosis: Mesmer Mesmerizes Mesmer, *American Journal of Clinical Hypnosis*, 37:1, 49-52, DOI: 10.1080/00029157.1994.10403109.

Miranda, M., Morici, J. F., Zanoni, M. B., and Bekinschtein, P. (2019). Brain-Derived Neurotrophic Factor: A Key Molecule for Memory in the Healthy and the Pathological Brain. *Frontiers in Cellular Neuroscience*, 13, 363. https:// doi.org/10.3389/fncel.2019.00363.

Müller, W. E., Sillani, G., Schuwald, A., and Friedland, K. (2021). Pharmacological basis of the anxiolytic and antidepressant properties of Silexan®, an essential oil from the flowers of lavender. *Neurochemistry International*, 143, 104899. https://doi.org/10.1016/j.neuint.2020.104899.

National Academies of Sciences, Engineering, and Medicine. 2017. The health effects of cannabis and cannabinoids: The current state of evidence and recommendations for research. The National Academies Press, Washington, D.C. doi: 10.17226/24625.

National Academies of Sciences, Engineering, and Medicine, Health and Medicine Division, Board on Population Health and Public Health Practice, and Committee on the Health Effects of Marijuana: An Evidence Review and Research Agenda. (2017). *The Health Effects of Cannabis and Cannabinoids: The Current State of Evidence and Recommendations for Research* (1st ed.). National Academies Press.

National Institutes of Health. *Office of Dietary Supplements - Magnesium.* National Institutes of Health, Office of Dietary Supplements. Retrieved February 6, 2022. https://ods.od.nih.gov/factsheets/Magnesium-HealthProfessional/.

Niaz, K., Zaplatic, E., and Spoor, J. (2018). Extensive use of monosodium glutamate: A threat to public health?. *EXCLI* journal, 17, 273–278. https://doi.org/10.17179/excli2018-1092.

Nojoumi, M., Ghaeli, P., Salimi, S., Sharifi, A., and Raisi, F. (2016). Effects of Passion Flower Extract, as an Add-On Treatment to Sertraline, on Reaction Time in Patients with Generalized Anxiety Disorder: A Double-Blind Placebo-Controlled Study. *Iranian Journal of Psychiatry*, 11(3), 191–197.

Palatnik, A., Frolov, K., Fux, M., and Benjamin, J. (2001). Double-blind, controlled, crossover trial of inositol versus fluvoxamine for the treatment of panic disorder. *Journal of Clinical Psychopharmacology*, 21(3), 335–339. https://doi.org/10.1097/00004714-200106000-00014.

Park C. (2013). Mind-body CAM interventions: current status and considerations for integration into clinical health psychology. *Journal of Clinical Psychology*, 69(1), 45–63. https://doi.org/10.1002/jclp.21910.

Perry, N., and Perry, E. (2006). Aromatherapy in the Management of Psychiatric Disorders. *CNS Drugs*, 20(4), 257–280. https://doi.org/10.2165/00023210-200620040-00001.

Pilkington, K., Kirkwood, G., Rampes, H., Cummings, M., and Richardson, J. (2007). Acupuncture for anxiety and anxiety disorders--a systematic literature review. *Acupuncture in Medicine: British Medical Acupuncture Society*, 25(1-2), 1–10. https://doi.org/10.1136/aim.25.1-2.1.

Piomelli, D., and Russo, E. B. (2016). The Cannabis sativa Versus Cannabis indica Debate: An Interview with Ethan Russo, MD. *Cannabis and Cannabinoid Research*, 1(1), 44–46. https://doi.org/10.1089/can.2015.29003.ebr.

Pratte, M. A., Nanavati, K. B., Young, V., and Morley, C. P. (2014). An alternative treatment for anxiety: a systematic review of human trial results reported for the Ayurvedic herb ashwagandha (Withania somnifera). *Journal of Alternative and Complementary Medicine*, 20(12), 901–908. https://doi.org/10.1089/acm.2014.0177.

Rock, E. M., and Parker, L. A. (2021). Constituents of *Cannabis sativa. Advances in Experimental Medicine and Biology*, 1264, 1–13. https://doi.org/10.1007/978-3-030-57369-0_1.

Rokhtabnak, F., Ghodraty, M. R., Kholdebarin, A., Khatibi, A., Seyed Alizadeh, S. S., Koleini, Z. S., Zamani, M. M., and Pournajafian, A. (2016). Comparing the Effect of Preoperative Administration of Melatonin and Passiflora incarnata on Postoperative Cognitive Disorders in Adult Patients Undergoing Elective Surgery. *Anesthesiology and Pain Medicine*, 7(1), e41238. https://doi.org/10.5812/aapm.41238.

Russo A. J. (2011). Decreased zinc and increased copper in individuals with anxiety. *Nutrition and Metabolic Insights*, 4, 1–5. https://doi.org/10.4137/NMI.S6349.

Shin, Y. K., Lee, S. Y., Lee, J. M., Kang, P., and Seol, G. H. (2020). Effects of Short-Term Inhalation of Patchouli Oil on Professional Quality of Life and Stress Levels in Emergency Nurses: A Randomized Controlled Trial. *The Journal of Alternative and Complementary Medicine*, 26(11), 1032–1038. https://doi.org/10.1089/acm.2020.0206.

Sommano, S. R., Chittasupho, C., Ruksiriwanich, W., and Jantrawut, P. (2020). The Cannabis Terpenes. *Molecules* (Basel, Switzerland), 25(24), 5792. https://doi.org/10.3390/molecules25245792.

Tan, A., Wang, M., Liu, J., Huang, K., Dai, D., Li, L., Shi, H., and Wang, P. (2020). Efficacy and safety of acupuncture combined with western medicine for anxiety: A systematic review protocol. *Medicine*, 99(31), e21445. https://doi.org/10.1097/MD.0000000000021445.

Tisserand, R., and Young, R. (2014). *Essential Oil Safety: A Guide for Health Care Professionals, second ed.*, Churchill Livingstone, London, U.K.

Volz, H. P., and Kieser, M. (1997). Kava-kava extract WS 1490 versus placebo in anxiety disorders--a randomized placebo-controlled 25-week outpatient trial. *Pharmacopsychiatry*, 30(1), 1–5. https://doi.org/10.1055/s-2007-979474.

Walker, A. F., Marakis, G., Christie, S., and Byng, M. (2003). Mg citrate found more bioavailable than other Mg preparations in a randomised, double-blind study. *Magnesium Research*, 16(3), 183–191.

White, A., and Ernst, E. (2004). A brief history of acupuncture. *Rheumatology* (Oxford, England), 43(5), 662–663. https://doi.org/10.1093/rheumatology/keg005.

Williamson A. (2019). What is hypnosis and how might it work?. *Palliative Care*, 12, 1178224219826581. https://doi.org/10.1177/1178224219826581.

Yang, X. Y., Yang, N. B., Huang, F. F., Ren, S., and Li, Z. J. (2021). Effectiveness of acupuncture on anxiety disorder: a systematic review and meta-analysis of randomised controlled trials. *Annals of General Psychiatry*, 20(1), 9. https://doi.org/10.1186/s12991-021-00327-5.

Zhou, Y., and Danbolt, N. C. (2014). Glutamate as a neurotransmitter in the healthy brain. *Journal of Neural Transmission* (Vienna, Austria: 1996), 121(8), 799–817. https://doi.org/10.1007/s00702-014-1180-8.

Chapter 7

Abdallah, C. G., Averill, C. L., Ramage, A. E., Averill, L. A., Alkin, E., Nemati, S., Krystal, J. H., Roache, J. D., Resick, P., Young-McCaughan, S., Peterson, A. L., Fox, P., and Strong Star Consortium (2019). Reduced Salience and Enhanced Central Executive Connectivity Following PTSD Treatment. *Chronic Stress*, 3, 2470547019838971. https://doi.org/10.1177/2470547019838971.

Dougherty, D. D., Brennan, B. P., Stewart, S. E., Wilhelm, S., Widge, A. S., and Rauch, S. L. (2018). Neuroscientifically Informed Formulation and Treatment Planning for Patients With Obsessive-Compulsive Disorder. *JAMA Psychiatry*, 75(10), 1081. https://doi.org/10.1001/jamapsychiatry.2018.0930.

Galovski, T. E., Blain, L. M., Mott, J. M., Elwood, L., and Houle, T. (2012). Manualized therapy for PTSD: flexing the structure of cognitive processing therapy. *Journal of Consulting and Clinical Psychology*, 80(6), 968–981. https://doi.org/10.1037/a0030600.

Goubert, D. P. (2020). *Learning Acceptance and Commitment Therapy: The Essential Guide to the Process and Practice of Mindful Psychiatry, first ed.* American Psychiatric Association Publishing, Washington D.C.

Kaczkurkin, A. N., and Foa, E. B. (2015). Cognitive-behavioral therapy for anxiety disorders: an update on the empirical evidence. *Dialogues in Clinical Neuroscience*, 17(3), 337–346. https://doi.org/10.31887/DCNS.2015.17.3/akaczkurkin.

Marcus, S. V., Marquis, P., and Sakai, C. (1997). Controlled study of treatment of PTSD using EMDR in an HMO setting. *Psychotherapy: Theory, Research, Practice, Training*, 34(3), 307–315. https://doi.org/10.1037/h0087791.

Shapiro F. (1999). Eye Movement Desensitization and Reprocessing (EMDR) and the anxiety disorders: clinical and research implications of an integrated psychotherapy treatment. *Journal of Anxiety Disorders*, 13(1-2), 35–67. https://doi.org/10.1016/s0887-6185(98)00038-3.

Shapiro F. (2014). The role of eye movement desensitization and reprocessing (EMDR) therapy in medicine: addressing the psychological and physical symptoms stemming from adverse life experiences. *Permanente Journal*, 18(1), 71–77. https://doi.org/10.7812/TPP/13-098.

Stultz, D. J., Osburn, S., Burns, T., Pawlowska-Wajswol, S., and Walton, R. (2020). Transcranial Magnetic Stimulation (TMS) Safety with Respect to Seizures: A Literature Review. *Neuropsychiatric Disease and Treatment*, 16, 2989–3000. https://doi.org/10.2147/NDT.S276635.

Tendler, A., Zohar J., Carmi L., Roth Y., and Zangen A. (2018). O14. Deep TMS of the Medial Prefrontal and Anterior Cingulate Cortices for OCD: A Double-Blinded Multi-Center Study. *Biological Psychiatry*, 83(Supple 9): S113-S114.

Wallis, O. C., and de Vries, J. (2020). EMDR treatment for anxiety in MS patients: A pilot study. *Multiple Sclerosis Journal*, 6(4), 2055217320974388. https://doi.org/10.1177/2055217320974388.

Chapter 8

Beck, A. T. (1976). *Cognitive Therapy and the Emotional Disorders, first ed.* International Universities Press, New York, N.Y.

Burns, D. D. (1980). *Feeling Good: The New Mood Therapy.* New American Library, New York, N.Y.

Cascio, C. N., O'Donnell, M. B., Tinney, F. J., Lieberman, M. D., Taylor, S. E., Strecher, V. J., and Falk, E. B. (2016). Self-affirmation activates brain systems associated with self-related processing and reward and is reinforced by future orientation. *Social Cognitive and Affective Neuroscience*, 11(4), 621–629. https://doi.org/10.1093/scan/nsv136.

Cohen, G. L., and Sherman, D. K. (2014). The psychology of change: self-affirmation and social psychological intervention. *Annual Review of Psychology*, 65, 333–371. https://doi.org/10.1146/annurev-psych-010213-115137.

Dahl, C. J., Lutz, A., and Davidson, R. J. (2015). Reconstructing and deconstructing the self: cognitive mechanisms in meditation practice. *Trends in Cognitive Sciences*, 19(9), 515–523. https://doi.org/10.1016/j.tics.2015.07.001.

Dunn, B. D., Stefanovitch, I., Evans, D., Oliver, C., Hawkins, A., and Dalgleish, T. (2010). Can you feel the beat? Interoceptive awareness is an interactive function of anxiety- and depression-specific symptom dimensions. *Behaviour Research and Therapy*, 48(11), 1133–1138. https://doi.org/10.1016/j.brat.2010.07.006.

Favre, P., Kanske, P., Engen, H., and Singer, T. (2021). Decreased emotional reactivity after 3-month socio-affective but not attention- or meta-cognitive-based mental training: A randomized, controlled, longitudinal fMRI study. *NeuroImage*, 237, 118132. https://doi.org/10.1016/j.neuroimage.2021.118132.

Hariri, A. R., Bookheimer, S. Y., and Mazziotta, J. C. (2000). Modulating emotional responses: effects of a neocortical network on the limbic system. *Neuroreport*, 11(1), 43–48. https://doi.org/10.1097/00001756-200001170-00009.

Kircanski, K., Lieberman, M. D., and Craske, M. G. (2012). Feelings into words: contributions of language to exposure therapy. *Psychological Science*, 23(10), 1086–1091. https://doi.org/10.1177/0956797612443830.

Ko, H., Kim, S., and Kim, E. (2021). Nursing Students' Experiences of Gratitude Journaling during the COVID-19 Pandemic. *Healthcare* (Basel, Switzerland), 9(11), 1473. https://doi.org/10.3390/healthcare9111473.

Kreiser, I., Moyal, N., and Anholt, G. E. (2019). Regulating Obsessive-Like Thoughts: Comparison of Two Forms of Affective Labeling with Exposure Only in Participants with High Obsessive-Compulsive Symptoms. *Clinical Neuropsychiatry*, 16(1), 25–32.

Lieberman, M. D., Eisenberger, N. I., Crockett, M. J., Tom, S. M., Pfeifer, J. H., and Way, B. M. (2007). Putting feelings into words: affect labeling disrupts amygdala activity in response to affective stimuli. *Psychological Science*, 18(5), 421–428. https://doi.org/10.1111/j.1467-9280.2007.01916.x.

Montero-Marin, J., Garcia-Campayo, J., Pérez-Yus, M. C., Zabaleta-Del-Olmo, E., and Cuijpers, P. (2019). Meditation techniques v. relaxation therapies when treating anxiety:
a meta-analytic review. *Psychological Medicine*, 49(13), 2118–2133. https://doi.org/10.1017/S0033291719001600.

Sears, S., and Kraus, S. (2009). I think therefore I om: cognitive distortions and coping style as mediators for the effects of mindfulness meditation on anxiety, positive and negative affect, and hope. *Journal of Clinical Psychology*, 65(6), 561–573. https://doi.org/10.1002/jclp.20543.

Singer, T., Kok, B. E., Bornemann, B., Bolz, M., and Bochow, C. (2015). *The ReSource Project: Background, Design, Samples, and Measurements, first ed.* Leipzig: Max Planck Institute for Human Cognitive and Brain Sciences.

Taren, A. A., Gianaros, P. J., Greco, C. M., Lindsay, E. K., Fairgrieve, A., Brown, K. W., Rosen, R. K., Ferris, J. L., Julson, E., Marsland, A. L., and Creswell, J. D. (2017). Mindfulness Meditation Training and Executive Control Network Resting State Functional Connectivity: A Randomized Controlled Trial. *Psychosomatic Medicine*, 79(6), 674–683. https://doi.org/10.1097/PSY.0000000000000466.

Thomassin, K., Morelen, D., and Suveg, C. (2012). Emotion Reporting Using Electronic Diaries Reduces Anxiety Symptoms in Girls With Emotion Dysregulation. *Journal of Contemporary Psychotherapy*, 42(4), 207–213. https://doi.org/10.1007/s10879-012-9205-9.

Valk, S. L., Bernhardt, B. C., Trautwein, F. M., Böckler, A., Kanske, P., Guizard, N., Collins, D. L., and Singer, T. (2017). Structural plasticity of the social brain: Differential change after socio-affective and cognitive mental training. *Science Advances*, 3(10), e1700489. https://doi.org/10.1126/sciadv.1700489.

Vinson, J., Powers, J., and Mosesso, K. (2020). Weighted Blankets: Anxiety Reduction in Adult Patients Receiving Chemotherapy. *Clinical Journal of Oncology Nursing*, 24(4), 360–368. https://doi.org/10.1188/20.CJON.360-368.

Wood, A.M., Froh, J. J., and Geraghty, A. W. (2010). Gratitude and well-being: A review and theoretical integration. *Clinical Psychology Review*, 30(7), 890–905. https://doi.org/10.1016/j.cpr.2010.03.005.

Wood, J. V., Perunovic, W. Q., and Lee, J. W. (2009). Positive self-statements: power for some, peril for others. *Psychological Science*, 20(7), 860–866. https://doi.org/10.1111/j.1467-9280.2009.02370.x.

Chapter 9

Bestbier, L., and Williams, T. I. (2017). The Immediate Effects of Deep Pressure on Young People with Autism and Severe Intellectual Difficulties: Demonstrating Individual Differences. *Occupational Therapy International*, 2017, 7534972. https://doi.org/10.1155/2017/7534972.

Bhavanani, A. B., Madanmohan, and Sanjay, Z. (2012). Immediate effect of chandra nadi pranayama (left unilateral forced nostril breathing) on cardiovascular parameters in hypertensive patients. *International Journal of Yoga*, 5(2), 108–111. https://doi.org/10.4103/0973-6131.98221.

Chen, H. Y., Yang, H., Meng, L. F., Chan, P. S., Yang, C. Y., and Chen, H. M. (2016). Effect of deep pressure input on parasympathetic system in patients with wisdom tooth surgery. *Journal of the Formosan Medical Association*, 115(10), 853–859. https://doi.org/10.1016/j.jfma.2016.07.008. org/10.4103/0973-6131.98221.

Draghici, A. E., and Taylor, J. A. (2016). The physiological basis and measurement of heart rate variability in humans. *Journal of Physiological Anthropology*, 35(1), 22. https://doi.org/10.1186/s40101-016-0113-7.

Dunn, B. D., Stefanovitch, I., Evans, D., Oliver, C., Hawkins, A., and Dalgleish, T. (2010). Can you feel the beat? Interoceptive awareness is an interactive function of anxiety- and depression-specific symptom dimensions. *Behaviour Research and Therapy*, 48(11), 1133–1138. https://doi.org/10.1016/j.brat.2010.07.006.

Eppley, K. R., Abrams, A. I., and Shear, J. (1989). Differential effects of relaxation techniques on trait anxiety: a meta-analysis. *Journal of Clinical Psychology*, 45(6), 957–974. https://doi.org/10.1002/1097-4679(198911)45:6<957::aid-jclp2270450622>3.0.co;2-q.

Field, T., Diego, M., Delgado, J., and Medina, L. (2013). Tai chi/yoga reduces prenatal depression, anxiety and sleep disturbances. *Complementary Therapies in Clinical Practice*, 19(1), 6–10. https://doi.org/10.1016/j.ctcp.2012.10.001.

Hasan, N., and Yang, H. (2019). Factors affecting the composition of the gut microbiota, and its modulation. *PeerJ*, 7, e7502. https://doi.org/10.7717/peerj.7502.

Kahana-Zweig, R., Geva-Sagiv, M., Weissbrod, A., Secundo, L., Soroker, N., and Sobel, N. (2016). Measuring and Characterizing the Human Nasal Cycle. *PloS One*, 11(10), e0162918. https://doi.org/10.1371/journal.pone.0162918.

Lehrer, P. M., and Gevirtz, R. (2014). Heart rate variability biofeedback: how and why does it work?. *Frontiers in Psychology*, 5, 756. https://doi.org/10.3389/fpsyg.2014.00756.

Manzoni, G. M., Pagnini, F., Castelnuovo, G., and Molinari, E. (2008). Relaxation training for anxiety: a ten-years systematic review with meta-analysis. *BMC Psychiatry*, 8, 41. https://doi.org/10.1186/1471-244X-8-41.

Marotta, A., Sarno, E., Del Casale, A., Pane, M., Mogna, L., Amoruso, A., Felis, G. E., and Fiorio, M. (2019). Effects of Probiotics on Cognitive Reactivity, Mood, and Sleep Quality. *Frontiers in Psychiatry*, 10, 164. https://doi.org/10.3389/fpsyt.2019.00164.

Rosenberg, S., Shield, B., and Porges, S. W. (2017). *Accessing the Healing Power of the Vagus Nerve: Self-Help Exercises for Anxiety, Depression, Trauma, and Autism*. North Atlantic Books, Berkeley, CA.

Saoji, A. A., Raghavendra, B. R., and Manjunath, N. K. (2019). Effects of yogic breath regulation: A narrative review of scientific evidence. *Journal of Ayurveda and Integrative Medicine*, 10(1), 50–58. https://doi.org/10.1016/j.jaim.2017.07.008.

Shaffer, F., and Ginsberg, J. P. (2017). An Overview of Heart Rate Variability Metrics and Norms. *Frontiers in Public Health*, 5, 258. https://doi.org/10.3389/fpubh.2017.00258.

Shaffer, F., and Meehan, Z. M. (2020). A Practical Guide to Resonance Frequency Assessment for Heart Rate Variability Biofeedback. *Frontiers in Neuroscience*, 14, 570400. https://doi.org/10.3389/fnins.2020.570400.

Shannahoff-Khalsa D. (1993). The ultradian rhythm of alternating cerebral hemispheric activity. *International Journal of Neuroscience*, 70(3-4), 285–298. https://doi.org/10.3109/00207459309000583.

Simon, N. M., Hofmann, S. G., Rosenfield, D., Hoeppner, S. S., Hoge, E. A., Bui, E., and Khalsa, S. B. S. (2021). Efficacy of Yoga vs Cognitive Behavioral Therapy vs Stress Education for the Treatment of Generalized Anxiety Disorder. *JAMA Psychiatry*, 78(1), 13. https://doi.org/10.1001/jamapsychiatry.2020.2496.

Singh, K., Bhargav, H., and Srinivasan, T. M. (2016). Effect of uninostril yoga breathing on brain hemodynamics: A functional near-infrared spectroscopy study. *International Journal of Yoga*, 9(1), 12–19. https://doi.org/10.4103/0973-6131.171711.

Steffen, P. R., Austin, T., DeBarros, A., and Brown, T. (2017). The Impact of Resonance Frequency Breathing on Measures of Heart Rate Variability, Blood Pressure, and Mood. *Frontiers in Public Health*, 5, 222. https://doi.org/10.3389/fpubh.2017.00222.

Szulczewski M. T. (2019). Training of paced breathing at 0.1 Hz improves CO_2 homeostasis and relaxation during a paced breathing task. *PloS One*, 14(6), e0218550. https://doi.org/10.1371/journal.pone.0218550.

Tompkins, T. A., Mainville, I., and Arcand, Y. (2011). The impact of meals on a probiotic during transit through a model of the human upper gastrointestinal tract. *Beneficial Microbes*, 2(4), 295–303. https://doi.org/10.3920/BM2011.0022.

Toussaint, L., Nguyen, Q. A., Roettger, C., Dixon, K., Offenbächer, M., Kohls, N., Hirsch, J., and Sirois, F. (2021). Effectiveness of Progressive Muscle Relaxation, Deep Breathing, and Guided Imagery in Promoting Psychological and Physiological States of Relaxation. *Evidence-Based Complementary and Alternative Medicine*, 2021, 1–8. https://doi.org/10.1155/2021/5924040.

Towers, A. E., Oelschlager, M. L., Patel, J., Gainey, S. J., McCusker, R. H., and Freund, G. G. (2017). Acute fasting inhibits central caspase-1 activity reducing anxiety-like behavior and increasing novel object and object location recognition. *Metabolism: Clinical and Experimental*, 71, 70–82. https://doi.org/10.1016/j.metabol.2017.03.005.

Tyagi, A., and Cohen, M. (2016). Yoga and heart rate variability: A comprehensive review of the literature. *International Journal of Yoga*, 9(2), 97–113. https://doi.org/10.4103/0973-6131.183712.

Vandeputte, D., Falony, G., Vieira-Silva, S., Tito, R. Y., Joossens, M., and Raes, J. (2016). Stool consistency is strongly associated with gut microbiota richness and composition, enterotypes and bacterial growth rates. *Gut*, 65(1), 57–62. https://doi.org/10.1136/gutjnl-2015-309618.

Weersma, R. K., Zhernakova, A., and Fu, J. (2020). Interaction between drugs and the gut microbiome. *Gut*, 69(8), 1510–1519. https://doi.org/10.1136/gutjnl-2019-320204.

Wei, M., and Groves, J. (2017). *The Harvard Medical School Guide to Yoga: 8 Weeks to Strength, Awareness, and Flexibility* (Illustrated ed.). Da Capo Lifelong Books, New York, N.Y.

Yang, B., Wei, J., Ju, P., and Chen, J. (2019). Effects of regulating intestinal microbiota on anxiety symptoms: A systematic review. *General Psychiatry*, 32(2), e100056. https://doi.org/10.1136/gpsych-2019-100056.

Chapter 10

Abramowitz, J. S., Deacon, B. J., and Whiteside, S. P. H. (2019). *Exposure Therapy for Anxiety, Second Edition: Principles and Practice*, The Guilford Press, New York, N.Y.

Bennett, M. P., and Lengacher, C. (2009). Humor and Laughter May Influence Health IV. Humor and Immune Function. *Evidence-Based Complementary and Alternative Medicine: eCAM*, 6(2), 159–164. https://doi.org/10.1093/ecam/nem149.

Buxton, R. T., Pearson, A. L., Allou, C., Fristrup, K., and Wittemyer, G. (2021). A synthesis of health benefits of natural sounds and their distribution in national parks. *Proceedings of the National Academy of Sciences of the United States of America*, 118(14), e2013097118. https://doi.org/10.1073/pnas.2013097118.

Chatterjee, D., Hegde, S., and Thaut, M. (2021). Neural plasticity: The substratum of music-based interventions in neurorehabilitation. *NeuroRehabilitation*, 48(2), 155–166. https://doi.org/10.3233/NRE-208011.

Craske, M. G., Treanor, M., Conway, C. C., Zbozinek, T., and Vervliet, B. (2014). Maximizing exposure therapy: an inhibitory learning approach. *Behaviour Research and Therapy*, 58, 10–23. https://doi.org/10.1016/j.brat.2014.04.006.

Fredborg, B., Clark, J., and Smith, S. D. (2017). An Examination of Personality Traits Associated with Autonomous Sensory Meridian Response (ASMR). *Frontiers in Psychology*, 8, 247. https://doi.org/10.3389/fpsyg.2017.00247.

Fredborg, B. K., Clark, J. M., and Smith, S. D. (2018). Mindfulness and autonomous sensory meridian response (ASMR). *PeerJ*, 6, e5414. https://doi.org/10.7717/peerj.5414.

Goldin, P. R., Thurston, M., Allende, S., Moodie, C., Dixon, M. L., Heimberg, R. G., and Gross, J. J. (2021). Evaluation of Cognitive Behavioral Therapy vs Mindfulness Meditation in Brain Changes During Reappraisal and Acceptance Among Patients With Social Anxiety Disorder. *JAMA Psychiatry*, 78(10), 1134. https://doi.org/10.1001/jamapsychiatry.2021.1862.

Goldin, P., Ziv, M., Jazaieri, H., and Gross, J. J. (2012). Randomized controlled trial of mindfulness-based stress reduction versus aerobic exercise: effects on the self-referential brain network in social anxiety disorder. *Frontiers in Human Neuroscience*, 6, 295. https://doi.org/10.3389/fnhum.2012.00295.

Huang, B., Hao, X., Long, S., Ding, R., Wang, J., Liu, Y., Guo, S., Lu, J., He, M., and Yao, D. (2021). The Benefits of Music Listening for Induced State Anxiety: Behavioral and Physiological Evidence. *Brain Sciences*, 11(10), 1332. https://doi.org/10.3390/brainsci11101332.

Janik McErlean, A. B., and Banissy, M. J. (2018). Increased misophonia in self-reported Autonomous Sensory Meridian Response. *PeerJ*, *6*, e5351. https://doi.org/10.7717/peerj.5351.

Kim, S. H., Kim, Y. H., and Kim, H. J. (2015). Laughter and Stress Relief in Cancer Patients: A Pilot Study. *Evidence-Based Complementary and Alternative Medicine: eCAM*, *2015*, 864739. https://doi.org/10.1155/2015/864739.

Louie, D., Brook, K., and Frates, E. (2016). The Laughter Prescription: A Tool for Lifestyle Medicine. *American Journal of Lifestyle Medicine*, 10(4), 262–267. https://doi.org/10.1177/1559827614550279.

Mantzios, M., and Giannou, K. (2018). When Did Coloring Books Become Mindful? Exploring the Effectiveness of a Novel Method of Mindfulness-Guided Instructions for Coloring Books to Increase Mindfulness and Decrease Anxiety. *Frontiers in Psychology*, 9, 56. https://doi.org/10.3389/fpsyg.2018.00056.

Mitterschiffthaler, M. T., Fu, C. H., Dalton, J. A., Andrew, C. M., and Williams, S. C. (2007). A functional MRI study of happy and sad affective states induced by classical music. *Human Brain Mapping*, 28(11), 1150–1162. https://doi.org/10.1002/hbm.20337.

Mora-Ripoll R. (2010). The therapeutic value of laughter in medicine. *Alternative Therapies in Health and Medicine*, 16(6), 56–64.

Morishima, T., Miyashiro, I., Inoue, N., Kitasaka, M., Akazawa, T., Higeno, A., Idota, A., Sato, A., Ohira, T., Sakon, M., and Matsuura, N. (2019). Effects of laughter therapy on quality of life in patients with cancer: An open-label, randomized controlled trial. *PLOS One*, 14(6), e0219065. https://doi.org/10.1371/journal.pone.0219065.

Poerio , G.L., Blakey, E., Hostler, T.J., and Veltri, T., (2018) More than a feeling: Autonomous sensory meridian response (ASMR) is characterized by reliable changes in affect and physiology. *PLoS One* 13(6): e0196645. https://doi.org/10.1371/journal.pone.0196645.

Smith, S.D., Fredborg, B.K., Kornelsen, J. 2019. A functional magnetic resonance imaging investigation of the autonomous sensory meridian response. *PeerJ*, 7:e7122 https://doi.org/10.7717/peerj.7122.

Strean W. B. (2009). Laughter prescription. *Canadian Family Physician*, 55(10), 965–967.

van der Wal, C. N., and Kok, R. N. (2019). Laughter-inducing therapies: Systematic review and meta-analysis. *Social Science and Medicine (1982)*, 232, 473–488. https://doi.org/10.1016/j.socscimed.2019.02.018.

Yim J. (2016). Therapeutic Benefits of Laughter in Mental Health: A Theoretical Review. *Tohoku Journal of Experimental Medicine*, 239(3), 243–249. https://doi.org/10.1620/tjem.239.243.

Index

A

acceptance and commitment therapy (ACT), 166–167

acting out, 106

acupuncture, 156–157

ADD. *See* attention deficit disorder

ADHD. *See* attention deficit hyperactivity disorder

affective labeling (journaling), 193–195

  example situation, 194

  journal prompts, 194

  naming of emotions, 193

  responses to prompts, 195

  self-reflection, 193

affirmations (journaling), 195–199

  believable affirmations, 197–198

  example situation, 196

  general affirmations, 198–199

  journal prompts, 198

  negative thoughts, 196

  positive affirmations, 196

  as self-care, 195

agency, definition of, 80

agreeableness (as super trait), 100

Ainsworth, Mary, 47

Allen, Jennifer, 238

all-or-nothing thinking, 203

alprazolam (Xanax), 116

alternate-nostril breathing, 214–215

alternative treatments. *See* complementary and alternative medicine

American Psychiatric Association, 115

anal personality, 97–98

analysis, journaling for. *See* journaling

animal hoarding, 66

animal magnetism (hypnosis), 158

antidepressants, 119–126

  brain shocks, 124

  discontinuation symptoms, 123, 126

  side effects, 120–126

    emotional blunting, 123

    gastrointestinal symptoms, 121–122

    increased anxiety, 120–121

    serotonin effect, 122

    sexual dysfunction, 122

    weight gain, 122–123

  withdrawal, 123–126

ANTS. *See* Automatic Negative Thoughts

anxiety disorders. *See* disorders

applied relaxation, 228

aromatherapy, 148–156

  bergamot (*Citrus bergamia*), 152

  delivery methods, 153

  dilutions guidelines, 154

  essential oils, 150, 153, 155

  essential oils, uses for, 156

  frankincense (*Boswellia carterii*), 152

  lavender (*Lavandula angustifolia*), 150

  neroli (*Citrus aurantium var amara*), 150

  olfactory nerve pathway, 150

  patchouli (*Pogostemon cablin*), 151

  recipes and tips, 261–265

    bath oil, 264

    calming oil blend combinations, 262–263

    oil blends, 262

    peaceful sleep oil, 263–264

    relaxing bath salt, 264

    room spray, 265

    single oils, 262

B

C

D

G

H

I

J

K

L

labeling, 203
laughter therapy, 241–243
  incongruity theory, 242–243
  release theory, 242
  superiority theory, 242
  therapeutic effects, 242
laughter yoga, 243–245
  basics, 243
  cell phone laughter (exercise),
    244
  childlike play, 244
  clapping and chanting, 243
  driving laughter (exercise), 244
  exercises, 244–245
  hula hoop laughter (exercise),
    245
  yoga breathing, 243–244
lavender (*Lavandula angustifolia*),
  141–142, 150
leaky gut, 221
Lexapro, 116
libido, suppressed, 20
libido theory (Freud), 97–98
life crises. *See* existential anxiety
Lightner, Candace, 108
Lightner, Cari, 108
Lipitor, 221–222
lizard brain, 4
lorazepam, 127
low sex drive, 20
Lyrica, 133

M

magnesium, 137–139
  common side effects, 139
  recommendation, 139
  recommended amount, 138
  sources, 138

magnetic resonance imaging
  (MRI), 174
magnifying and minimizing, 204
mandala designs, 241
marijuana. *See* cannabis
mature defenses, 108–109
  humor, 108
  sublimation, 108
  suppression, 109
MBSR program. *See* Mindfulness-
  Based Stress Reduction program
McCrae, Robert, 100
medical condition, anxiety due to,
  50–53
  cardiovascular disorders, 51
  endocrine diseases, 51
  metabolic disturbances, 52
  neurological illness, 52
  respiratory illnesses, 52
medications. *See* prescription
  medications
meditation, 186–190
  attentional meditations, 186
  body scan, 187–188
  breathing meditation, 187
  constructive meditation,
    188–189
  deconstructive meditation, 189
  session length, 190
Mesmer, Franz Anton, 158
metabolic disturbances, 52
metformin, 222
microbiome. *See* probiotics and
  microbiome
midazolam (Versed), 142
mindfulness, 180–183
  acceptance, 181
  attention, 180–181
  awareness, 181
  components, 180–181
  conscious listening, 182–183
  conscious reaction, 181

N

O

P–Q

R

S

T–U

V

W–X

Y

Z